Diodore of Tarsus:
Commentary on Psalms 1–51

Society of Biblical Literature

Writings from the Greco-Roman World

John T. Fitzgerald, General Editor

Editorial Board

David Armstrong
Elizabeth Asmis
Brian E. Daley, S.J.
David G. Hunter
David Konstan
Michael J. Roberts
Johan C. Thom
Yun Lee Too
James C. VanderKam

Number 9

Diodore of Tarsus:
Commentary on Psalms 1–51

Volume Editor
Everett Ferguson

Diodore of Tarsus:
Commentary on Psalms 1–51

Translated with an Introduction and Notes by
Robert C. Hill

Society of Biblical Literature
Atlanta

DIODORE OF TARSUS:
Commentary on Psalms 1–51
Copyright © 2005 by the Society of Biblical Literature.
All rights reserved.

No part of this work may be reproduced or transmitted in any form or by any means, electronic or mechanical, including photocopying and recording, or by means of any information storage or retrieval system, except as may be expressly permitted by the 1976 Copyright Act or in writing from the publisher. Requests for permission should be addressed in writing to the Rights and Permissions Office, Society of Biblical Literature, 825 Houston Mill Road, Suite 350, Atlanta, GA 30329, USA.

Library of Congress Cataloging-in-Publication Data

Diodore, of Tarsus, Bishop of Tarsus, d. ca. 392.
[Diodori Tarsensis Commentarii in Psalmos. English]
Diodore of Tarsus : commentary on Psalms 1-51 / translated with an introduction and notes by Robert C. Hill.
     p.   cm. — (Writings from the Greco-Roman world ; v. 9)
Includes bibliographical references and indexes.
ISBN 1-58983-094-6 (paper binding : alk. paper)
  1. Bible. O.T. Psalms I–LI—Commentaries—Early works to 1800. I. Hill, Robert C. (Robert Charles), 1931– II. Title. III. Series.

BR65.D393D5613 2005
223'.207—dc22   2004030353

05 06 07 08 09 10 11 12   5 4 3 2 1

Printed in the United States of America on acid-free, recycled paper conforming to ANSI/NISO Z39.48-1992 (R1997) and ISO 9706:1994 standards for paper permanence.

Table of Contents

Acknowledgments — vii

Abbreviations — ix

Introduction

   1. Life and Works of Diodore — xi
   2. Authenticity of the *Commentary* — xii
   3. Diodore's Text of the Psalter — xv
   4. Diodore's Approach to Scripture — xvii
   5. Diodore's Style of Commentary — xx
   6. Diodore, Interpreter of the Psalms — xxiv
   7. Diodore as Spiritual Director — xxx
   8. The Christology of the *Commentary* and Other Theological Accents — xxxiii
   9. Diodore's Achievement in the *Commentary on the Psalms* — xxxiv

Diodore, *Commentary on Psalms 1–51*

   Preface — 1
   Psalm 1 — 5
   Psalm 2 — 7
   Psalm 3 — 10
   Psalm 4 — 12
   Psalm 5 — 16
   Psalm 6 — 19
   Psalm 7 — 21
   Psalm 8 — 25
   Psalm 9 — 29
   Psalm 10 — 33
   Psalm 11 — 36
   Psalm 12 — 38
   Psalm 13 — 40
   Psalm 14 — 41
   Psalm 15 — 44
   Psalm 16 — 45
   Psalm 17 — 48
   Psalm 18 — 51
   Psalm 19 — 59
   Psalm 20 — 64
   Psalm 21 — 66

Psalm 22	69
Psalm 23	74
Psalm 24	75
Psalm 25	77
Psalm 26	80
Psalm 27	82
Psalm 28	85
Psalm 29	86
Psalm 30	89
Psalm 31	93
Psalm 32	98
Psalm 33	100
Psalm 34	103
Psalm 35	107
Psalm 36	112
Psalm 37	115
Psalm 38	121
Psalm 39	124
Psalm 40	128
Psalm 41	131
Psalm 42	134
Psalm 43	137
Psalm 44	138
Psalm 45	142
Psalm 46	148
Psalm 47	150
Psalm 48	152
Psalm 49	154
Psalm 50	159
Psalm 51	165
Select Bibliography	171
General Index	175
Index of Biblical Citations	177
Index of Modern Authors	181

Acknowledgments

This volume on Diodore of Tarsus appearing now in the series Writings from the Greco-Roman World, and subsequent ones on Theodore of Mopsuestia and Theodoret of Cyrus, will hopefully contribute to a greater appreciation of the way the Old Testament was read in Antioch. That, at least, is my intention and hope.

I am grateful to the General Editor of the series, John T. Fitzgerald, and to the Editorial Director of the Society of Biblical Literature, Bob Buller, for acceptance of this work. For refinement of the text, and for expansion of my own grasp of the Fathers in Antioch and beyond, I am indebted to Everett Ferguson, who kindly edited the volume.

ROBERT C. HILL

Abbreviations

AB	Anchor Bible
Aug	*Augustinianum*
Bib	*Biblica*
CCSG	Corpus Christianorum: Series graeca
CPG	*Clavis patrum graecorum.* Edited by Maurice Geerard. 5 vols. CCSG. Turnhout: Brepols, 1974–87.
DTC	*Dictionnaire de théologie catholique.* Edited by A. Vacant et al. 15 vols. Paris: Letouzey et Ané, 1903–50.
EnchSym	*Enchiridion Symbolorum, Definitionum et Declarationum*
FC	Fathers of the Church
GO	Göttinger Orientforschungen
HeyJ	*The Heythrop Journal*
ITQ	*Irish Theological Quarterly*
JECS	*Journal of Early Christian Studies*
JTS	*Journal of Theological Studies*
KlT	Kleine Texte
LXX	Septuagint
MSU	Mitteilungen des Septuaginta-Unternehmens
NJBC	*The New Jerome Biblical Commentary*
NS	new series
OrChrAn	Orientalia christiana analecta
OTL	Old Testament Library
PG	Patrologia graeca
PL	Patrologia latina
RSR	*Recherches de science religieuse*
SC	Sources chrétiennes
StPatr	*Studia Patristica*
TRE	*Theologische Realenzyklopädie*
VTSup	Vetus Testamentum Supplements

Introduction

1. Life and Works of Diodore

Diodore's name is associated principally with Tarsus, a see in Cilicia over which he presided from 378 until his death a decade and a half later. But he was a native of Antioch, and it was there he so developed his reputation as an exegete as to be called to conduct the city's house of religious formation, or ἀσκητήριον, having among his distinguished pupils John (later bishop of Constantinople, to be awarded the sobriquet Chrysostom) and Theodore (later bishop of Mopsuestia, to be known as The Interpreter). The former would in his *Laus Diodori*[1] refer to his teacher glowingly as "this wise father of ours," and the latter pay him the sincerest form of flattery in more closely adhering to his exegetical principles. It was Theodore, too, with whom Diodore would be bracketed in condemnation by the Lateran council of 649.[2] There was a tragic irony in this condemnation of a man who had been the fearless opponent of Julian the Apostate in his futile attempt to restore pagan worship to Antioch in 362–363 and declare Christ an impostor (and Diodore *Nazaraei magus*), who was banished by Julian's successor Valens in 372, and whose role at the council of Constantinople in 381 and in the development of its creed earned him for his orthodoxy the accolade of the emperor Theodosius in confirming the council decrees.[3]

The regrettable upshot of this condemnation of "the father of Nestorianism"[4] was the loss to posterity of most of his numerous works. Both church historians Socrates and Sozomen mention Diodore's many books on the Bible, if slightly implying an emphasis on the literal sense of the text[5]—an emphasis appearing also in an extant hermeneutical maxim of his which survives in a

---

[1] PG 52:764.
[2] Cf. *EnchSym* 519.
[3] *Cod. Theodos.* xvi 1.3, cited by Johannes Quasten, *Patrology* (3 vols.; Westminster, Md.: Newman, 1950–60), 3:397.
[4] The claim of Cyril of Alexandria, *Contra Diodorum et Theodorum* 17 (PG 76:1149).
[5] Socrates, *Historia ecclesiastica* 6.3 (PG 67:665–68); Sozomen, *Historia ecclesiastica* 8.2 (PG 67:1516), who (on the basis of Socrates) remarks, "I was told that (Diodore) left many books of his own writings, and composed commentaries on the surface meaning of the divine words."

fragment of his *Quaestiones* on the Octateuch, "We (in Antioch) far prefer τὸ ἱστορικόν to τὸ ἀλληγορικόν (as practiced in Alexandria)," and which presumably suffuses his missing work on the difference between Antioch's favored hermeneutical approach of θεωρία and that of ἀλληγορία (as misunderstood by Diodore and his own mentor Eustathius).[6] It is fortunate that Diodore's *Commentary on the Psalms* has survived the flames of prejudice (under someone else's name) and has been (at least partially) edited by Jean-Marie Olivier.[7] This work and his well-documented reputation are sufficient, in Olivier's judgment, to establish Diodore as "le véritable fondateur" of the distinctively Antiochene historical method of reading Scripture, even if to the scholar-priest Lucian (martyred in 312) goes the title of "l'initiateur" of the Antiochene school.[8] Olivier's judgment we shall have to assess for ourselves on the evidence of the English translation, now appearing for the first time below.[9]

2. Authenticity of the *Commentary*

As Diodore's sole surviving work, the *Commentary on the Psalms* is thus clearly of great importance as illustrating the exegetical principles of the school he founded—even if "exegesis" is also a term we may use only with qualifications.[10] It comes to us, whole or in part, in eight manuscripts of the tenth to the fifteenth centuries in two lines of direct transmission, the earlier represented by the best and earliest manuscript, Parisinus Coislinianus 275, the

---

[6] Cf. Christoph Schäublin, "Diodor von Tarsus," *TRE* 3:764–65.

[7] *Diodori Tarsensis commentarii in Psalmos*, vol. 1: *Commentarius in Psalmos I–L* (CCSG 6; Turnhout: Brepols, 1980). For ease of reference, page numbers of the text of this edition are included in the translation below.

[8] *Commentarii*, ciii. To speak of a "school of Antioch" should not imply "a local habitation and a name," in the way we find Quasten, *Patrology*, 2:121–23, speaking of the school of Caesarea which became Origen's refuge after his exile from Egypt. Rather, we mean by the term a fellowship of like-minded scholars joined by birth, geography, and scholarly principles, even if in this case Didore did exercise a magisterial role.

[9] For a fuller account of Diodore's life and works, see Schäublin, "Diodore von Tarsus," 763–66.

[10] Cf. John N. D. Kelly, *Golden Mouth: The Story of John Chrysostom. Ascetic, Preacher, Bishop* (Ithaca, N.Y.: Cornell University Press, 1995), 94: "Neither John, nor any Christian teacher for centuries to come, was properly equipped to carry out exegesis as we have come to understand it. He could not be expected to understand the nature of the Old Testament writing."

latter by a family of manuscripts including Parisinus graecus 168.[11] An anomaly that still preoccupies at least one eminent scholar is the fact that in the latter manuscript no name is appended,[12] while in the former the work bears the name of Anastasius III, metropolitan of Nicea (a title that was not current prior to the ninth century). In the introduction to his critical edition of the *Commentary* (which unfortunately did not reach beyond the first third of the Psalter), Jean-Marie Olivier on the basis of earlier research[13] demonstrates that the work is clearly Antiochene, that the principles espoused in its preface and adopted in the following exegesis are faithful to those exemplified in that lost work mentioned above on the difference between θεωρία and ἀλληγορία, that its failure to register christological polemic later arising from Apollinarianism and Nestorianism is due to its having been composed early in Diodore's career while he was still head of the *asketerion,* and that its authorship by Diodore was suppressed for the obvious reason of his later poor standing after condemnation as Nestorian along with Theodore by church councils (which led also to the destruction of almost all of Theodore's works).[14]

Such argumentation for the authenticity of the *Commentary* as a work of Diodore's has proved conclusive for scholarship generally.[15] The degree to which Theodore embraces its overall approach and reproduces countless individual elements, even at times verba-

[11] Olivier surveys and evaluates the manuscript tradition of the *Commentary* in his introduction, *Commentarii,* xi–lxxii.

[12] Robert Devreesse raises doubts about authenticity and manuscript tradition (*Les anciens commentateurs grecs des psaumes* [Studi e Testi 264; Vatican City: Bibliotheca Apostolica Vaticana, 1970], 302–11). Olivier retorts (*Commentarii,* lxxviii) in regard to the latter that Diodore's work comes to us in direct manuscript tradition, unlike the reconstituted text by Devreesse of Theodore's work, *Le commentaire de Théodore de Mopsueste sur les psaumes (I–LXXX)* (Studi e Testi 93; Vatican City: Biblioteca Apostolica Vaticana, 1939).

[13] Notably by L. Mariès in a series of studies culminating in "Etudes préliminaires à l'édition de Diodore de Tarse 'Sur les Psaumes,'" *RSR* 22 (1932): 385–408, 513–40.

[14] Cf. Olivier, *Commentarii,* ciii–cviii. Beyond the reconstituted text of Theodore's commentary on Pss 1–81, we have in Greek only his *Commentary on the Twelve Prophets,* a text edited by Angelo Mai in 1832 that appears in PG 66:124–632, a critical edition appearing in 1977 by Hans N. Sprenger, *Theodori Mopsuesteni commentarius in XII prophetas* (GO, Biblica et Patristica 1; Wiesbaden: Harrassowitz, 1977).

[15] Cf. *CPG* 3818 (the further rubric, "Pss LI–CL paratur," is inaccurate, the publishers advising that editor Olivier is producing nothing more). Marie-Josèphe Rondeau arrives at the same conclusion as Olivier, positing a date before 378 or

tim, and to which the later more mature and measured Theodoret, under the influence also of Alexandrian commentators, will subject to scrutiny the positions of both these Antiochene predecessors, confirms its provenance for a close reader.[16] The composer makes little reference to current events that would enable us to pinpoint its date; when he reads Ps 19:12–13, "Purify me from my hidden sins, and spare your servant from external influences," he recalls a situation known to his readers in which some of the faithful lapsed under torture in time of persecution—at the time of Julian?

> By *hidden sins* he refers to the situation with lust in which we are overcome, and by *external influences* to what befalls us unexpectedly from without, normally called accidental by the uninitiated—or rather, to put it more plainly, what befalls us by way of temptation and an onset of the devil, as for example what happened in the case of the martyrs, when all of a sudden persecution came upon them in a time of tranquillity, then they fell under the power of the authorities, then they were subjected to torture and often, though having good intentions, they succumbed to the great number of tortures and fell into the indeliberate sin of denial. What was not of their doing, therefore, but originated and befell them from without he calls *external influences*.

There is internal evidence as well that the commentator is still exercising a magisterial position in scriptural and moral matters, distinctions being drawn and rules stated in the manner of a master to his neophytes (called "brothers," ἀδελφοί, in the preface). He lectures on the basic moral imperative—do good and avoid evil—in comment on Ps 37:3, delivers a systematic classification of sins mortal and venial in connection with Ps 19:12–13 cited above, and Ps 45:14 prompts in him an encomium of virginity and its "esteemed role in the church." Chrysostom in his homilies on the Psalms to the congregation(s) in his διδασκαλεῖον[17] will not adopt the manner of a mentor in the way true of Diodore, who anticipated the compliment by rarely moralizing on the psalmists' moral axioms, leaving that to a preacher like his more celebrated pupil.

---

even 372 (*Les commentaires patristiques du Psautier du IIIe au Ve siècles* [OrChrAn 219–220; Rome: Pont. Institutum Studiorum Orientalium, 1982-85], 1:93–102).

[16] For details, cf. the introductions to my translations of these two works.

[17] For evidence of this venue for Chrysostom's fifty-eight homilies on the Psalms, see the introduction to my *St. John Chrysostom: Commentary on the Psalms* (2 vols.; Brookline, Mass.: Holy Cross Orthodox Press, 1998), 1:8–9.

3. Diodore's Text of the Psalter

This internal evidence, then, confirms the generally accepted attribution of the *Commentary* to Diodore. There is also the fact that the commentator is clearly reading as his biblical text the Greek version in use in Antioch, a version made by—or, more likely, revised by—Lucian,[18] and hence often referred to as Lucianic. We know of its existence from Jerome, who speaks of three forms of the Septuagint current in his time, including a version adopted in Antioch-Constantinople "which Origen and Eusebius of Caesarea and all the Greek commentators call the popular text, and which by most is called the Lucianic text."[19] Though this term is not acceptable to all scholars,[20] the individual features of the Antioch text have been documented by the editions emanating from the Göttingen project,[21] a text coming to light from the commentaries of the Antiochene Fathers—Diodore and his successors Chrysostom, Theodore, and Theodoret[22]—and hopefully rendering unacceptable the use of "Septuagint" as a univocal term.[23] Diodore in this work

---

[18] Paul Kahle would see the Antioch text as a translation separate from the Alexandrian version generally known as the Septuagint, Lucian's revision of it occurring centuries later (*The Cairo Genizah* [2nd ed.; Oxford: Blackwell, 1959], 256–57). Natalio Fernández Marcos, *The Septuagint in Context: Introduction to the Greek Versions of the Bible* (trans. Wilfred G. E. Watson; Leiden: Brill, 2001), 57, finds to the contrary that "in the case of the LXX a process like that of the Aramaic Targums did not occur"—though he will still speak of the LXX as "a collection of translations" (xi, 22). Sidney Jellicoe agrees that a Lucianic version made directly from the Hebrew is unlikely in view of the general ignorance of that language (*The Septuagint and Modern Study* [Oxford: Clarendon, 1968], 160–61).

[19] Cf. *Praef. in Paral.* (PL 28:1324–25), *Ep.* 106.2 (PL 22:838).

[20] It is acceptable to David S. Wallace-Hadrill, *Christian Antioch: A Study of Early Christian Thought* (Cambridge: Cambridge University Press, 1982), 30, and to Benjamin Drewery, "Antiochien," *TRE* 3:106. Fernandez Marcos speaks interchangeably of Lucian, Lucianic, and Antiochian recension. Dominic Barthélemy prefers "Antiochien" (*Les devanciers d'Aquila* [VTSup 10; Leiden: Brill, 1963], 126–27), as does Jean-Noel Guinot, *L'Exégèse de Théodoret de Cyr* (Théologie historique 100; Paris: Beauchesne, 1995), 171–72.

[21] Cf. Alfred Rahlfs, *Septuaginta: Vetus Testamentum graecum*, vol. 10: *Psalmi cum Odis* (2nd ed.; Göttingen: Vandenhoeck & Ruprecht, 1967).

[22] Cf. Fernandez Marcos on "The Antiochene Text of the Greek Bible," *Scribes and Translators: Septuagint and Old Latin in the Books of Kings* (VTSup 54; Leiden: Brill, 1994), 28: "One of the reasons for the uncertainty concerning the Lucianic recension of the Octateuch was the lack of critical editions of the Antiochene Fathers."

[23] For some evidence that such usage is still current with (Western) biblical commentators, see my article, "*Orientale lumen*: Western Biblical Scholarship's

is less helpful to text critics than the others for the reason that he is less interested in subjecting his text to criticism than they, as we shall see. Olivier admits that he depends on Diodore's comment on a particular verse to retrieve the biblical text in use,[24] which can be a fallible exercise; on several occasions a reader—who has the advantage of reference also to Theodoret's complete commentary[25] and the partially extant commentaries of Theodore and Chrysostom[26] (if not all critically edited)—observes that reconstructed text and commentary on it do not cohere. Further, the editor seems unaccountably to have omitted the text of Ps 49:18a, "Because his soul will be blessed in his lifetime," along with Diodore's comment on it. It has not been a concern of this translator to note all the distinctive readings of the LXX text in use by Diodore; this exercise has been undertaken by Olivier in the introduction to his edition.[27] Comparison with the text used by the other Antiochenes, however, suggests that Diodore's differs from theirs at Pss 7:6 (though with support from Chrysostom); 18:19 (a clause occurring that is unknown to the Hebrew); 35:12 (a word occurring that is unknown elsewhere), 35:25; 46:5.[28] We are reminded, however, that we have available a critical edition only of one-third of the full *Commentary*.

It is to this local form of the Greek version, then, that Diodore turns to comment on this part of the Old Testament for his readers—unspecified, but seemingly at least the student body of the *asketerion* in Antioch, though Theodoret will confirm its reaching a wider readership. (Diodore's New Testament text—likewise "popular," κοινή, in Jerome's terms—also reveals individual features, adverted to in the text below.) His Greek Bible begins with Genesis—or Κοσμοποιία as he calls it, and Theodore Κτίσις—and includes deuterocanonical books like the Maccabees, Baruch, Sirach, and the Wisdom of Solomon.[29] The Psalter of this Bible he

---

Unacknowledged Debt," in *Orientale Lumen Australasia—Oceania: Proceedings 2000* (ed. Lawrence Cross; Melbourne: Australian Catholic University, 2001), 157–72.

[24] *Commentarii*, xcv.
[25] PG 80:857–1998.
[26] PG 55:39–498.
[27] *Commentarii*, xcvi.
[28] Attention is drawn to these instances in the text below.
[29] It may be that the Antiochenes' canon did not include the book of Esther; none of them cites it directly. In comment on Ps 66:3, Theodore cites from Josephus almost verbatim the text of Esth 8:14–17, an unlikely citation if his Bible

regards as one book, βιβλίον—"the book of the divine Psalms"—not the five books into which it has been divided in our more recent Bibles;[30] and it is basic to his interpretation of the Psalms and his assessment of the authenticity of the titles that the Psalter comes to him as a rather haphazard reassembly of the collection by Ezra in the wake of its loss at the time of the exile. He sees no significance in the doxology concluding Ps 41 that modern commentators recognize as a device signaling the closure of the first of the five books.

4. Diodore's Approach to Scripture

Rationalist though his attitude is to the Bible's compilation and the import of the psalm titles,[31] Diodore is in no doubt of the divine inspiration of the biblical authors, προφῆται all, and of David in particular. From the opening of the preface he assures us of the Psalms' value to us because inspired (a pastoral application we shall lament not finding more frequently): "The Holy Spirit, who guides all human affairs, gives voice through most blessed David to his own response to our sufferings so that through it the sufferers may be cured." When he arrives at the opening verses of that Ps 45 that prompted reflection on biblical inspiration by so many of the Fathers, he analyzes that charism (leading Chrysostom, Theodore, and Theodoret to do likewise),[32] highlighting in typically Antiochene accents the contribution the author brings to the impulse of the Spirit. He paraphrases v. 1c, "My tongue the pen of a rapid scribe," in these terms, "I bring to bear also my tongue to the extent possible so as to serve the thought coming from grace in the way that a pen follows the lead of a writer's thought," where both elements are nicely balanced, the human contribution upheld yet delicately nuanced with the phrase "to the extent possible"—a balance which becomes typical of Antiochene dyophysite thinking also on the

---

contained that book. Theodoret, who likewise seems unfamiliar with Esther, does include 1–2 Esdras and 3 Maccabees.

[30] Diodore checks his reading of Ps 7:13b against "some of the Psalters," suggesting that this biblical collection was available as a separate volume, suited to liturgical use, for instance.

[31] G. Bardy will balk at the use of this term, preferring "raisonnable": "Le mot rationaliste ne conviendrait ici" ("Diodore," *Dictionnaire de spiritualité* [17 vols. in 21; Paris: Beauchesne, 1937–95], 3:991).

[32] Cf. my article, "Psalm 45: A *Locus Classicus* for Patristic Thinking on Biblical Inspiration," *StPatr* 25 (1993): 95–100.

incarnate Word,[33] soteriology, morality, and spirituality, where divine and human must be held together.[34]

Reading his text of "the book of the most divine Psalms" in his local Greek version, Diodore suffers the handicap of all his peers of being unfamiliar with the language of the original. This handicap predictably imposes a range of limitations on his commentary. He is, for instance, unable to detect the alphabetic structure of certain psalms, though (e.g., in Pss 34; 37) he senses the effect this can have on the psalmist's movement of thought, ἀκολουθία, which in the absence of linguistic skills becomes his primary criterion for evaluating the text. Like many a teacher, unwilling to admit to imperfect knowledge, he will rule on textual details when he should be more tentative (a habit Theodore will learn from him); when Ps 19 opens with the celebrated verse, "The heavens tell of the glory of God," Diodore assures his readers that the plural is normal Hebrew practice, citing for contrast Ps 115:16, where—unfortunately for him—the Hebrew term is again in the plural.

> Stating singular things as plural is a Hebrew idiom, especially in the case of heavenly things, either on account of their importance or also by another custom. Elsewhere he illustrates this more clearly by speaking in this case not in the plural but in the singular, "The heaven is the Lord's heaven," in the sense of dedicated, and he goes on, "but the earth he has given to human beings."

He is unable to detect the many shortcomings of the LXX in rendering the Hebrew text, as we shall see, and even to recognize a scribal error, such as occurs in Ps 48:9, where his local text reads, "We suspected, O God, your mercy in the midst of your people," a scribe obviously having copied ναοῦ, "temple," as λαοῦ, "people" (though admittedly his successors will do no better, Chrysostom coming up with an awful solecism at this point).

Textual errors such as these or obscure expressions of the

---

[33] See the citation below of his comment on Ps 45:7 in regard to Diodore's Christology.

[34] Failure to acknowledge such a theological basis to the Antiochene approach to Scripture, which is then presented simply as an arbitrary "project" or "strategy" (that "failed"), somewhat impairs the analysis of John J. O'Keefe, "'A Letter That Killeth': Toward a Reassessment of Antiochene Exegesis, or Diodore, Theodore and Theodoret on the Psalms," *JECS* 8 (2000): 83–104. Strangely, Chrysostom is omitted from the study. O'Keefe might also have noted that the citation of 2 Cor 3:6 adopted as a monitum in his title the Antiochene Theodoret had already adduced in introducing his *Commentary on the Song of Songs* (PG 81:37).

psalmist are no problem for Diodore, despite his inability to seek enlightenment from the Hebrew: he simply rationalizes what he finds before him. When Ps 31 in his text has the word ἐκστάσεως appended to the title, he does not do as Theodoret will do and check a copy of the Hexapla to find that the word occurs only in some LXX manuscripts; instead, he hazards a guess: "What did 'perplexity' mean to the person who gave the title? That person would have had a better idea; but in my view it implies the actual astonishment of the author at God's surprising actions." More than his successors he trusts these hunches of his, applying rationalist principles to matters such as the ordering of the psalms and their titles, which in his view (he tells us in the preface) "are in most cases faulty, the compilers of the psalms mostly guessing at their connection and not placing them by meaning."

Yet, as is evident in his firm commitment to the divine inspiration of the biblical authors, his rationalism is not total, and does not extend to questioning the authorship of the psalms, the issue not even being raised in the preface: they are all David's, even if all but a few rest on a factual basis, ἱστορία, that the author was inspired to foresee. When the title of Ps 39 makes mention of Jeduthun, he dismisses the possibility that this attribution may involve authorship: "It is likely that it was given by David to Jeduthun, a temple singer, for singing—though the composition of the psalms was by David and no one else." Psalm 14 he gratuitously sees referring to the eighth-century events involving Sennacherib and the Rabshakeh; far from letting the possibility arise that this could suggest multiple authors of the Psalms at various times, he simply observes, "Now, it is worth marveling at the grace given to David of foretelling so many years before not only the events but also people's ways of thinking at that time." For him προφητεία can be both retrospective and prospective, but more properly the latter (as he asserts in the preface).

Diodore will communicate to his pupils an approach to Scripture as a moral text; it is not primarily doctrinal, even less ascetical or mystical—an approach, of course, that does not promote full appreciation of the Psalms in particular. He begins his work with an endorsement by the author of the Pastorals to this effect: "Scripture teaches what is good, reproves sins, corrects omissions, and thus brings a person to perfection; in fact, he goes on to say, 'so that the person who belongs to God may be ready, prepared for every good work' (2 Tim 3:16–17)." The Psalms are thus text rather than song composed for recital within the liturgy, whether of Old or of New Testament. Diodore does not share with modern commentators an interest in liturgical *Sitze im Leben*; even the mention of singing to the accompaniment of musical instruments in places like Ps 33:2 does not lead him to such a comment—though he is prompted to explain the question-and-answer form of Ps 24 on the grounds that "the verses had to be recited antiphonally." His accent, as we shall see further in looking at his hermeneutics, falls rather on ἀλήθεια, πράγματα;[35] the Psalms may be approached as historical documents for edification, as he observes of Ps 5.

> Some commentators believe from this that the psalm was composed from the point of view of the church.... Let them take it thus if it is their pleasure to think that way, and console themselves if they have no interest in accepting the factual indications. It always behooves the historical commentator, however, to give nothing priority over the facts (ἀλήθεια) and not to hinder those wanting to give encouragement from such things.

This is one lesson that Theodore remembered from his time in the *asketerion,* though he and particularly Chrysostom would improve on their mentor in choosing to document the psalmists' sentiments more widely from elsewhere in Scripture, Diodore rarely doing so.

5. Diodore's Style of Commentary

With such an approach to the nature of the Scriptures and the Psalter in particular, then, Diodore comes to the task of commentary on the text for "the brethren" and perhaps other readers. With alternative approaches no doubt in mind that used the text only as a springboard, he cites it as a first principle in his preface that "attention must be paid to the actual text of the psalms." His accent is going to be on comprehension, as Chrysostom and Theodoret will likewise insist in light of their experience of people's imperfect

---

[35] Frances Young reminds us that Antioch's accent on πράγματα represented a reaction against Origen's approach to the biblical text (*Biblical Exegesis and the Formation of Christian Culture* [Cambridge: Cambridge University Press, 1996], 162–63). Diodore had learned this accent from Eustathius, bishop of Antioch at the time of the council of Nicea, who had accused Origen of concentrating rather on *onomata* (cf. E. Klostermann, ed., *Origenes, Eustathius von Antiochien und Gregor von Nyssa über die Hexe von Endor* [Bonn: A. Marcus and E. Weber, 1912], 16).

understanding of a psalm's overall meaning, διάνοια; he tells his readers in the preface that "they should grasp the movement of thought (ἀκολουθία) and 'sing with understanding,' as the text says (Ps 47:7), from the depths of their mind and not superficially and at the level of lips alone." In the manner of his school, he begins commentary on each psalm with a statement of its theme, ὑπόθεσις, usually interpreted καθ' ἱστορίαν, and its purpose, σκοπός; as he says in introducing Ps 40, "The fortieth psalm has a Babylonian theme. Blessed David's purpose is to show the Israelites benefiting greatly from the prolonged hardship, and the actual text makes the psalm clearer."

If there is nothing novel about Diodore's accent on ἀλήθεια and πράγματα in the text, neither is there in a grammatical and rhetorical approach.[36] Though lacking a knowledge of Hebrew, he feels free to remark on Hebrew idiom with unwarranted confidence. He is constantly claiming the LXX has effected a change in tense or mood of verbs without his ever referring to the Hebrew, ἀκολουθία being his guiding criterion; ten times in the course of a few verses (Ps 40:13-16) he arbitrarily makes changes to mood and tense because (as modern commentators also remark) the psalm has undergone a change of direction that possibly suggests two compositions (not a possibility he can entertain)—and yet the recurrence of vv. 13-17 later in the Psalter as Ps 70 escapes him. There is, of course, an element of eisegesis in this. He dismisses as otiose the LXX's attempt to reproduce the Hebrew particle *akh-*, as in his comment on Ps 39:6:

> *Yet everything is futility, every living person*: not even all the possessions amassed nor all humankind, if measured by their lifetime, from Adam to the last human being—not even this measure is anything in comparison with the measure of your life, Lord. *At any rate, man goes about like a painting, of course* (v. 6). *Yet* and *of course* add nothing to the thought, being a slovenly translation from the Hebrew.

---

[36] It is a basic premise of Schäublin that Diodore's pupil Theodore is influenced in particular by pagan rhetoricians in adopting this approach: "Theodor sein Rüstzeug als Interpret der paganen Grammatik verdankt" (*Untersuchungen zu Methode und Herkunft der antiochenischen Exegese* [Theophaneia: Beiträge zur Religions- und Kirchengeschichte des Altertums 23; Köln: Hanstein, 1974], 158). Diodore, if not Theodore's other mentor Libanius, evidently played a role as well. Cf. Young, who attributes Antioch's hostility to Origenist allegory to a different educational system, παιδεία (*Biblical Exegesis*, 170-71).

The particle does in fact "add to the thought." On the other hand, it is only when he reaches Ps 40:10 that he remarks on the device of parallelism ("the dominating principle" of biblical poetry, in Mitchell Dahood's words)[37] that has escaped attention thus far, his grasp of Hebrew prosody being imperfect. Proper adoption of a grammatical and rhetorical exegesis clearly requires linguistic and other skills that Diodore does not possess.

Commentary will often begin with a remark on the title, usually disparaging, especially if it does not reflect the factual basis, ἱστορία, previously determined by the commentator. Psalms 27–30 Diodore—or the "others" to whom he acknowledges a debt in the preface—takes as referring to events involving King Hezekiah and the Assyrian invaders. Having commented on them in light of this conviction, he concludes (in a pejorative tone that Theodore will adopt and intensify toward all his predecessors except his mentor), "This is the commentary and the actual content of these four psalms. The psalms' titles, on the other hand, are quite ridiculous, and you would be unable to control yourself if you considered the superficiality of the titles."[38] Yet he is beyond detecting the solecisms the LXX had committed in rendering many of the cryptic phrases in the titles (often liturgical directions), only avoiding trouble when he chooses to ignore the title (as Theodore wisely will never cite a psalm title). In the title to Ps 45, for example, the LXX has seen in the Hebrew term *shoshanim*, "according to the lilies" (presumably a cue to the musicians from a popular melody), the verb *shanah*, "to change," and like other Antiochenes Diodore rationalizes this false lead: "'To the end. For those to be changed. For the sons of Korah, for understanding. A song for the beloved.' 'Those to be changed' means those taking a turn for the better. So the psalm title means that this psalm is recited for those taking a turn for the better in later times when the Son of God appears" (a christological interpretation that is rare in him).

While his Antiochene successors, especially Chrysostom and Theodoret, will submit the text of the Psalter to a degree of criticism, at least to the extent of citing alternative translation of obscure expressions from the ancient versions associated with the names of Aquila, Symmachus, and Theodotion to be found in a

---

[37] *Psalms* (AB 16–17A; Garden City, N.Y.: Doubleday, 1966–70), 1:xxxiii.
[38] *Commentarii*, 170.

copy of the Hexapla, and in the case of Syriac-speaking Theodoret by recourse to the Peshitta,[39] Diodore is reluctant or unable to do so.[40] We have mentioned his ignorance of the original language of the Psalms; and when Ps 29:8 reads in his LXX, "The Lord will shake the wilderness of Kadesh," he remarks, "He calls the holy place *Kadesh*, which in Syriac is normally Kaddeis, referring to the same holy place," his solitary reference to Syriac being no more convincing than Theodore's, though both commentators should have been able to cite the pentateuchal occurrences of Kadesh. Throughout commentary on the entire Psalter he checks his LXX text against the alternative versions only at nine places,[41] generally that of Symmachus and then mainly to confirm the LXX rather than gain clarification from an alternative rendering. He finds difficulty, for instance, in the local LXX version of Ps 17:13: *"Rescue my soul from the ungodly, your sword from foes of your hand.* There is some elliptical expression in these verses that causes obscurity, his meaning being, Rescue my soul from the ungodly sword of the foes of your hand." He is reading "sword" here in the genitive (as does Aquila, he might have discovered), whereas other forms of the LXX read the accusative, as Theodoret finds, and Theodore is aware also of a form in the dative—but Diodore has not taken pains to throw light on the textual difficulty. Olivier is probably right to conclude that he does not have access to a copy of that rich textual resource, the Hexapla, a deficiency his pupils will remedy.

With these linguistic and textual blind spots, Diodore finds his basic tool for arriving at a text's meaning in ἀκολουθία, the author's movement of thought as he judges it; we have seen him freely adjusting verb tenses and moods to suit. Psalm 3 contains three occurrences of the Hebrew rubric *selah*, which the LXX renders διάψαλμα; Origen had given it a meaning "always," which Aquila had encouraged and Chrysostom will favor (in commentary on Pss 140; 143); but again Diodore follows his own hunch, citing ἀκολουθία (modern commentators admitting defeat).

---

[39] Michael P. Weitzman holds that the Peshitta version of the Psalms already existed and had attained authoritative status by around 170 (*The Syriac Version of the Old Testament* [Cambridge: Cambridge University Press, 1999], 253).

[40] When his text of Ps 7:13b reads, "He made his arrows for those on fire," Diodore remarks that "some of the Psalters" had a somewhat different reading, his successors knowing one or the other. It is still not a copy of the Hexapla to which he turns.

[41] Olivier lists eight of these; a ninth could be added, of Aquila on Ps 3:4 (*Commentarii*, xcix).

As I said, therefore, the occurrences of διάψαλμα and the songs of διάψαλμα are changes in rhythms and styles, not alterations in ideas. The movement of thought also reveals this: after the reference διάψαλμα you never find the following thought in opposition to what precedes, being instead sequential and consistent. Hence it is clear that the occurrence midstream of διάψαλμα involved no interruption to the thought of the text, instead perhaps altering the rhythm in keeping with the norms of music and rhythm applying at the time.

On the other hand, though not sensitive to the Psalms' cultic context, Diodore can recognize different genres within psalms (with the exception of apocalyptic, a problem for someone interpreting καθ' ἱστορίαν). Psalm 51 is characterized by modern commentators as a liturgy or some such form, and Diodore similarly responds to the author's distinctive style, remarking, "He presents his whole discourse as if God personally were present and judging." He also speaks in the preface of different genres of psalms, though predictably classifying them mainly on the basis of point of view, πρόσωπον, of the historical characters for whom David speaks.

Diodore, we remarked, comes through as exercising a magisterial role, as one would expect of the head of the Antioch *asketerion,* and he wins our respect for his methodical presentation. He has a special interest in the topic of theodicy; when it surfaces in Ps 19, he systematically clarifies the issues for his students. "Of those people denying providence there are many different kinds: some absolutely deny providence, others confine it to heaven, still others to the things of earth and the common lot of humankind, not actually to each person individually altogether. Among the latter there emerges a variety of differences, but among those claiming independent existence the godlessness is one and the same without exception." From the opening of comment on the first psalm he shows he is not generally inclined to be expansive, his paraphrase at times being so concise as to rival Theodoret's συντομία, and to leave the reader looking for more. Yet at times his explanation of an obscure point can be as prolix and tautological as Theodore more consistently will prove to be.

6. Diodore, Interpreter of the Psalms

If Diodore did not have every exegetical skill to transmit to his students, there was one conviction he was intent on leaving them with, and that was the way the Psalms should be interpreted. This hermeneutic was doubtless one of the things that "I also in my own case had received from others," as he puts it in the preface; and Theodore was clearly convinced of its validity, Chrysostom less so (Theodoret at a later stage tapping into "others" of a different ilk). While he generally does not engage in polemic (as Theodore is wont to do) with interpreters of a different mind, he is clearly aware of and unsympathetic to their hermeneutic, classing them in the preface as "self-opinionated innovators" because they do not follow Paul's procedure in Gal 4:22–5:1 as he flatters himself he is doing. He is aware of levels of meaning in the Psalter and of the way to distinguish and prioritize them.

> We shall treat of it historically and textually and not stand in the way of a spiritual and more elevated sense. The historical sense, in fact, is not in opposition to the more elevated sense; on the contrary, it proves to be the basis and foundation of the more elevated ideas. One thing alone is to be guarded against, however, never to let the discernment process be seen as an overthrow of the underlying sense, since this would no longer be discernment but allegory: what is arrived at in defiance of the content is not discernment but allegory.

The options for a commentator are literal, κατὰ τὴν λέξιν, and historical, κατὰ τὴν ἱστορίαν,[42] on the one hand, and on the other the method of discernment, θεωρία,[43] in looking for a spiritual sense, κατὰ τὴν ἀναγωγήν. There is no opposition between the two approaches, he claims, as long as the latter does not erode the former. The hermeneutical principles are clear; unfortunately, we have seen that their expositor is not equipped to do justice to his text, and his interest in the "more elevated" spiritual meaning is rarely evident, while the process of θεωρία—strangely for an author

---

[42] The difficulty with Diodore's antithesis between the two approaches here and in his axiom cited above, "We far prefer τὸ ἱστορικόν to τὸ ἀλληγορικόν," is that the terms are not clearly defined. Young notes that Antioch's understanding of the term was not "historical" in the modern sense (*Biblical Exegesis*, 168); and Schäublin likewise: "Freilich, was heist in der Sprache der Antiochener 'historisch'? Ihre erhaltenen Schriften teilen keine Definition des ἱστορικόν mit, und einigen Bemerkungen Diodors vermag man blos eine sehr allgemeine Abgrenzung gegenüber der Allegorese zu entnehmen" (*Untersuchungen*, 156).

[43] Cf. A. Vaccari, "La θεωρία nella scuola esegetica di Antiochia," *Bib* 1 (1920): 3–36; P. Ternant, "La θεωρία d'Antioche dans le cadre de sens de l'Ecriture," *Bib* 34 (1953): 135–58, 354–83, 456–86; Bradley Nassif, "'Spiritual Exegesis' in the School of Antioch," in *New Perspectives in Historical Theology* (ed. B. Nassif; New York: Harper & Row, 1978), 342–77.

of a work on the subject[44]—is touched on again only in comment on Ps 8:6 ("You put all things under his feet") in the case of a failure of Jewish readers to discern a christological reference there.

We have been warned, then, that the historical sense of the Psalms is, in Diodore's view, "the basis and foundation of the more elevated ideas"—should these attract the commentator's attention as well. To this position he remains consistently faithful throughout the work. With the titles dismissed as a later and "faulty" appendage, he is free to discover a historical reference in all but a few psalms (Pss 1; 37; 49 being allowed a general applicability), even if this means doing scant justice to that "literal" reading he specified and being guilty of eisegesis to bring the text into line with a predetermined ἱστορία,[45] or factual basis. The net result is that if readers were thinking that they would find help in the *Commentary* for depthing the spiritual riches of this classic and applying them to situations in their own lives, they would be disappointed in discovering the "more elevated sense" and such needs to be neglected.[46]

In his preface Diodore blandly and gratuitously declares that the Psalms in almost all cases are prophetic in the sense of referring to historical events concerning David and Saul, Hezekiah and the Assyrians, the Jews and the Babylonian exile, the Maccabees, and in one case Jeremiah (Ps 35). "These also belong to the prophetic (προαγορευτικός) genre: some mention disasters due to occur to the nation on account of the multitude of sins, others unprecedented marvels following on the disasters. They were all composed in different styles to match the different kinds of coming events." When he comes to the moving expression of personal confidence that is Ps 27, beginning "The Lord is my light and my salvation: whom shall I fear?" Diodore simply includes it with a group of psalms dealing with Hezekiah's troubles with the Assyrians, and neglects its potential for readers wishing to apply it to personal situations.

---

[44] Socrates and Sozomen both contrast Diodore's attention to the "mere letter of the divine Scriptures" or "surface meaning of the divine words" with his avoidance of their θεωρία (PG 67:668,1516).

[45] Diodore will draw the longbow to fix upon details (like mention of a sick bed) in Ps 41 to attribute it to Hezekiah's situation.

[46] One therefore wonders how it is that Bardy can commend his subject for his "vie spirituelle et son souci d'apostolat" ("Diodore," 993)—the latter the identical phrase he used without much greater warrant of Theodoret's commentary on Scripture ("Théodoret," *DTC* 15:312).

The twenty-seventh, twenty-eighth, twenty-ninth, and thirtieth psalms have the same theme, composed from the viewpoint of blessed Hezekiah and directed against the Assyrians. The inspired author David prophesied and adopted this theme on the other's part (πρόσωπον), using his very words in prophecy and displaying his feelings.

Psalm 23 likewise, beginning "The Lord is my shepherd," which in Artur Weiser's words "has gained immortality by the sweet charm of its train of thought and its imagery, and by the intimate character of the religious sentiments expressed therein," Diodore simply declares "is by those returning from Babylon," his terse paraphrase reflecting nothing of "the sentiments of an almost childlike trust"[47] that have made it a favorite of all who know the Psalter.

It is not that Diodore has no capacity for appreciating the imagery of lyrical poetry. It is just that, once it is determined (gratuitously) that a poem rests on a certain ἱστορία, its expressions have to be approached literalistically. Hence, when in Ps 48, that "hymn celebrating the beauty and impregnability of Zion,"[48] v. 8 says in hyperbolic fashion, "God established it forever," Diodore has to interject, "*Forever* does not mean for the whole of time: how could it, when the city was later besieged both by Antiochus and by the Romans?" And to prove his point he cites Ps 21:4, "He asked life of you, and you gave him length of days forever," which he has already taken to refer to Hezekiah's illness, and by a mathematical exercise he demonstrates that an extra fifteen years of life in the king's case similarly does not amount to "forever."[49] If pathos and hyperbole thus fail to receive due appreciation, so too does apocalyptic, that genre that presents the reader with an eschatological scenario requiring "a willing suspension of disbelief," which to a commentator intent on finding a predetermined ἱστορία is anathema; when the opening verses of Ps 46 (a psalm which Diodore has already determined is dealing with conflict between Ahaz and the northern kingdom) depict "the cosmic upheaval . . . of the great

---

[47] *The Psalms* (trans. H. Harwell; OTL; London: SCM, 1962), 227.

[48] Dahood, *Psalms,* 1:289.

[49] Wallace-Hadrill would object to "literalism" being applied to the Antiochenes (though he never goes back beyond his pupils to Diodore): "Literalism is a term which could be used of some of the cruder minds of Origen's time, of certain Arabian sects, for example, and of some millenarist groups, but it hardly fits the Antiochenes. There is nothing crudely literal-minded about insisting that an ancient text should be seen primarily in its own terms" (*Christian Antioch,* 32). O'Keefe might heed this monitum.

final catastrophe,"⁵⁰ he resists any recognition of the wider horizons. In other words, the vision and artistry of the psalmists is scaled down to suit the narrowly historical interpretation of the commentator.

Diodore's faithful pupil Theodore (predictably not receiving the nod from his other master Libanius to succeed him in the role of rhetor as did Chrysostom)⁵¹ responds rigidly to his master's voice in this regard, if we are to judge from what remains of his own Psalms commentary and from the more fully extant work on the Twelve Prophets. Chrysostom will find history not such suitable grist to his moral mill in his διδασκαλεῖον, while Theodoret will learn from predecessors of a different bent that the Psalms can also be taken as a text for understanding the significance of Jesus. For predictable reasons Diodore is reluctant to see Jesus in focus in the Psalms, it being difficult for one interpreting them καθ' ἱστορίαν to see πράγματα realized in his case as far as the New Testament presents them.⁵² Psalm 22, beloved by all the Evangelists for its testimonia of the passion, he cannot allow to be messianic; the resemblance is only superficial.

> Similarities in facts emerged also in the case of Christ the Lord, especially in the passion, such that some commentators thought from this that the psalm is uttered on the part of the Lord. But it is not applicable to the Lord: David is seen to be both mentioning his own sins and attributing the sufferings to the sins.

That presents a problem for a dyophysite Antiochene: the question of suffering can impugn divine impassibility; in the words even of Theodoret (who nevertheless embraces the psalm's messianic dimension), "this is the most baffling thing of all," while not surprisingly Theodore judges those finding any christological application here "guilty of no little rashness." Diodore fails to appreciate the Evangelists' use of Old Testament texts as testimonia, submitting them to his literalistic scrutiny; and so he disputes

---

⁵⁰ Dahood, *Psalms*, 1:279.

⁵¹ The invitation, which we learn of from Sozomen in his *Church History* 8.2 (PG 67:1513), Chrysostom could not accept. For details of Theodore's sometimes servile dependence on Diodore, see Robert C. Hill, "His Master's Voice: Theodore of Mopsuestia on the Psalms," *HeyJ* 45 (2004): 40–53.

⁵² Diodore, and more rigidly Theodore after him, especially in the *Commentary on the Twelve Prophets,* generally set their hermeneutical perspective within the boundaries of the Old Testament. Schäublin would say this position results from the influence of pagan rhetoricians like Aristarchus, who required "Homer to be clarified from Homer" (*Untersuchungen*, 159).

the reference by all of them to vv. 16–17 of that Ps 22, citing in opposition the evidence of John 19:36 and Exod 12:46. "This did not happen in the Lord's case: even if the first clause *They dug my hands and my feet* applies, the second does not, *They numbered all my bones*; we are told they did not break a bone of his, according to Scripture. So the statement, They scrutinized my total capacity and my every action and subjected them to examination, applies to David." Even pupil Theodore will prove able to recognize accommodation for what it is when he meets it.[53] Psalm 45, by contrast, not calling impassibility into question, is wholeheartedly accepted as messianic.

> This psalm seems to refer to the Lord Jesus, not to Solomon, as Jews claim: even if under pressure they transfer most of the content to Solomon for being expressed in human fashion, yet the verse *Your throne, O God, is forever and ever, the rod of your kingship a rod of equity* completely shuts their mouth, since Solomon was not called God and did not reign forever. Instead, Christ alone as God also adopted the human condition for our sake and, being God and king forever, also retained his own status by nature.

The Jewish claim to the psalm—a claim also subjected to literalistic review—helps him retrieve its christological meaning.[54]

A principal reason why Diodore, as leader of the exegetical school of Antioch, is inclined to subordinate the Psalms' spiritual meaning is that he sees allegory involved, an unacceptable alternative. This emerged in his insistence in the preface, we saw, on his fidelity to Paul's way in Galatians of interpreting the story of Hagar and Sarah in Gen 16:15; 21:2, 9 without allegorizing it (Paul would disagree). He likewise reacts badly to interpretation of an obscure phrase "on the eighth" in the title of Ps 6 (a liturgical rubric on which modern commentators differ) as involving

---

[53] Though not so often or so perceptively, Diodore can acknowledge the NT's accommodation of a psalm text, as in the case of Ps 40:6–8 appearing in Heb 10:5–7.

[54] Diodore is thought (with Theodore) to be the object of Theodoret's criticism in his preface to his own *Commentary on the Psalms* (PG 80:860) for an overly Jewish approach—which probably means nonchristological. (For Diodore's nomination, see Guinot, "L'*In Psalmos* de Théodoret: Une relecture critique du commentaire de Diodore de Tarse," *Cahiers de Biblia Patristica* 4 [1993]: 103.) To be sure, Diodore only occasionally balks at some such expression as Ps 9:11, "Sing to the Lord dwelling in Sion," which he paraphrases as "Glorify the Lord who is adored in Sion," and he does not elaborate on the psalmist's strictures against insincere temple worship in Ps 50.

numerology on the part of some commentators, which betokens allegory and is thus anathema to an Antiochene.

> The title of the sixth psalm, "To the end, in hymns, on the eighth. A psalm of David," it is not possible to interpret, nor is there any need to bring to the fore the old wives' tales of the practitioners of allegory. They, in fact, refer mention of "the eighth" to numerology, coming up with ideas as their trade suggests and causing the readers to go grey in the process of wearing themselves out over perfect and imperfect numbers.

In effect, he does in the preface open the way for a typological interpretation, though calling it "discernment," offering an example that has the backing of Heb 11:4; 12:24 (a necessary condition for an Antiochene): "Rejecting (allegory) once and for all, then, we shall not stand in the way of responsibly discerning (ἐπιθεωρεῖν) and bringing ideas to a more elevated sense, such as by comparing Abel and Cain to the synagogue of the Jews and the church, and trying to show that while the synagogue of the Jews is flawed like Cain's sacrifice, the church's gifts are acceptable as were Abel's at that time, when he offered to the Lord the unblemished lamb according to the law."[55] In fact, however, we do not find Diodore practicing typology on any of the psalm texts.[56]

7. Diodore as Spiritual Director

The net result of this tight focus on ἱστορία by the commentator in almost every psalm is that their general applicability—the feature, after all, that makes them a spiritual classic, at least to modern tastes—is reduced, and that Diodore's efficacy as a spiritual director (not to say guru, a role no Antiochene would assume) is considerably undercut. Psalm 25 he will claim—against the evi-

---

[55] Chrysostom likewise feels free to use a typological approach to biblical texts while conscious that his audience would not tolerate an allegorical approach. In his third homily on Isa 6 (SC 277:122) on King Uzziah's effrontery in presuming to arrogate to himself priestly functions, he declines to cite Isa 14:14 (words addressed there to the king of Babylon) to support his presentation of the devil's similar hybris for the reason that "those not happy to accept allegories will reject our testimony," and so has recourse to plain statement from 1 Tim 3:6.

[56] Young, while within her rights to maintain that "'typology' is a modern coinage" (*Biblical Exegesis*, 193), is clearly at odds with the facts to assert that "'typology' is a modern construct. Ancient exegetes did not distinguish between typology and allegory" (152). Chrysostom, we have just seen, knew that his audience appreciated the difference quite well.

dence—to be composed on the part of the exiles; but he soon has to abandon the effort and recognize it as expressing sentiments proper, in the words of Weiser, to "a pensive soul earnest in its piety,"[57] the result being that his commentary degenerates into terse paraphrase. Likewise Ps 32, one of the early church's seven penitential psalms, does not long tolerate commentary from the viewpoint of Hezekiah, and Diodore soon abandons the attempt. Only rarely, as with Ps 37, will he admit of a psalm that "of old it applied to Jews specifically and now to all human beings in common," in which case his commentary proves to be jejune by comparison with Chrysostom's (where extant) and Theodoret's.

The phrase used above of our assessment of Diodore's success as spiritual director—"at least to modern tastes"—ought be kept in mind. If we do not advert to the accent placed on comprehension pure and simple by both Chrysostom and Theodoret as well in their approach to work on the Psalter, we are in danger of applying solely contemporary criteria to an approach of a different age. At first flush, the attitude of Diodore as leader of the *asketerion* to the spiritual dimension of the Psalms strikes us as an anomaly, not only regrettable but culpable;[58] in our view, with our expectations—and probably to readers of another "school" in his time—it impairs his value as a spiritual director. As he rigidly rejected an approach to the biblical text that he called "self-opinionated" and perhaps identified with followers of Origen, so he had no time for the style of spirituality some would class as "mystical"; as Louis Bouyer says, "the mysticism expressed in the forms of thought inherited from Origen proved itself unassimilable," and so Antioch went on to develop an "asceticism without mysticism."[59] In this process Diodore's reaction proved severe, and to his readers within and beyond the *asketerion* it could be thought impoverishing; his Antiochene successors would soften its impact—yet they themselves would not disavow its impersonal stance, obviously finding it appropriate (as we do not). Diodore began, we saw, by claiming the Psalms are not doctrinal but moral in nature, filling that instructive and corrective role the author of the Pastorals recognized in all

---

[57] *Psalms*, 238.

[58] In his *Church History* 6.3 (PG 67:665), Socrates make a point of saying Chrysostom and Theodore came under Diodore's tutelage "in regard to ascetical matters."

[59] *The Spirituality of the New Testament and the Fathers* (trans. Mary Perkins Ryan; London: Burns & Oates, 1963), 449, 446.

Scripture (2 Tim 3:16–17, the text that opens his preface)—though in fact his commentary focuses more on the factual basis to any parenesis, its ἱστορία. He will lecture on the morality of sin, involving the role of γνώμη and free will (προαίρεσις), in commenting on the second half of Ps 19 (conceded by modern commentators to be a separate work). His moral accents are typically Antiochene,[60] stressing the balance between divine grace and human effort in behavior,[61] a balance true also of biblical composition.

But a reader could have gained as much from the didactic Pastorals themselves; the Psalms offer the reader (or worshiper) more—lyrical expression of hope and despair, love and longing, trust and abandonment, sin and forgiveness, suffering and relief—all the stuff of spiritual awareness and growth. Diodore in his time and to his tastes, however, is not willing or not able to give more. Psalms such as 25 ("To you, Lord, I lifted up my soul") and 32 ("Happy are those whose transgressions are forgiven") that express such moving sentiments are generally given short shrift; rare it is for a verse to elicit anything like an insight into intimacy with God, as in comment on Ps 36:9: "He continues, *Because with you is a fountain of life; in your light we shall see light*: thanks to you it is possible for us both to live and to be enlightened unto piety: *In your light* we see you, as if to say, through piety leading to you we experience you." Bishop Theodoret's repeatedly sacramental interpretation of psalm verses is also missing, needless to say. Today we find the psalmists' intimacy neglected by Diodore, while on the other hand appreciating his unwillingness to concede a New Testament eschatology to the psalmists adopted by the bishop of Cyrus and some modern commentators on verses like Pss 21:4 and 27:13.[62] In short, expectations of modern Western readers of the Psalter evidently differ markedly from those in Antioch of Diodore's time.

---

[60] Psalm 51 Diodore denies is, as the title claims, the consequence of David's sin, instead "by and large suiting every person who confesses and asks for lovingkindness." In commentary on it he makes no statement on the fall, on any original sin, or on any impairment of human nature as the result of such sin.

[61] As often happens with the Antiochenes, the balance can at times tip in favor of the human element. Diodore remarks of the good person beatified in Ps 1, "To such a person everything comes simply and easily, God working and cooperating with him"—not vice versa. Cf. my article, "A Pelagian Commentator on the Psalms?" *ITQ* 63 (1998): 263–71.

[62] In regard to his views on eschatology, however, we note that he was not in a position to impart to his pupils an understanding of the OT notion of Sheol, as emerges in commentary on Pss 28; 30; 40; 49. Hence their ignorance of it.

8. The Christology of the *Commentary* and Other Theological Accents

Scholars such as Mariès and Olivier who upheld the attribution of this work to Diodore had to deal with the objection that this "father of Nestorianism" could hardly be responsible for a work betraying such an orthodox Christology, and that it must have been composed in the wake of Chalcedon.[63] Given Diodore's limited hermeneutical perspective, we are not surprised to find him resisting a christological application in the first fifty-one psalms included in Olivier's critical edition. (Psalm 110, which elicited from Chrysostom a diatribe against a rogues' gallery of heretics, prompted a similar response from Diodore; but it lies beyond those pages.) While Rondeau speaks of the "effacement du Christ locuteur chez Diodore,"[64] in the case of Ps 45 we saw him making an exception (if only to resist Jewish claims); when after an assertion of the central figure's royal and even divine status v. 7 reads, "God your God anointed you with the oil of gladness beyond your partners," thus grouping him with other gifted figures, Diodore feels a distinction called for.

> He uses the phrase *beyond your partners* in this way, that while the others who were anointed were anointed with oil of prophecy or priesthood or royalty, he was anointed with the Holy Spirit. Here again he makes mention of the incarnation (οἰκονομία), or how he was able to call the same person God in one case as in the above verse *Your throne, O God, is forever*, and in another case *God your God anointed you*. In the above case, however, he referred to nature; here he introduces the incarnation.

He thus distinguishes between equality in nature and the human condition assumed by Jesus, upholding the two natures while denying subordination (which is all of a piece with other of Diodore's theological positions, we have noted). We find him resisting an Arian subordinationist interpretation also of Ps 2:8.

In a work where the accent falls on interpretation καθ' ἱστορίαν, it is not surprising if christological and trinitarian issues—even if in the air at the time—are not canvassed by the commentator for the

---

[63] Cf. Olivier, *Commentarii*, cv–cvi.
[64] *Les commentaires*, 2:303.

benefit of his students and other readers.⁶⁵ He is clearly as opposed to finding trinitiarian thinking in Old Testament authors as Theodore will be, and it is not with his encouragement that Theodore and Theodoret will find such a reference in Ps 51:11, "Do not remove your holy spirit from me." He is equally reluctant in the case of Ps 30:8: "This expression *I shall cry to you, Lord, and make my petition to my God* Scripture is in the habit of using; such an expression is not an interchange of persons, nor in fact is he speaking of the Lord and God as different, unless one were to suspect that with inspired vision he is hinting at the Father and the Son."

9. Diodore's Achievement in the *Commentary on the Psalms*

It is not for light on current theological debate, then, that we turn to the *Commentary on the Psalms* recently established as authentically Diodore's. Rather, it is for the insight this work uniquely gives us into the approach to Scripture by "le véritable fondateur" of the Antiochene school of exegesis, in the words of its editor. If we regret that Olivier has not been able to complete the task of preparing a critical edition of the whole of this solitary extant work, we are content that these fifty-one psalms elicited from Diodore an illuminating exposition of principles in the preface and an adequate demonstration of their application to the text of the Psalter, throwing ample light on the degree to which his pupils Theodore and John Chrysostom, together with Theodoret, were respectively indebted to him and also succeeded in slipping some of his limitations. The pupils have not left us an introduction to their commentaries in which they may have exposed their exegetical and hermeneutical principles; and in the preface left by the bishop of Cyrus we do not recognize the magisterial figure seen in master Diodore.

It has to be admitted on the basis of this work that he was clearly not a textual critic even of their standard; he was unable to impart to them a knowledge of the language of the Psalms' composition, and seems not to have had available, or troubled to access, a copy of the Hexapla to supplement the shortcomings of his local Antiochene Septuagint text (which, nevertheless, he further illus-

---

⁶⁵ Rowan Greer makes no reference to this work in building a case (against Alois Grillmeier) for Diodore's Christology to be seen as truly Antiochene ("The Antiochene Christology of Diodore of Tarsus," *JTS* NS 17 [1966]: 327–41).

trates) with alternative versions of the Psalter's numerous obscurities—a deficiency his successors will rectify. He left his alumni with the impression that a commentator on the sacred text, even if at one remove from the author's original thought, should feel free and even confident not only to explicate it but also to adjust it if ἀκολουθία suggested the need. Theodoret's response to Pauline teaching on the gratuity of divine grace, which Antioch thought in need of modification, would show how risky this license could be.[66]

It is not so much for the limited exegetical skills that Diodore brings to the task of commentary, however, that this work is significant, but for the hermeneutical convictions that inform it and that will come to be thought typically Antiochene, even if not all exponents of the method will prove rigidly committed to them. If nothing more than his preface to the *Commentary* had survived, we should be grateful for the light it sheds on the Antiochene approach to "the book of the divine Psalms." From the outset his accent is on comprehension—an accent his successors will respect; he is insistent that people "should grasp the movement of thought and sing with understanding" (a phrase we find verbatim in Chrysostom and Theodoret). While this general aim is commendable, if partial, however, Diodore does not come to work on the Psalter without hermeneutical baggage inherited from his predecessors, the "others" to whom he acknowledges a debt in the preface. From them, including doubtless Eustathius, Diodore imbibed an antipathy to that method of interpreting the biblical text that he associated with the term allegory; and admittedly some corrective was required. Yet, to judge from his work on this spiritual classic, that hostile reaction to (Origen's?) alternative hermeneutical method resulted in his being less open to its spiritual dimension, even if notionally upholding the process of θεωρία by which a reader might arrive at it.[67] We saw above that, though sensitive to the psalmists' employment of a range of literary genres (apocalyptic excepted), this master of the *asketerion* in Antioch depressed the spiritual aspirations and sentiments that they were so evidently

---

[66] See my article "Theodoret Wrestling with Romans," *St Patr* 34 (2001): 347–52.

[67] P. Ternant maintains that by θεωρία Antioch meant their scriptural hermeneutic as opposed to Alexandria's ἀλληγορία, which they took as a denial of any factual element in the text at all: "Par θεωρία Antioche entendait signifier se propre position, et par ἀλληγορία celle de l'adversaire" ("La θεωρία d'Antioche dans le cadre de sens de l'Ecriture," 137–40).

voicing—all to keep a tight focus on the ἱστορία of every psalm but a few.

Fortunately, two of his successors in Antioch in practice will not accept this constraint—Theodore the egregious exception—though none of them would ever succeed in depthing the Psalter's pastoral and even mystical content (to use a word anathema to Diodore) to the satisfaction of modern readers. As the work deserved to escape the flames of prejudice on the part of his theological opponents, so we have to admit it exemplifies not only the broad lines but also the real shortcomings of Antioch's spiritual exegesis of the inspired Word. The fact that only his *Commentary on the Psalms* has survived intact of all Diodore's encyclopedic work on the Bible is therefore not an unmixed blessing to modern attempts to retrieve the principles and practice of Antiochene exegetes of the Old Testament; there is danger this *Commentary* could be taken as a paradigm. For their approach to Torah and Former Prophets we are left to read the *Quaestiones* of Theodoret on the Octateuch and on Kingdoms and Chronicles;[68] with nothing of Chrysostom surviving beyond his Genesis homilies and only fragments of Theodore,[69] we find in Theodoret here (unlike the Psalter) a heavy reliance on Diodore's work on this one-third of the Bible that is more congenial to an Antiochene and more responsive to the principles of the

[68] Cf. the critical editions of both works: Natalio Fernández Marcos and Angel Sáenz-Badillos, *Theodoreti Cyrensis Quaestiones in Octateuchum* (Textos y estudios "Cardenal Cisneros" 17; Madrid: Consejo Superior de Investigaciones Cientificas, 1979); Natalio Fernández Marcos and José Ramon Busto Saiz, *Theodoreti Cyrensis Quaestiones in Reges et Paralipomena* (Textos y Estudios "Cardenal Cisneros" 32; Madrid: Consejo Superior de Investigaciones Cientificas, 1984). See also Guinot, *L'Exégèse de Théodoret de Cyr*, 748–97, for the degree of dependence of Theodoret on Diodore in commentary on Torah and Deuteronomist. Devreesse has collected fragments of Diodore's work on Octateuch and Kingdoms from the catenae in *Les anciens commentateurs grecs de l'Octateuque et des Rois* (Studi et Testi 201; Vatican City: Biblioteca Apostolica Vaticana, 1959). The volumes on the Pentateuch in the recent Ancient Christian Commentary on Scripture series under the general editorship of Thomas C. Oden (Downers Grove, Ill.: InterVarsity Press, 2001–) could do with not only acknowledging the variety of Septuagintal forms used by the Greek Fathers they cite, especially in the light of work by Fernández Marcos and others, but also including reference to Diodore of Tarsus in their "Biographical Sketches." There it is instead Theodore who is anomalously listed as "founder of the Antiochene, or literalistic, school of exegesis," Diodore's influential work on the Octateuch, of which fragments survive, escaping citation.

[69] Cf. Devreesse, *Essai sur Théodore de Mopsueste* (Studi e Testi 141; Vatican City: Biblioteca Apostolica Vaticana, 1948), 5–27, for extant fragments of Theodore's work on the Octateuch.

school's founder. If modern readers find that these principles do not measure up to the spiritual riches offered by the psalmists, they should reserve final judgment on their adequacy until they are acquainted also with Antioch's approach to Moses and the Deuteronomist.

Commentary on Psalms 1–51

Preface

"All Scripture is inspired by God," according to blessed Paul, "and useful for teaching, for reproving, for correcting, for training in righteousness." It teaches what is good, reproves sins, corrects omissions, and thus brings a person to perfection; in fact, he goes on to say, "so that the person who belongs to God may be ready, prepared for every good work."[1] You would not be wrong to infer that this general commendation of the divine Scripture applies to the book of the divine Psalms. After all, it gives gentle and kindly instruction in righteousness to those willing to learn, reproves willful people in a caring manner and without harshness, and corrects whatever chance failings befall us when our choices are awry.

We do not appreciate this when we sing the psalms, however, so much as when we find ourselves in the very affairs on account of which we are brought to feel the need of the psalms. So while any people who have recourse only to the thanksgiving psalms on account of life's joys are most fortunate, nevertheless since it is not possible for us, being human, to avoid experiencing difficulties and encountering necessities, which befall us from without and also from within our own selves, our souls recognize in the psalms a most helpful remedy, finding in them an apt basis for the conversations they are wont to have with God. The Holy Spirit, who guides all human affairs, gives voice through most blessed David to his own response to our sufferings so that through it the sufferers may be cured. It happens this way, at any rate, when initially we hastily undertake the singing of the psalms casually and apply ourselves to them superficially, but on encountering problems and troubles we then come to our senses and apply ourselves when our wound itself almost of its nature elicits the proper response, (4)[2] and the remedy is adopted in turn and overcomes the precise ailment.

This biblical text—I mean the Psalms—being so indispensable, therefore, I thought it right to publish, just as I also in my own case

---

[1] 2 Tim 3:16–17, the Koine text reading "prepared" in place of "equipped."
[2] For ease of reference, we have inserted into the text the page numbers of the Olivier edition.

had received from others, a precise outline of its contents, the genres befitting the psalms, and a commentary on the text, in case the brethren at the time of singing the psalms be likely to be confused by the sentiments, or by failing to understand them give their minds to other pursuits. Instead, they should grasp the movement of thought and "sing with understanding," as the text says,[3] from the depths of their mind and not superficially and at the level of lips alone.

The overall theme of the psalms, then, is divided into these two parts, the moral and the doctrinal. The moral part is itself divided: certain psalms correct individual behavior, some dealing with the race of the Jews alone, others with people in general; the individual commentaries will make clear which these are. Likewise in the individual commentaries the doctrinal content is divided into two: some psalms are addressed to those who believe things came into being of themselves, other ones to those claiming these things do not fall under providence. While the person who teaches that they exist of themselves also logically interprets them as not falling under providence, the one who denies providence does not necessarily claim also that they came into being of themselves; instead, they admit there is a creator of everything, of whatever kind they admit, but make no allowance at all for a providence of his or of any kind, or restrict it to heavenly affairs. To people under this impression the psalms supply proof that things have the same person as both God and Creator, and that his providence reaches even to most insignificant things, nothing being without a share in what is brought into existence by him and in providence for the future. After all, it is unlikely that God would be capable of creating insignificant and lowly things, on the one hand, and on the other take no interest in providing for (5) trifling things and neglect them, since he had not deemed it unworthy to be their creator on account of his exalted station. The person reading my individual commentaries will therefore recognize these psalms.

There is also another theme in the psalms, the Babylonian captivity; there is a group on that subject as well, or rather many groups. Some psalms are composed from the viewpoint of those about to go off into captivity, others of those actually there, others on the part of those hoping to return, others of those already returned.

---

[3] Ps 47:7 (in the numbering of the Hebrew and of modern versions, followed also in the text below); cf. 1 Cor 14:15.

There are also other psalms recounting events in the past, where the author recounts the happenings in Egypt and in the desert for the benefit of those coming later.

There are also Maccabean psalms: some of them are composed specifically from the precise viewpoint of Onias or someone similar, others from the general viewpoint of those Israelites still suffering persecution. There are others specifically applicable to Jeremiah and Hezekiah. These also belong to the prophetic genre: some mention disasters due to occur to the nation on account of the multitude of sins, others unprecedented marvels following on the disasters. They were all composed in different styles to match the different kinds of coming events, with the Holy Spirit providing remedies ahead of time for the afflicted.

There is danger, however, that we may cause those eager to catch a glimpse of the detailed commentary on the psalms themselves to have qualms by being occupied with the diversity of their content. (6) Be this as it may, attention must be paid to the actual text of the psalms, remembering only this fact (which you are aware of, brethren) that all inspired genres are divided into three—future, present, and past. There is, on the one hand, the inspired composition of Moses, who recounts events in Adam's time and later ages, while on the other there is the discovery of what is hidden, as happened in the case of Peter's detecting the theft by Ananias and Sapphira.[4] Prophecy, strictly speaking, however, forecasts the future, and perhaps many generations later; for instance, the prophets mentioned the coming of Christ, and the apostles the nations' response in faith and the Jews' rejection.

One must therefore begin from the outset by using the order found in the actual book of Psalms, not the order of the events themselves; the psalms do not occur in order, instead each occurring as it was found. This is demonstrated in many of the psalms, especially from what is inscribed as a title to the third psalm, "A psalm of David, when he fled from his son Absalom," and in the title to the one hundred and forty-fourth psalm, "A song to Goliath." Now, who does not know how more ancient is the story of Goliath than that of Absalom?[5] The psalms have incurred this problem from the book's being lost in the Babylonian captivity and found later in the time of Ezra, not however as a whole book but scattered in ones and

---

[4] Cf. Acts 5:1–11.
[5] Diodore treats this question of the compilation of the Psalter into its present form on the basis of the apocryphal 2 Esdr 14.

twos and perhaps also threes, and being assembled as they were found, not as originally recited. Hence the titles, too, are in most cases faulty, the compilers of the psalms mostly guessing at their intention and not citing them out of close knowledge. (7)

Nonetheless, as far as possible we shall with God's grace give a commentary also on the erroneous parts without avoiding the actual reality; instead, we shall treat of it historically and literally and not stand in the way of a spiritual and more elevated insight. The historical sense, in fact, is not in opposition to the more elevated sense; on the contrary, it proves to be the basis and foundation of the more elevated meanings. One thing alone is to be guarded against, however, never to let the discernment process be seen as an overthrow of the underlying sense, since this would no longer be discernment but allegory: what is arrived at in defiance of the content is not discernment but allegory. The apostle, in fact, never overturned the historical sense by introducing discernment despite calling discernment allegory,[6] not through ignorance of the terms but to emphasize that, even if the name allegory is chosen for the ideas, the meaning gained through discernment should never be at the expense of what is by nature historical. Self-opinionated innovators in commenting on the divine Scripture, by contrast, who undermine and do violence to the historical sense, introduce allegory, not in the apostle's sense, but for their own vainglory making the readers substitute one thing for another—for example, by taking abyss as demons, a dragon as the devil, and the like (not to add folly to folly).

Rejecting that once and for all, then, we shall not stand in the way of responsibly discerning and bringing ideas to a more elevated sense, such as by comparing Abel and Cain to the synagogue of the Jews and the church, and trying to show that while the synagogue of the Jews is flawed (8) like Cain's sacrifice, the church's gifts are acceptable as were Abel's at that time, when he offered to the Lord the unblemished lamb according to the law.[7] You see, far from nullifying the historical sense or disqualifying discernment, it is middle ground and the fruit of experience, in keeping with the historical

---

[6] Diodore seems to be referring to Paul's use of (what he at least calls) allegory in Gal 4:22–5:1, which the commentator seems to say is rather an instance of θεωρία, which properly does not erode the historical value of Hagar and Sarah in Gen 16:15; 21:2, 9—something that occurs with allegory, he claims.

[7] Diodore feels encouraged to adopt this interpretation of the Gen 4 rivalry with some (implicit) encouragement from the author of Heb 11:4; 12:24.

and the fuller sense; it rids us of pagan habits of saying one thing and meaning another and introducing absurdities, while not drawing us to Judaism and suffocating us by forcing us to settle for the literal sense alone and attending only to it, but allowing us to proceed further to a more elevated understanding.

In short, the person about to read the commentary on the divine psalms ought be aware of this.

Psalm 1

The first psalm, then, is both moral and general in scope, instructing not any particular person but people in general. Now, if it mentions *law* (v. 2), it does not oblige us to think only of the written law but of the innate natural law, which is not coercive, as the Manichees say, but instructing the person prepared to learn. So do not allow the identity in terms to give rise to misunderstanding: law that is natural and linked to nature is referred to, which is not temporary, like a person's having a sense of humor, having two feet, going grey in old age. It is implanted in all people and in every individual person; it is not temporary or subject to alteration, being also called a natural law because by it we can learn and distinguish what is for the better, like knowing that God exists, that it is good to respect parents and not to harm others. It is nature, in fact, that teaches each person this as if giving orders not to do to another what one would not want to suffer from someone else. (9) So when you read *And on his law he will meditate day and night* (v. 2), it is clear that he means this law by which we distinguish what is bad and what is good. Even if he employs the term involving similarity of name, no harm is done to the thought, since the person meditating on the one law or the other is definitely acting properly.

Blessed the man who did not walk in the counsel of the ungodly (v. 1), that is, the one who was not involved in ungodly purposes. Ungodly purposes mean thinking there is no God or forming the impression that, while he exists, he exercises no providence for what exists. *And did not take his place in the way of sinners*, such as someone who did not commit the sins people do or, if sinning, did not persist in it but swiftly extricated himself (by *way* referring to behavior, like the verse, "Blessed the blameless in the way," that is, in behavior).[1] *Or rest on the seat of the corrupt.* By *corrupt* he refers

---
[1] Ps 119:1.

not only to sinners themselves but also to those involving others in similar behavior. So he blesses the person who shuns the company of such people; "evil associations corrupt good behavior," according to the apostle.[2] *Or rest on the seat of the corrupt*: having directed us away from bad behavior, he leads us toward better.

In fact, he proceeds, (10) *But his choice is for the law of the Lord* (v. 2), the word *choice* meaning interest, concern, attention. *And on his law he will meditate day and night*, as if to say, always. So he is saying, Blessed is the one who does not follow the godless, who hates sins, who shuns *the corrupt* and devotes himself to meditating on the divine law and always persists in fruitful meditation. What such a person is like, in fact, he goes on to explain. *He will be like the tree planted by the water channels, which will produce its fruit in due season, and its leaf will not fall* (v. 3): as the tree close to water is seen to be fruitful in due season on account of constant irrigation and continues to appeal by the beauty of its foliage, so too will be the person who gives his mind to meditation on good things like irrigation, and from it he can constantly bear good fruit. *Whatever he does will prosper*. He moved from the figure to the reality: taking a tree as an example, he moved to the archetype itself—I mean the person—saying, To such a person everything comes simply and easily, God working and cooperating with him.

While this is the way such people are, he is saying, what of the godless and sinners? *Not so are the ungodly, not so. Instead, they are like dust, which the wind sweeps from the face of the earth* (v. 4): just as (11) in reference to the righteous he mentioned stability and permanence, so in the case of the ungodly evanescence and instability, dust being affected by the swirling of the winds and having no position of its own. So what is the result? *For this reason the ungodly will not have a place to stand in judgment, nor sinners in the council of the righteous* (v. 5). He represented the ungodly as self-condemned, with no possibility of their catching sight of the court where there is perhaps the possibility of gaining pity as a result of the judge's great indulgence. So he is saying, Neither will the ungodly see the judge nor will sinners take part in the assembly of the righteous. *Because the Lord knows the way of the righteous* (v. 6). By *Because he knows* he referred not to knowledge but to relationship and care, as if to say, God in fact makes his own the doings of the righteous.

---

[2] 1 Cor 15:33, Diodore not adverting to the proverb's being borrowed by Paul from the pagan Menander.

And the way of the ungodly will perish: the pursuits of the ungodly will be consigned to ruin along with those responsible for them.

This first psalm, then, is moral, and is of benefit to everyone prepared to give themselves to meditation on the good.

Psalm 2

The second psalm is a prophecy to do with the Lord. He mentions in the first verses the groundless frenzy of the Jews against him, (12) and the fact that they would betray him to Herod and Pilate, and that the Lord would come to no harm from it.[1] On the contrary, it would even redound to his glory; he would save those believing in him and crush the unbelieving with his powerful rule (referring to this as *an iron rod*). The author therefore begins as though inveighing bitterly in these words, *For what purpose did nations rage, and peoples form empty plots?* (v. 1), that is, what was the cause, or what grounds did they have for such awful hatred? *Rage* means precisely the neighing that horses make when also pawing the ground, even without anyone's intervening to irritate them, instead their own brutish character prompting them to hostility and an attack on any undeserving person. So *why did nations rage and peoples form empty plots?* By *nations and peoples* he means either the Israelites themselves or those of Herod's company in being Gentiles, and by *peoples* the Jews. *Empty* was a nice addition: such a performance brought them no result.

There is a clearer reference in what follows to Herod and Pilate. *The kings of the earth presented themselves, and the rulers came together in concert* (v. 2). The term *presented themselves* means, They set themselves to this, as Paul also says, "Present your bodies (13) as a living sacrifice, holy and pleasing,"[2] that is, set aside your bodies. *Against the Lord and against his Christ.* Here he brought out that the one who acts lawlessly against Christ and against the Lord commits no less a sin against his Father as well. So what was their claim in their all colluding? The meaning is given here with an ellipse of the word "saying," as often happens in Scripture, as we shall proceed to demonstrate. He goes on, *Let us break their bonds, and thrust away*

---

[1] Diodore opts for a christological interpretation on the basis of the quotation of vv. 1–2 by the Jerusalem community at the release of Peter and John from detention (Acts 4:23–31).
[2] Rom 12:1.

from us their yoke (v. 3). He took "saying" not as being said but as occurring in fact, just as also in Jeremiah God said at some time in reproaching the Israelites, "You said, I shall not serve you,"[3] meaning, You lived in such a way as to wish to shake off your service of me. So he takes "said" for granted, meaning, They all conspired as if saying in their mind *Let us break their bonds* and so on.

So much for them: what of the Lord God? *He who dwells in heaven will ridicule them, and the Lord will sneer at them* (v. 4): but the one who is superior to the schemers will render their scheme ridiculous (*sneering* being a release of breath through the nostrils for setting at nought people who are raging to excess). Not only will he reduce their affairs to ridicule and reproach, he is saying, but they will also experience the most intense wrath on his part. He goes on, in fact, (14) *Then he will speak to them in his wrath, and in his anger he will confound them* (v. 5). Once again *Then he will speak* has reference to action in the sense that he will cause them to have the experience of the wrath and anger of those confounding and disturbing them. What of the Lord? *But I have been established as king by him on Sion his holy mountain* (v. 6): then the victim will say to those responsible for the action, Whatever you do and whatever your frenzy, a king has been appointed, who gives evidence of the beginning of his reign from Sion, and announces to all the will of God. In fact, he proceeds to say, *Announcing the Lord's decree. The Lord said to me, You are my son, today I have begotten you* (v. 7). Once again here he used the word *said* of events in the sense, The Father's nature made me a son: it was not that a decree transferred the dignity of sonship to me, but his being itself imprinted on me a stamp of the person of the Father.[4] Now, the word *today* refers to the present time in terms of human affairs; but what is present to us implies something further, conveying both future and past. With God, on the other hand, where time is not a factor, the three meanings are taken together, namely, present, future, and past. So he means that in his case *today* and eternity are identical and not to be distinguished.

Ask it of me, and I shall give you the nations for your inheritance and the ends of the earth as your possession (v. 8). The presentation (15) is as follows: the phrase *Ask and I shall give you* means, You can obtain the inheritance of all things by nature. To whom does he say *Ask*? The Arians claim it is the Son. When did he say this to him,

---

[3] Jer 2:20.
[4] A phrase Diodore takes from Heb 1:3.

after the creation of the world or before the making of all that exists? I mean, if before creation, how could he ask for what did not exist? and how did the Father hand over to him lordship of nations when it was not available? The claim is ridiculous. If, on the other hand, it was after creation that he said it to him, and clearly all that exists are creatures and products of the Son, how did the Son not have lordship of them when he was by nature lord of their making and creator? But as I said, the presentation deals with the Lord's incarnation: all that is said of him regarding the descent touches on the incarnation and the divine plan, not his existence from the beginning or his lordship.

You will tend them with an iron rod (v. 9). By *iron rod* he refers to a strong and effortless rule. *You will smash them like pottery.* He did well to contrast the weakness of the adversaries with the strong rule, by earthen *pottery* referring to the Jews, on the one hand, and on the other by *iron* to the reign of the one crucified by them. What the iron rod does to the earthen pots is clear and is seen happening in the case of Jews: while they had hope of reshaping, they were referred to as clay, as in Jeremiah when the clay fell (16) from the hand of the potter, God took what had fallen and reshaped it on the basis of his skill, and went on to say, "Surely I can reshape you like this potter?"[5] But when they were later baked hard in the wrong shape and from clay turned into pots, he threatens them with being smashed beyond repair. So what follows?

The author now recommends to everyone what is to their advantage in the words, *Kings, now take heed; be instructed, all who judge the earth* (v. 10): so learn, everyone of any prominence throughout the earth, what God has decreed. To do what? *Serve the Lord with fear, and rejoice in him with trembling* (v. 11): submit to him, serving with joy, happy in the rightness of your submission. *Take advantage of instruction in case the Lord should be angry and you fall from the right path* (v. 12): embrace sound teaching and do not forsake such reasonable behavior. *Since his wrath is enkindled in a flash, blessed are all who trust in him*: wrath is destined to take possession of all the transgressors, while you will then appreciate my advice when wrath overtakes human affairs whereas you are proof against this experience by taking the initiative to hope in the savior. (17)

---

[5] Jer 18:6.

Such, then, is the second psalm. Now, you ought to realize that in the Hebrew the first and second psalms are not divided, being combined into one.[6] The number of one hundred and fifty, however, is preserved in the ninth: the ninth psalm is divided by it into two, whereas in our text it is kept as one whole one. So the division there compensates for the combination here to give the right number.

Psalm 3

The third psalm has an appropriate title arising from the theme to do with Absalom, at the time when it was not only Absalom who rebelled against his father, but on his account all with allegiance to Absalom and hostility to David. After all, it was not possible that in such a long period of rule he would not at some time have people hostile and envious. Hence he begins the psalm in this fashion. *Lord, why have those who oppress me become so numerous?* (v. 1): hostility to me comes not from one but from many. *Many rise up against me.* And what is worse, *Many say to my soul, For him salvation does not lie with his God* (v. 2): hostility on their part is not so hard for me to bear as their insinuation of the cause; they reason that I am not being helped by you as usual. *But you, Lord, are my defense, my glory, you lift up my head* (v. 3): but you, Lord, faithful to yourself, are supporting me where I fall and glorifying me when I am unjustly maligned by them. *My head* means beginning and kingship: Hebrew uses the one word for beginning and head; you can see this more clearly in the book of the creation of the world, where the Seventy said, "In the beginning God made heaven and earth," whereas Aquila said, "At the top God made heaven and earth."[1]

From this point the psalm continues in sequence, *I cried aloud*

---

[6] It is not the case with our Hebrew Bible (contary to the opinion of Olivier, *Commentarii*, xcvii) that a wisdom psalm and a royal psalm are combined into one. Where did Diodore, who did not know Hebrew, find it so? He does not seem to be consulting a copy of the Hexapla, we noted; nor is he aware of how Hebrew and LXX also differ in their division of Pss 114–116, 147.

[1] Diodore, of course, is referring to the opening of Genesis, which he calls Κοσμοποιία, and Theodore will call Κτίσις. He is right in saying that the Hebrew term in the psalm verse, *ro'sh*, can mean head and beginning; but he is perhaps unaware that the term in Gen 1 that Aquila (the first of the alternative translations cited)—mistakenly—renders as "head" is *re'shith*, which has the latter meaning. (Modern scholars, however, suggest Gen 1:1 should rather read, "When God . . .")

to the Lord, and he gave ear to me from his holy mountain (v. 4). Διάψαλμα. One tense replaces another in the verses, and this is found in many places in the psalms; the meaning is, in fact, Lord, support me and glorify me and so on, and when I cry to you, hearken to me (using the past for the future). It is also necessary to indicate the difference between the term διάψαλμα (19) and the song of the διάψαλμα, or in short what their meaning is. While διάψαλμα means a change of tune and alteration of rhythm, then, and not a shift in thought, as some commentators believed, so does song of the διάψαλμα, since frequently singers changed the tunes according to the availability of instruments. So it indicates alternation in styles and rhythms, not change in ideas. It is, in fact, ridiculous to mention anything else, though some commentators have come up with extraordinary notions, like the Spirit coming upon the author at one time and withdrawing at another, which did not happen—perish the thought.[2] I mean, the Holy Spirit did not grant the authors the grace of addressing the text in the manner the demons do to those unaware of what they are saying; rather, he implanted in their mind complete understanding, and on receiving this knowledge they gave voice to it to the extent of their capability, not uttering what they did not understand in the manner of the seers, but having complete knowledge of the force of their words.

As I said, therefore, the occurrences of διάψαλμα and the songs of διάψαλμα are changes in rhythms and styles, not alterations in ideas. The movement of thought also reveals this: after the reference διάψαλμα you never find the following thought in opposition to what precedes, being instead sequential and consistent. Hence it is clear that the occurrence midstream of διάψαλμα involved no interruption to the thought of the text, instead perhaps altering the rhythm in keeping with the norms of music and rhythm applying at the time.

Let us, however, see what follows in the psalm. *I lay down and slept; I awoke because the Lord will defend me* (v. 5). The sequence (20) is logical here as well, although the tense is likewise changed, the meaning being, Even if in the meantime I was humbled (*sleep* here meaning humbling), yet on your part support me and awaken me. If it happens, what will be the result? *I shall not fear countless number of people assailing me all about* (v. 6). Since he had said at the beginning *Why have those who oppress me become so numerous?* he

---

[2] This was the view of Eusebius.

went on to say, Continue, Lord, to care for me as usual, and *I shall not fear* even *countless numbers* rising up and surrounding me.

Arise, Lord, save me, my God (v. 7): so do this, Lord. *Because you have smitten all those who hate me without cause.* Again the tense is changed, the meaning being, Strike all who hate me without reason. *You broke the teeth of sinners*, that is, break the power of those who sin against me (*teeth* here meaning power and force). *Salvation belongs to the Lord, and your blessing on your people* (v. 8): it is clear that salvation lies within your power—not only mine but also that of all your people. (21)

Psalm 4

The fourth psalm is a rebuke of those presuming that created things are beyond providence, blessed David supplying a proof from his own situation and that of people in general. He cites his own person, in fact, as righteous and blameless so as to present all who are likewise without blame enjoying as much as he is seen to receive in his own case, and to conclude from this that it is due to their own sin that people not so blessed do not participate in it to the same extent as they. In other words, it is the greatest form of providence that all alike—sinful and righteous—are not granted the identical lot; instead, each benefits from God's oversight according to individual merit, especially since everyone's enjoying the same goods equally would be an effect no longer of providence but of confusion and lack of discrimination.

So much, then, for consideration of his own case; from that of people in general in turn he says that from the beginning he established human nature in a condition of need, not of self-sufficiency; he made it not independent in existence but needing a supply of nourishment from without, which both holds the living being together and brings it to being, depending on the creator's decision. So he selected the more basic items of human nourishment and cited them as God's generous provision to everyone—namely, grain, wine, and oil—and tries to show that it was a mark of the greatest providence to supply those in need with what is required for sufficiency and continuance. The detailed commentary will make all this clearer. (22)

Now, this psalm bears a title, "To the end, with hymns. A psalm as a song of David." Remember my saying at the beginning that in placing the psalm titles they guessed at their content, getting some right, others wrong. So in this case they seem to have been right, in my view, in referring to this psalm which includes a treatment of providence as a hymn: it is truly a hymn of praise to God to express the belief that all people fall under God's supervision and their affairs come under providence from him. The divine Scripture does not usually use introductions: the skill of the orators introduced them individually so as to give a supplementary report of what was about to be said; but on coming across the above device, the divine Scripture began the same practice.

Hence, here as well, as though dealing with adversaries, right from the first verse he responds in the words, *The God of my righteousness hearkened to me when I called upon him* (v. 1). As though some adversaries were claiming that what is done here below is of no interest to God, and he does not hearken to those who call upon him, accordingly he at once claims in his turn, as though refuting them, Often when I called upon him he hearkened to me—and hearkened to me when my request was right. By *my righteousness* he refers not to his life but to his request, suggesting that to those who make right requests he is found responding promptly. Sometimes, on the other hand, he does not hearken to people when they are themselves responsible for not being heard (23) on account of not making a right or beneficial request. He cites his own case here to include all who have such an attitude—I mean righteous and blameless—and then in his wish to show what a right request it is: passing over many others, he classes all right requests under this one.

What in fact does he go on to say? *In tribulation you gave me space.* There are therefore two forms of tribulation: we either inflict tribulations and sufferings on ourselves as a result of mismanagement, or we fall foul of them despite our best intentions. The former tribulation requires us to show endurance and patience, the sufferers being aware that there is nothing harmful in what comes from God, and it is they themselves who reap the thorns they personally sow. The righteous request, by contrast, is a case of the latter tribulation of which we fall foul despite our best intentions, when as often happens we are the victim of brigands, we suffer shipwreck, or we come close to death by illness, in all of which cases the righteous request brings joy. It is in regard to them that David confirms that often when he was involved involuntarily in distress and begged God's assistance, he was not only rescued but even was vouchsafed more generous providence—the sense of *given space*, since though tribulation constricts and depresses the soul, relief and joy expand and elate it. The reversal, too, is good: whereas in the first verse he addresses his adversaries, in the second he makes a change and converses with God, bringing out that he is not lying in what he says; he would not have spoken with confidence to the God who knows everything. He then goes on, *Have mercy on me and hearken to my prayer.* The tense is changed here again, his meaning being, You had mercy on me and heard my prayer; (24) you pitied my falling into involuntary tribulations and helped me.

After addressing this to God, he turns his attention once more to stupid people in the words, *Mortals that you are, how long will you be slow of heart? Why do you love futility and search for deceit?* (v. 2): since God readily assists and helps those making a righteous petition, why are you slow and hard of heart like iron or stone, willingly involving yourselves in futility and deceit? Their *deceit*, in fact, was in claiming God does not exercise providence, and their *futile* thinking was the conviction that the judge does not exercise surveillance. This thought constantly overtakes sinners: they think they will not pay the penalty, rejecting the judge's role along with his providence. This is not so, however, he is saying, not so; you will come to the opposite conviction. Namely? *Know that the Lord has made his holy one an object of wonder* (v. 3): that over those dedicated to him (the sense of *holy ones*) God exercises supervision, makes them glorious, and causes them to be an object of wonder. *The Lord will hearken to me in my cry to him*: and so it is possible for any such person to cry aloud with confidence, because God hearkens to me when I call on him.

Having to this point delivered a sufficient rebuke and taught that God exercises providence and surveillance over what exists, on the one hand, and on the other he makes himself accessible to those making righteous requests and turns from those bent on lawlessness, he removes further opposition between these groups by exhorting them in the words, *Are you angry? Do not sin* (v. 4). He says *Are you angry?* as a question: If you are angry, (25) he is saying, put up with it, but by your anger do not make things worse. In fact, with their claiming, We are reduced to anger at the things that happen when we see life's inequities, and we adopt this attitude in anger, David exhorts them in the words, When you are angry, do not sin further by thinking providence does not occur; instead, realize that much of what happens surpasses your understanding, and it is better to submit to the one who is both aware and capable of everything. After all, if we allow surgeons to burn and cut the sick person on account of their skill, and do not get upset at their art despite the pain of the operation, how much more so, when we fall foul of more grievous and trying events which God like a skillful surgeon either applies to us or allows, like burning or the knife, do we not submit to such great skill by convincing ourselves that he does everything for our benefit, especially since nothing but good was likely to happen? So *Are you angry?* he asks; *do not sin.*

How so? Give the remedy also for this, blessed author. *Repent in bed for what you say in your heart*: even if you entertain such resolves while your anger is in control, repent and entertain different ideas when you are granted respite (the meaning of *bed*) and your thoughts are at rest, anger no longer causing them to be restive. (26) *Offer the sacrifice of righteousness, and put your hope in the Lord* (v. 5): even if you are so disposed in respect of offenses already committed, offer hope in him for the future as a sacrifice of righteousness to him. *Sacrifice of righteousness* was well said, since whereas the former thoughts were unjust, the latter replaced them with righteousness and recommended hope in the one who knows everything.

Again in the next verse he introduces another juxtaposition of theirs. *Many say, Who will show us good things?* (v. 6): while some with such thoughts in mind from anger will have adequate healing in repentance, therefore, others who are not angry and who require a more reasonable proof and desire to be independent of providence, as it were, say to us, Display the actual good effects of providence and parade them before our eyes. Hence he goes on, *The light of your countenance, Lord, has left its mark on us.* He did well to say *has left its mark on us*: tokens of your providence in us are visible to those who perceive them properly—and perhaps even to those who do not perceive them properly if we appreciate that it is not possible to live without signs of your providence. Of what kind are these? *You have brought joy to my heart. They grew prosperous from the fruit of their grain, wine, and oil* (v. 8): the forms of your providence are inscribed and indelibly etched, as it were, on each person's heart; after all, who is the provider and who the supplier of what is needed from without for life? (27) In fact, perhaps it was for this reason also that you put us in a state of need, so that we might not forget the provider of what we need and receive. After all, you were capable firstly of making us feel no need, and then of giving us some nourishment sufficient for several days; you were not prepared to do this, however, causing us instead to look for it each day so that you might have the opportunity for supply, and those receiving it daily might not forget you as the giver. So who will set at nought, he asks, the manifest signs of your providence, or prove totally unmindful of it?

To me, on the other hand, Lord, grant peace of mind, feeling no confusion or imagining what is marked by your providence to be devoid of it. He goes on, in fact, *In peace I shall lie down and in the same instant go to sleep* (v. 8): so let it be my good fortune to enjoy peace, respite, and rest in these righteous thoughts. *Because you alone, Lord, have given me grounds for hope*: grant me with this hope alone to endure and to abide in this frame of mind, this being of benefit and great value to those so inclined.

Psalm 5

The title to the fifth psalm reads, "To the end, for the woman receiving an inheritance. A psalm for David." Some commentators believe from this that the psalm was composed from the point of view of the church, especially as it mentions the rejection of some people and their replacement by others, in the words, *A man of blood the Lord abhors, whereas I in the abundance of your mercy shall enter your house, I shall bow down toward your holy temple* (28) *in awe of you* (vv. 6–7). Let them take it thus if it is their pleasure to think that way, and console themselves if they have no interest in accepting the factual indications. It always behooves the historical commentator, however, to give nothing priority over the facts and not to hinder those wanting to give encouragement from such things. Declining to take the psalm to suit those desiring to interpret it as they wish, I for my part shall conduct the commentary historically, as I also learned to do, with the text undergoing no violence at our hands, in my view, unlike the way of those who elsewhere misrepresent its theme.

So the actual commentary is based on history, the psalm dealing with Babylon; I remarked at the beginning, remember, that there are different occasions for which the Babylonian psalms were composed. In this case, then, he speaks from the viewpoint of the people in captivity, deriving benefit from the misfortunes, asking to return and occupy their own lands, and promising to reform in the future and no longer give attention to idols, and instead to give undivided attention to the temple and to acknowledge that while vice was responsible for the captivity, virtue and repentance were responsible for the return and the reform.

Hence he begins this way, *Give ear to my words, Lord, understand my cry. Attend to the sound of my prayer* (vv. 1–2). He says the same thing three times; the repetition is the mark of someone ardently concerned for their request, people very desirous of something often having no qualms about repeating themselves. *My king and my God. Because I shall pray to you, Lord.* This comes from people already showing benefit and promising further improvement: I shall no longer be devout to the idols, he is saying; I know that you are my king and my God, and I shall not address my petitions to anyone else. (29) *In the morning you will hear my voice, in the morning I shall plead my case to you and you will take note of me* (v. 3). By *in the morning* Scripture normally refers to promptness. So he means, You will promptly hearken to me and make me plead my case to you in the temple in Jerusalem in your sight. You see, since he acknowledged the true God, he naturally went on to say that such a God would both hearken and provide rapid support, not being deaf and dumb like the idols, capable only of a tardy consolation of the petitioners, or rather none at all. It therefore belongs to the true God also to lend help to those who rightly want justice done.

Hence he goes on, *Because you are not a God who wills wickedness. The evildoer will not dwell with you, nor the lawless abide before your eyes* (vv. 4–5): righteous as you are, you cannot bring yourself to see anything wrong or put up with the transgressor; instead, such people you keep at a distance. It is, in fact, characteristic of the living God who is provident for human affairs not to be in ignorance of those in trouble who are perishing and wasting as a result of their own wickedness. Hence he goes on, *You hated all the workers of iniquity, you will destroy all the speakers of falsehood. A man of blood and deceit the Lord loathes* (vv. 6–7): extremely hateful to you are the lawless, the dishonest, the bloodthirsty, and the deceitful.

But I, in the abundance of your mercy, shall enter your house, I shall bow down toward your holy temple in awe of you (v. 7); so since I am (30) now rid of such an attitude—I was brought to my senses by my sufferings—it would be right to be granted help and recover your holy temple, on the one hand, and on the other to worship there so that justice may prevail. After all, if you keep transgressors at a distance, you will also welcome without question those who have reformed. This, in fact, is the reason why he invokes God's righteousness at this point in the words, *Lord, guide me in your righteousness* (v. 8): so exercise your righteousness and guide me to the city and the holy temple for two reasons: for your righteousness, and secondly on account of the taunts of the foe, who believe that we do not enjoy providence and that it is offered equally to those breaking your law and to those who practice virtue.

Hence he proceeds, *Because of my enemies direct my path before you. There is no truth in their mouths, their heart is frivolous* (vv. 8–9).[1] Why do the enemy behave this way? Because what they intend and say is frivolous, he is saying. What kinds of things? Listen. *Their throat is an open grave, they deceive with their tongues*: their speech is rather of bloodshed, and they bring most severe punishment on themselves in the belief that you exercise no providence over human affairs, and there is no judge of what is done and said by individuals. Hence he goes on, (31) *Condemn them, O God* (v. 10). It should also be understood (this is a good place to mention it) that when he uses the verb in the sense of condemnation, he uses the accusative, as you will find throughout Scripture without exception. *Let them come to grief through their own plotting*: let those believing you are not a judge fall victim to such awful folly. *By the measure of their own impieties drive them out, because they have provoked you, Lord*: just as those with such ideas are guilty of impiety, treat them accordingly, Lord; those who believe you are not a just judge provoke you in no small way.

Let all who hope in you rejoice (v. 11): just as those people rightly pay the penalty for their wrongful desires, so on being reformed we deserve to experience the opposite, joy and happiness and justified boasting. He goes on in fact, *They will exult forever, and you will dwell in them*, that is, you will abide with them (meaning the city of Jerusalem, by God's good pleasure). *Because you will bless the righteous* (v. 12). By *the righteous* here he refers to the people by comparison with the people of Babylon, since they hoped in God, (32) whereas the others thought God does not have an eye to human affairs. He also supplies a conclusion: *Lord, you crowned us as with a shield of approval.* The phrase *You crowned us* stands for Crown us, one tense taking the place of the other here. So he is saying, Crown us, encircle and surround us with your approval and lovingkindness as with a shield.

---

[1] Where the final clause in v. 8 reads "my path," other forms of the LXX read "your path," like our Hebrew.

Psalm 6

The title of the sixth psalm, "To the end, in hymns, on the eighth. A psalm of David," it is not possible to interpret, nor is there any need to bring to the fore the old wives' tales of the practitioners of allegory.[1] They, in fact, refer mention of "the eighth" to numerology, coming up with ideas as their trade suggests and causing the readers to go grey in the process of wearing themselves out over perfect and imperfect numbers. This not being the way to go, then, people with a more sober idea of "the eighth" claim instead it is the Lord's day since the eighth day is the same as the first. If this were the case, however, I still cannot understand why the psalm does not keep to hymns, but instead involves confession and declaration of sin and is a petition for freedom from current misfortune, even though the title says "in hymns, a psalm of David."

For this reason, then, we leave the whole title to those prepared to guess at it, and outline the psalm's real theme, which is as follows. Some psalm genres were recited by blessed David (33) on the sin with Bathsheba, sometimes containing confession and admission of the sin, sometimes begging for relief from the misfortunes inflicted on him for the sin. When he experienced human weakness and fell victim to a twofold and most serious sin, you see, as a pious man he attributed to the sin every trial and pain of soul and disaster befalling him: the greater the trials, the greater they proved occasions of piety to him. This sixth psalm, then, is one of that kind of psalm; from verse-by-verse commentary you will gain a more precise knowledge of the degree of devotion with which he confesses to God and implores him.

Lord, do not censure me in your anger, nor discipline me in your wrath (v. 1). Here he is not asking for punishment to be averted; instead, along with the blows he asks the judge for indulgence so that the infliction of the trials may mean his coming to his senses and being reformed, not simple imposition of a penalty, since

---

[1] As in Ps 12, the mention of "the eighth" leads some modern commentators to see a musical direction about octaves on the basis of its occurrence also in 1 Chr 15:21, a book in which liturgical music is given prominence. Sigmund Mowinckel, *The Psalms in Israel's Worship* (2 vols.; New York: Abingdon, 1967), 1:9, on the other hand, denies that the music of the Israelites was based on an octave scale, preferring to observe that the number eight plays an important part in many ritual acts. The psalm is the first of the seven psalms known from the early church as penitential psalms—as Diodore implies?

whereas the one bringing us to our senses applies punishment moderately, the person giving vent to anger and rage strikes mercilessly and without love. It is obvious to those with understanding how much gentleness he requires of the judge in not asking for punishment to be averted. Hence the following also comes from someone winning the master over to compassion; he goes on, in fact, *Have mercy on me, Lord, because I am weak* (v. 2): with nothing valid to say in opposition to the penalties except weakness, I ask to be given mercy lest the misfortunes prevail over my unsound condition and not result in (34) any improvement, my death preceding the reform that comes from suffering. *Heal me, Lord, for my bones are quivering, and my soul is severely shaken* (vv. 2–3). He says the same thing again: by *my bones* he means my strength and my soul. Once again here he adds *severely*, seeking relief from suffering to excess, not asking for suffering in accord with his strength to be averted. The fact that he wants an excessive degree to be averted he indicates by saying in what follows, *You, Lord, how long?* You aggravate it and draw it out, Lord, and make it still more severe so that my mind is already giving way (the meaning of the above phrase *my soul is severely shaken*).

Turn, Lord, rescue my soul, save me for your mercy's sake (v. 4): treat me lovingly, not because I am worthy but because it becomes you to grant me this, such as I am. *There is no one to remember you in death. In Hades will anyone confess to you?* (v. 5). Allow me an opportunity for thanksgiving, Lord; the extent of the calamities leaves me without the possibility of singing hymns of thanksgiving for the future. *I grew weary with my groaning* (v. 6): I was tired of groaning. Groaning is a feeling of pain; but if pain becomes extreme, it cancels even the feeling, and when feeling comes to an end, there is no opportunity for hymns of thanksgiving. (35) *Each night I shall drench my bed, flooding my bedding with my tears.* In the verbs *I shall drench* and *I shall flood* one tense has been substituted for another once more, future taking the place of present. The flow of thought suggests, I groan constantly, flood my bedding, and douse my bed with tears. *My eye was affected by anger* (v. 7)—by your anger. He means, in fact, Even my sight is now affected and dimmed by your anger with me. *I grew old in the midst of all my foes*: my foes, on the other hand, spent time taunting me (*I grew old* meaning for a long time, giving the sense, They did not desist from heaping taunts on me).

Depart from me, all you evildoers (v. 8). Here again he uses

Depart elliptically, his meaning being, Provide me, Lord, with the ability to say to the foe, *Depart from me*, since I have received help from God. Hence he goes on, *Because the Lord had hearkened to the sound of my weeping*. As in the case of *depart*, this also means, Provide me, Lord, with the ability to say, Depart *because the Lord hearkened to the sound of my weeping* and so on. *The Lord heard my request, the Lord accepted my prayer* (v. 9). To this point (36) the phrase Provide me has been said in reference to the foe. With this done, then, what follows? *Let all my foes be ashamed and confused* (v. 10): if this will be my lot from you, Lord, they will be put to shame, the current mockers experiencing alarm and uncertainty, as it goes on to say. *Let them be thrown back and quickly put to extreme shame*: let this happen completely and quickly, since it becomes you to grant such a thing, merciful as you are, and to be ever mindful of me as a recipient of your kindness.

Psalm 7

"A psalm of David, which he sang to the Lord on the words of Hushai, the Benjaminite." This is the title of the seventh psalm. It seems to me appropriate: those applying the titles did not have recourse to guessing in every case, as I mentioned; instead, in places they supplied the right title, as in this case. Blessed David, you see, sang this psalm on the scheming of Hushai, which had got the better of Ahithophel and led to his demise. When David's son Absalom, remember, rebelled against his father's reign and gained control of Jerusalem, the palace in it, and his father's wives, Ahithophel advised him to follow up his initial successes with the pursuit of (37) David before the people's spirit ebbed with the passage of time. Hushai came on the scene and claimed that this advice was wrong and that mistakes should be feared on the grounds that David's experience in war was sufficient to make a difference and drive off an attacker. Hushai's scheme gained the day over Ahithophel, this being God's decision. For this reason Ahithophel took it amiss and did away with himself. For this to happen, then, and for Hushai's words to gain the day, David beseeches God in the words, *Lord my God, in you have I hoped, save me*. You would gain a more precise knowledge of this by reading carefully the book of Kings.[1]

[1] Cf. 2 Sam 16–17.

Lord my God, in you have I hoped, save me (v. 1): while my son trusts in numbers, weapons, horses, and above all the audacity and frenzy of those with him, I hope in you alone, who are capable of saving me not only from him but also from all those conspiring with him against me. Hence he goes on, *from all my pursuers and rescue me.* Then to bring out Absalom's strength and power, and the lowly condition of himself and those with him, he continues, *Do not snatch my soul like a lion, with no one to rescue me or save me* (v. 2).

He then supplies as well the reasonableness of his plea. (38) *Lord my God, if I have done this* (v. 3). *This* was well put: he is saying the same thing in demonstrative fashion in the sense of what I suffer: If I did this to the king before me. *If there is wrong on my hands*: if I did wrong and snatched the kingship from another person to whom it belonged. *If I have repaid evil for evil* (v. 4): if I did not rise above even justified vengeance against the adversary; while it is permissible for someone encountering a schemer to apply vengeance with justification, I did not choose to. So if I did not persevere even to the point of enduring everything to avoid transgressing your laws, what then? *Let me then end up empty-handed before my foes* (v. 4): let me be defenseless against my foes, and not only defenseless: may I even suffer from them what they desire to see happening to me. He goes on, in fact, *Let the foe then hunt down my soul and seize it, and trample my life into the ground* (v. 5), that is, give me over to death. *And bury my glory in the dust*: if I have anything glorious or regal, let this also be confined and enclosed with me in the grave.

And the sequel, *Rise up, Lord, in your wrath; be exalted in the boundaries of your foes* (v. 6): arouse yourself in anger, therefore, Lord, (39) against the wrongdoers, and show yourself to be more exalted and superior to the foe. He did well to refer to his enemies as God's enemies in endeavoring to transgress God's boundary set to David's reign.[2] *Awake, Lord my God, in the command you gave*, that is, implement your own command: you commanded the wrongdoer to be punished; so since these people are doing wrong, arise and enforce the command you gave against wrongdoing. *An assembly of people will surround you; over it return on high* (v. 7): if this happens, your host will surround the tent with thanksgiving (*you* meaning his tent). The clause *Over it return on high* means, For

---

[2] Diodore's text seems to be reading "your foes," like Chrysostom's but unlike Theodoret's or other forms of the LXX. The LXX finds "boundary" in a similar Hebrew form for "arrogance" (unbeknown to Diodore).

this beneficence you are shown to be exalted and powerful against the lawbreakers. *The Lord will judge peoples* (v. 8): you are lord, judge, and arbiter of the peoples. *Judge in my favor, Lord, in your righteousness*: since you for your part are the one who makes the division between those who are wicked and those who are not, decide in my favor in this matter according to what is right to you, *and according to the innocence in me*: just as I for my part did no evil (referring to it here as *innocence*), so grant me this. (40)

Let the wickedness of sinners be brought to an end (v. 9): put an end to the wickedness of those sinning against me and bring it to a close, checking them all. *And you will direct the righteous*: act to support those whose thoughts are on righteousness. *God who tests hearts and entrails justly. My help is from God who saves the upright of heart* (vv. 9–10): the fact that I am not lying and do not feign honorable conduct in your sight you know, since it is you who tests thoughts and enters the recesses of the mind, and even to the very entrails where the thoughts of the mind take their beginning; you know that I am making a just request for help from you, since you are in the habit of saving those who keep free of wickedness. *God is a righteous judge, strong and long-suffering* (v. 11). Since above and below he called upon God's righteousness and adjured him as righteous, and it would not have been a mark of a righteous God to postpone the punishment of the transgressors, the author takes it on himself to account for the delay, saying that while he is a just judge, delay in punishing is not an oversight or weakness but long-suffering of set purpose, as it were. Hence he proceeds, *Who does not give free rein to his wrath every day*: if long-suffering were not associated with his justice, there would have been nothing to stop him punishing day in day out, since sinners always provide grounds for just punishment. Sinners, however, should not for this reason be disposed to indifference: those of right mind (41) rightly respect long-suffering as a threat and take delay in wrath as an aggravation of punishment; this should also be the attitude of those on whom the imposition of judgment does not fall promptly.

He proceeds, in fact, *If you are not converted, he will wield his sword; he bent his bow and had it at the ready, and with it he prepared means of death* (vv. 12–13). By *prepared* here he means firmly arranged; elsewhere by *ready* he means settled and firm, as in the verse, "Preparing mountains in his strength,"[3] that is, settling and

---

[3] Ps 65:6.

firming, though here readiness implies firmly and compactly. By *means of death* he refers to all the shafts and swords, in a figurative manner implying the punishment from God that is fixed and unremitting. *He made his arrows for those on fire.* Some of the Psalters have "he made those on fire;"[4] but neither the one nor the other does any harm to the meaning: if it has "he made those on fire," the meaning is that they consume those being punished, and if "he made them for those on fire," it has the sense, For those due to be punished the arrows of punishment are made and prepared.

He had to this point spoken of God's justice and long-suffering, and said that it would be fair for David himself to receive loving-kindness in that foes for the time being enjoy long-suffering with a view to conversion, but if unwilling they will turn the long-suffering into aggravation of punishment. At this point he now speaks of the wickedness of Ahithophel himself in giving evil advice, accepting evil proposals, and in proceeding to put extreme evil into practice, and says that all this reverted on his own head. Now, if the first part of the psalm contains a prayer for these events (42) while the latter part contains a narrative of the events as having happened already, there is no call for surprise: the genre of inspired composition is like this, and especially in the case of blessed David himself. You see, for what the prophets require from God in the case of the occurrence of events they receive grace and knowledge of the future and announce it as though already in the past; you would find this occurring not only in the psalms but also in all the other authors, where in the same way there occur prayers that they may take place and accounts of them as already having happened when God pleases to bring them to pass. This he makes available to the prophets, as I said, the grace of announcing what has not yet happened.

In this case as well, then, David in the first part prays to God that Ahithophel's advice might be found impractical, and in the final part announces the event as though already happened in the words, *Lo, he felt the pangs of bearing iniquity, conceived distress and brought forth lawlessness* (v. 14). *Pangs* are the pains of childbirth; but since conception leads to those pangs, he means in the two

[4] Chrysostom (though citing also a still different reading) and Theodoret go with Diodore's reading (and the LXX generally); Theodore (Greek text not extant) seems to reproduce the alternative reading. Perhaps the meaning is unaffected, as Diodore claims, because in either case the phrase is obscure. "Psalters" in particular would be numerous, and the chances of varied readings greater than in other biblical texts.

clauses, He conceived wickedness and gave birth to it, painful as it was to him in generating it and to those on whom it would be inflicted. *He dug a pit and excavated it* (v. 15). By *pit* here he means the depth of wickedness. He did not leave unexplored, he is saying, a single depth of such pondering of wickedness (taking as a figure of the actual event the case of people digging pits and not stopping short of depth before reaching the level required). This person, too, he is saying likewise went to the depths of wickedness, leaving nothing unplumbed by his thoughts.

But what happened as a result of God's help? (43) *And he fell into the depths he had made*: he was caught up in his own wickedness. *His trouble will come back on his own head* (v. 16): his wicked schemes reverted to him, now destroyed by the depraved schemes themselves that he had generated. *And on his own crown will descend his wrongdoing*: all his unjust schemes against me came down upon his own head, that is, on himself (by *crown* referring to his own person). *I shall confess to the Lord in keeping with his righteousness, and sing to the name of the Lord Most High* (v. 17): now that this has happened, what more is properly left me to do than give thanks to the God who is responsible for it all? I shall sing hymns to him that befit such wonderful kindness.

Psalm 8

"To the end, on the winepresses. A psalm of David." The words of this psalm bear no close relationship to the reference in the title. I mean, even granting that "on the winepresses" means on the gathering of the fruit (of the vine, presumably), I cannot conceive why on earth he would mention everything else coming under human control—birds, quadrupeds, reptiles—and make a particular point of (44) omitting mention of the fruit at the focus of attention.[1] So let us for our part pass over such pedantic nonsense and treat of the real theme of the psalm. It is, then, a hymn of praise uttered by blessed David under the influence of the Spirit for God the Word made man. The Lord himself also, in fact, brought this out in citing many of the verses at certain times of the incarnation,

---

[1] Diodore applies his rationalist principles to the psalm title, thus unwittingly being preserved from following the lead that the less skeptical Chrysostom and Theodoret find in the LXX version of the Hebrew term *gittith*, thinking to see there *gat*, winepress, though modern commentators disclaim an exact understanding of it—perhaps to do with musical instruments again or a particular tune.

and especially the verse *Out of the mouths of babes and sucklings you have perfected praise* (v. 2). This was demonstrated also by the events themselves when the Lord also took possession of the holy place to acclamation befitting God: after the Jews out of envy rebuked those doing good things and crying out, the Lord, to show that it is possible for anyone not be overcome by the evil of wicked people, by a divine activity prompted infants at the breast to recite such hymns of praise. Unreceptive as they were of the Jews' rebuke on account of their immature age, yet prompted by the divine activity, they gave voice to the hymn, with the result that those then at a loss to understand what was going on directed the blame at the Lord himself and said to him, "Do you not see what they are doing?" to which the Lord replied, "Yes."[2] After all, was the one responsible for the activity likely to deny it? He could not bring himself, however, to make the infants stop calling out because of the Jews' rage, the result being that instead he announced that even if the babies kept silence, which was impossible, he would show them a greater marvel in making the stones and all inanimate things speak up and cry aloud the glory of the one present. (45)

So far so good. If, however, the psalm goes on to hint at the human being in general in saying *You put all things under his feet* (v. 6) and listing them as *sheep and all cattle* and further *the beasts of the field* and the rest, it should be understood that he includes them all in the reference to some. But if the Jew under pressure were to contend that the reference is rather to the ordinary person, not to Christ, let it thus also be known that even at the beginning all such things were subjected to the ordinary human being for this reason, that he was an image of God the Word, who was due to become man in later times.[3] The conclusion from all quarters is that either the psalm refers to the Lord himself incarnate, or on his account is applied to his image. Proof that commentary on the text convinces adversaries even against their will that the reference is to the Lord incarnate in person you would gain from the consistent message of the words.

---

[2] Influenced by the Evangelists' citation of v. 2 of the psalm in the mouth of Jesus, Diodore concedes a christological dimension to it, and proceeds to develop the Gospel incident by conflating the accounts in Matt 21:8-17 and Luke 19:37-40, also giving newborn babes a role the Evangelists leave to children.

[3] The conclusion is thought legitimate also by modern commentators such as Weiser (*Psalms*, 144), who like Diodore sees an implicit reference to Gen 1:26, observing of v. 6, "We can speak here of man being created 'in the image of God and after his likeness.'"

Lord our Lord, how wonderful is your name in all the earth! (v. 1). Blessed David it is who is saying to the Lord incarnate that firstly all the earth will acknowledge the mystery and marvel at it, for it was by becoming man that he began giving signs of divinity from the earth. And since after this he was also taken up into heaven in his own flesh, the author follows the order of events in going on, *Because your magnificence is exalted above the heavens*: beginning from the earth, your glory surpassed (46) the heavens "so that he might fill all things."⁴ Now, what great sign of his glory in particular did he register on earth? *Out of the mouths of babes and sucklings you have perfected praise* (v. 2): while some of the other marvels sometimes happened also in the other biblical authors, for the first time in this case nature witnessed the utterance of articulate sounds on children's tongues, through immature organs, surpassing the understanding and appreciation of mature people, since now also for the first time it experienced a divine visit. *On account of your enemies so as to destroy enemy and avenger*: you did all this in the sight of your foes the Jews, so that on seeing what they do not wish they may suffer worse pains; and by the event enemy and avenger was destroyed. The Jew, you see, was in reality enemy of the law, not accepting the lawgiver when present, and yet he pretended to be its avenger.

Because I shall see the heavens, the works of your fingers (v. 3): it is no surprise if this was the effect of your artistry, the mouths of infants being opened and the dissimulation of such enemies being destroyed; it was, after all, those fingers achieving it that also smoothly sculpted the sky at the beginning. (47) *Moon and stars which you have put in place.* He obviously includes all things, sun and the rest, by mentioning the stars in particular. *You have put in place* refers to their production being achieved at the outset in such a way as to abide for as long as the maker decides. *What is the human being, after all, for you to be mindful of him, the son of man for you to have regard for him?* (v. 4) This shows the inspired author admiring, not enquiring about, the great degree of glory investing the human being, who at no time hoped to be vouchsafed such things. That is to say, God the Word's taking the "form of a slave"⁵ instead of some other better nature showed the extraordinary degree of beneficence toward the human being. So his intention is to indicate that all the privileges that belonged to the Lord's flesh—that is, to the perfect

⁴ Eph 4:10.
⁵ Phil 2:7.

human being—as a result of the union with God the Word are held in common by human nature.

You have brought him a little lower than the angels, you crowned him with glory and honor (v. 5). It is clear that by the *little lowering* he refers to death, since while the angel lives forever, the human being dies in accord with the law of nature. If, however, this is taken in reference to any human being,[6] the *lowering* is found to be not only *little* (48) but also great, especially if you consider the condition of the generation of Adam, of Abel, of Noah, and of Abraham by comparison with the angels abiding forever. Its proper application, however, is to the incarnation of the Lord, who by the interval of the three days gave evidence of the difference from the angels in regard to death, even though it was foreshortened, and by rising in turn from the dead was shown to be Lord of all.[7] He goes on, in fact, to say, *With glory and honor you crowned him, and appointed him over the works of your hands. You put all things under his feet* (vv. 5–6): having personally tasted death for a time, and for our sake at that, he was crowned with greater glory than the angels and established as lord of the dead themselves, and not only of them but also of every being seen and unseen. The phrase *You put all things under his feet* Paul, in fact, explains more clearly in saying, "In subjecting all things to him, God left nothing outside his control."[8] The psalm, however, implies the same thing more distinctly by saying *over the work of your hands*, with the result that there is no work of God which is exempt from the authority of the one appointed Lord.

Now, the apostle, as though addressing the faithful, comments more distinctly on the whole passage, claiming that this psalm refers to no one else than the Lord himself made man. He continues by referring to the verses of the psalm, "We see Jesus as the one made a little lower than angels by suffering death crowned with glory and (49) honor" (clearly referring to his lordship of all, his immortality and immutability) "so that apart from God he might

---

[6] For Theodoret the phrase makes reference to death as a result of the fall—a phrase that appears in the Paris manuscript of this work at this point.

[7] Myles Bourke, "Hebrews," *NJBC*, 924, comments on the use of the phrase from v. 5 in Heb 2:7: "The Greek words βραχύ τι can mean either little in degree or little in time; the first is their meaning in the psalm, but Heb takes them in the second sense. Jesus was for a little while made lower than the angels, in the days of his earthly life, but now he is crowned with glory and honor." Diodore follows this movement of thought. "The condition" of Adam and others perhaps touches on their longevity.

[8] Heb 2:8.

taste death for everyone," or, as some texts of the apostle have it, "so that by the grace of God he might taste death for everyone." Nothing in the text, in fact, impairs the meaning: if "by the grace of God" the flesh tasted death, it was clearly apart from God that it tasted death; and if "apart from God" it tasted death, obviously it was by the grace of God that it tasted death. Nevertheless, we must be governed by a translation that does no violence to the verse.[9]

A sufficient explanation of *You put all things under his feet,* then, as has been said, is that, in the apostle's words, "he left nothing outside his control." But because blessed David was addressing Jews who were incapable of being elevated by the statement or of knowing what was to come, he proceeds to some listing of items which at that time moved even the Jews to adequate thanksgiving in the belief that the hymn was composed for their sakes, since through them they realized they were masters of cattle and sheep. So he does this and as well adds the listing of the lowly creatures without undermining the sense of *You put everything under his feet*: even the listing of the most insignificant things is not a reversal of what was confessed—rather a confirmation, since even the most insignificant things in the listing are not exempt from the extent of the lordship.

Accordingly, having gone on to say, *Sheep and all cattle, and also the beasts of the field* (v. 7), that is, the tame and the wild, he proceeds, (50) *Birds of the air and fish of the sea, the creatures that travel the ways of the seas* (v. 8), as if to say, the mighty and the lowly. He rounds off the psalm with the hymn in the beginning, adding, *Lord our Lord, how wonderful is your name in all the earth!* (v. 9). He ratifies a fine opening with a fine conclusion.

Psalm 9

"To the end, on the son's secrets. A psalm of David." Those who attached the title to the ninth psalm meant it to indicate that the psalm contains thanksgiving for the good things God granted the people. Some of them he personally was alone aware of, and did not take account of the liberality, by "son" here referring to the people of the Israelites. By God's "secrets" Scripture normally refers to the good things coming from him, which were not known to human beings before this, as is clear from what the people say

---

[9] Diodore cites the verse with the final clause in the form known to Chrysostom, but is aware also of the form employed (not here) by Theodore and Theodoret. Modern commentators are puzzled by the force of the clause.

also in the fifty-first psalm, "You revealed to me the hidden and uncertain things of wisdom,"[1] there too meaning, You granted your people laws and instructions which people previously did not know.

As we said, then, even if the title given by the inscribers is obscure as to content, nevertheless it seems to approximate to the true meaning, except for an omission, (51) the fact that this ninth psalm has been divided into two in the Hebrew.[2] That is likely to be the case, since this psalm seems to have two themes: its first part contains thanksgiving for God's ransoming them from neighbors and enemies against the odds at different times, whereas the other part of the psalm levels a clear accusation against the disdainful treatment by the wealthy of the poor members of the people, the beginning of the second part being as follows, *Why, Lord, do you stand far off? why do you look down on us in good times and bad? When the godless acts disdainfully, the poor person is inflamed* (Ps 10:1–2). And so in the Hebrew, as I say, this ninth psalm of ours is numbered as two. The number of one hundred and fifty, however, is made up this way, as I said before,[3] that we take the first and second psalms as two whereas the Hebrew takes both as one, just as in this case we by contrast see this ninth psalm as one when they see it as two; the division of this ninth psalm makes up for the joining of the first and the second.

Now, the textual commentary will make clear what I say. If, however, on hearing "son" some people think Christ the Lord is referred to here, the sequel in particular does not allow this meaning to be taken, the author mentioning enemies and weapons and liberation and tyrannical nations. If, on the other hand, someone were to interpret metaphorically weapons and foes and nations as the demons, and claim that the coming of Christ is liberation from them, such a person would perhaps be responsible for a rather discerning explanation, to which we do not object, while for our part not giving it preference to the facts themselves and truth itself.

I shall confess to you, Lord, with all my heart (v. 1): I shall (52) give thanks to you from the depths of my mind. Now, what is the

---

[1] Ps 51:6. Diodore is unaware that the LXX is wide of the mark in seeing in the Hebrew *Muth Labben* (a technical term unfamiliar to modern commentators) the roots of words for death, secrets, son.

[2] Diodore is unable to refer to the alphabetic structure of the Hebrew original to confirm the accuracy of the LXX's judgment in maintaining the psalm as one. He is also unaware of how Hebrew and LXX differ in the division also of Pss 114–116, 147.

[3] Cf. Diodore's remarks at the close of comment on Ps 2.

form of the thanksgiving? *I shall recount all your marvels*, those giving thanks normally recounting the forms and reasons for thanksgiving. *I shall rejoice and be glad in you* (v. 2): I shall do so, not to discharge a requirement, but out of joy and happiness with the event. The divinity, in fact, takes satisfaction in such thanksgiving when the thanks are the fruit of independent feeling and not performance of some obligation. *I shall sing to your name, Most High.* He says the same thing again.

What is it, pray, for which you are thus giving thanks? *When my enemy turns backwards* (v. 3): because you put my foes to flight so as to be driven back. *They will lose their strength and vanish from sight. They will lose their strength* means, They lost their strength, one tense replacing another. He goes on, in fact, *Because you were responsible for my judgment being fair, seated on your throne as a righteous judge* (v. 4): you gave judgment in my favor, seated regally on your own throne, judging and condemning the adversaries. So for what were you responsible, Lord, seated on your throne and judging? *You rebuked nations, and the godless perished, you canceled his name forever and ever* (v. 5): you gave judgment after finding them to be guilty of wrongdoing and us (53) to be wronged, and you so treated them that, far from bearing your rebuke, they were completely destroyed—weapons, cities, kindred, and all. Hence he goes on, *The enemies' swords failed utterly* (v. 6), that is, they perished along with their weapons. *And you destroyed cities*: you destroyed their cities as well. *The memory of them has disappeared resoundingly* (connecting the kindred also with them). *Resoundingly* was well put: The result being, he is saying, that their ruin came to the ears also of those far off yet to be.

And the Lord abides forever (v. 7): for your part, Lord, on the contrary, with those people destroyed, you continued to exercise rule and strength, making your throne and reign more stable. Hence he goes on, *He established his throne in judgment*. The term *established* means founded and strengthened, as in another place, "Establishing mountains in his strength,"[4] that is, founding. *And he will judge the world in righteousness* (v. 8): it is not surprising if you judged these nations by right standards—our neighbors, I mean: you it is who delivers judgment on the whole world in due course and passes just sentence on each person. Hence he proceeds, (54) *He will judge peoples in rectitude*, that is, it is you who judges everyone in rectitude.

[4] Ps 65:6.

The Lord became a refuge for the needy, a help at the right time in tribulations (v. 9): after passing judgment and condemnation on them, therefore, and bringing ruin on them, you provided the opposite to us when brought low, and proved a refuge and help to us in need, especially when we required help from you. *Let those who know your name hope in you* (v. 10): for this reason all with reverence for you can be confident. *Because you did not forsake those seeking you, Lord*: you prevailed upon everyone to be of this mind by saving those who hope in you.

Sing to the Lord dwelling in Sion (v. 11): everyone, therefore, glorify the God who is worshiped in Sion. *Announce his exploits among the nations*: by your singing proclaim also to those at a distance what he did in our favor. *Because he who required their blood remembered*: your claim is that the God who avenges those who fear him, far from bearing peaceably the wrongs done his servants, took vengeance. (55) *He did not forget the cry of the poor*: neither the poverty nor the lowliness of the wronged led him to neglect justice.

Have mercy on me, Lord, see my humiliation by my foes (v. 13). *Have mercy on me* stands for You had mercy on me and rescued me from the foe, the tense being changed again. *You who lift me up from the gates of death*, that is, You who lifted me up and rescued me from death—and it was right for you to do so, Lord. Why? *So that I may proclaim all your praises in the gates of the daughter of Sion* (v. 14):[5] so that you may give me opportunity for thanksgiving in the place in which I was saved.

He then in turn resumes the account of the enemies' disasters. *Nations are stuck fast in the ruin they made* (v. 15). By *nations* he once more means the neighboring peoples, that is, They fell into their own traps, while we were saved against the odds. *Their foot caught in the trap they hid*: after setting traps, they were snared themselves, as though held fast by the foot so that their troubles were inescapable. *By making judgments the Lord is known* (v. 16): from this it is clear that God gives thought to justice in everything. How and in what manner? (56) *By the works of his hands the sinner is caught*: because all sinners fail to escape his hands or his punishments.

Let the sinners be sent off into Hades (v. 17). He asks, What did he do? He bade the sinners among them to die. *All the nations who give no thought to God*: he does the same thing also to all the other

---

[5] Olivier does not include in the text the final clause of the verse, "I shall rejoice in your salvation," on which Diodore (like his successors) seems to comment.

nations who have no interest in justice and in God's command. *Because the poor will not be forgotten in the end* (v. 18): so that all the nations may know that, even if by some permission his people suffered and were humbled, yet he will not forget his own forever. *The perseverance of the needy will not be lost forever*: instead, he trains his own in perseverance, and when he sees them persevering properly, the patience he produces in them is not without purpose.

Then he also addresses a prayer. *Rise up, Lord, do not let a human being prevail* (v. 19): please, Lord, always be like this to those who give no thought to you, lest they think human beings are capable of anything even without reference to your oversight. *May the nations be judged in your presence*: instead, distinguish between the nations that do wrong and those that are wronged. (57) *Appoint them a lawgiver, Lord* (v. 20): appoint yourself to lay down the law to sinners and also to those not sinning, bringing salvation to the latter and ruin to the former. *Let the nations know they are human*: all the nations will learn that even if they excel in workmanship and are distinguished for warlike skills, they are still human beings in need of support from you in everything.

Psalm 10

Why, Lord, do you stand far off? (v. 1). At this point he begins the second part,[1] in which he censures the grasping and disdainful among the people. After well saying *Why, Lord, do you stand far off?* he went on *Why do you ignore us in good times and bad?* You forbear to assist the poor person robbed and oppressed, he is saying, as though far away and not seeing what is going on. What is the result of this? *When the godless acts disdainfully, the poor person is inflamed* (v. 2). *The poor person is inflamed* was well put: finding no one to help and with the grasping person besetting him, his mind burns at the thought that you are not observing human affairs. *They are caught up in the schemes they have devised*: what comes of your forbearance, Lord? While the lowly person is inflamed and suffers intolerably, disdainful and grasping people have accomplices (58) and henchmen in the wrongs they commit, and are addressed as brave and manly and brilliant and the like by their toadies and flatterers.

---

[1] Cf. the opening to commentary on Ps 9 for Diodore's reasons for thinking that the LXX has committed an oversight in not following the Hebrew in dividing the psalm (as our modern versions do).

Hence he proceeds, *Because the wicked is commended in the desires of his heart* (v. 3): not only is such a person not reproved, but he is even commended by the flatterers as exercising courage sufficient to rebuff the plaintiffs. In his bitter complaint the author did well to go on, *And the wrongdoer is praised. The sinner provoked the Lord; in the intensity of his wrath he will not seek him out* (vv. 3–4): then for this reason the grasping person will not be conscious of provoking God: in his wish to give vent to his anger and desires, he becomes so caught up in his passion as to be unaware that there is someone who has an eye to human affairs. Hence he continues, *God is not before his eyes*: he acts as if God were not surveying what happens.

His ways are defiled at every moment (v. 5): for this reason he is constantly involved in lawless actions. *Your judgments are kept from his view*: he does not even want to admit that you are a just judge dealing with each person at the due time in accord with their behavior. *He will gain dominion over all his foes*: with no thought for this, the disdainful person believes he controls and dominates inferior people. (59) *He said in his heart, in fact, I shall not be moved from one generation to the next, suffering no harm* (v. 6). He says *suffering no harm* to mean By harm: He thinks he will always enjoy prosperity, he is saying, and is subject to no change or alteration, there being no one to pass judgment.

His mouth is full of cursing, bitterness, and deceit (v. 7): far from refraining from sinfulness and injustice in speech, he even lies and deceives and does everything harmful to the inferior person. *Under his tongue lies trouble and hardship.* He says the same thing in a different way. *He lies in hiding with the rich* (v. 8): conspiring with his fellows and accomplices, however, he prepares an ambush for the lowly. *To slay the innocent by stealth*: to bring death to the guiltless. *His eyes are on the needy*: like a lion after its prey he keeps a sharp eye on the person vulnerable to injustice (as stated in the following verse). *Like a lion in its den he lies in wait under cover* (v. 8). He goes on to explain why he lies in wait and what he intends. *He lies in wait to snatch the poor, to snatch the* (60) *poor by luring him; he will bring him down in his trap* (vv. 8–9). He did well to liken the grasping person with a lion, a rapacious beast: just as it lurks with the intention of snatching the weaker animals, dragging them away, bringing them to their den and eating them, such is the way these people also behave against the poor.

He goes on to explain what would therefore happen to them,

such as they are. *He will stoop and fall while having dominion over the needy* (v. 10). The clause has the force of a wish in place of *He will stoop and fall*, his meaning being, When such a person plans to get the better of the poor person and thinks such a person has already collapsed, then with trap at the ready as it were, the grasping person himself will fall in and pay the penalty for his lawlessness. Why? *He said in his heart, in fact, God has forgotten* (v. 11): he did everything because the particular thought he had in mind was that God is not interested in what happens. *He turned away his face from ever looking at the outcome*: since the grasping person has this idea that God turned away his face so as not to observe what happens, he has no qualms about proceeding to be grasping.

The sequel, however, indicates that the foregoing has the force of a wish; he goes on, *Rise up, Lord my God, let your hand be uplifted* (v. 12)—in other words, For this reason, Lord, therefore, rise up as though from sleep, and show the retribution from you to be superior to their intentions; (61) while punishing them, take pity on the wronged. He proceeds, in fact, *Forget not your needy ones forever*. He then goes on to supply also the reason why he prays for the grasping to be punished and the needy helped. *Why did the godless one provoke God? He said in his heart, in fact, He will not require an account* (v. 13): this is the particular reason the grasping person deserves to be punished, his thinking there is no God who requires an account. *You are looking, because you perceive hardship and anger* (v. 14). The expression is back to front, meaning, You look at hardship and perceive anger: it is not true, as the grasping person believes, that you do not observe what happens; instead, you see both the hardship of the victim and the frenzy of the grasping, as emerges from the grasping person falling into your hands and your bringing him to justice. He goes on, in fact, *So as to give him into your hands*: perceiving this, you forbear and bide your time; instead of any lack of interest in the needy on your part, there is deep concern and care. He goes on, in fact, *The poor, after all, is left in your care; you were a help to an orphan*. By *poor* and *orphan* here he refers metaphorically to the wronged in being for a time bereft of a helper.

Break the arm of the sinner and evildoer (v. 15): break the power of the grasping (62) so that they may be doubly punished, for desiring to commit robbery and being thwarted by weakness. *His sin will be looked for, and will not be found on account of it*. By *his sin* is meant the possessions and wealth which he wrongly amassed. He will look for them at the time of his misfortune, he is saying, and he will not find them, nor will he gain any profit from them. The phrase *on account of it* means either his greed or his intention. *The Lord is king forever, and forever and ever* (v. 16): in order that you, Lord, may be seen to reign justly for all the age, giving a just verdict in favor of everyone who is badly mistreated. *You will perish, nations, from his earth.* He refers to the grasping as *nations* here for not living according to the Mosaic law, and instead perhaps living by no laws like savages: Such people, he is saying, cannot inhabit God's earth.

You hearkened to the longing of the needy, Lord (v. 17): God, who takes the part of the wronged, does not allow the grasping to dwell in the same place. *Your ear attended to the readiness of their heart.* By *the readiness* he means the stability and hope which the wronged showed in you in persevering. (63) *Judge in favor of orphaned and humbled so that a human being may not go further in boasting on the earth* (v. 18): you paid heed and gave thought, Lord, and deemed it right to help those badly mistreated, on the one hand, while also utterly removing the grasping from your earth to prevent a grasping mentality emerging against the more needy.

Psalm 11

"To the end. A psalm of David." David uttered this psalm on his own part when pursued by Saul. And since he was continually given the advice to move from place to place, with Saul on the point of arriving in the places where he was hidden, he says to those keeping him on the run, *In the Lord I trust: how will you say to my soul, Move to the mountains like a sparrow?* (v. 1). Even if movement is necessary, he is saying, nevertheless let it be known that I do not hope to secure safety from those with whom I am constantly in opposition except by hoping in God, who can provide me with safety in every place (*How will you say to my soul* meaning, Why do you urge me). *Because, lo, the sinners have bent the bow* (v. 2), as though they are reporting and telling of the need for him to be constantly on the move because of the schemers (64) having prepared every form of death (*bow* and *arrows* referring to the schemes). *They have prepared arrows for the quiver to shoot in the dark at the upright of heart. In the dark* means, as though in the dark: *dark* is a moonless night, so *dark* is lack of moonlight.[1]

---

[1] The Greek term in the text is σκοτομήνη, not simply σκότος, and so Diodore touches on the reference to the moon, μήνη, disposing of the point in a few words, as will Theodoret (unlike the prolix Theodore).

Having to this point quoted the words of those recommending movement to him, he now proceeds to address God. *Because what you completed they laid low* (v. 3), that is, Your works they are anxious to divest me of in some fashion: what you achieved in me—that is, anointing me and fitting me for kingship—they are anxious to destroy and to thwart your intentions as far as possible. *But what did the righteous man do?* In other words, I did nothing wrong to the person of Saul, and on that basis I am more righteous than he is, suffering unjustly at his hands. For this reason, then, I deserve to receive help from you, the God dwelling both in the temple and in heaven (as he goes on to say). *The Lord is in his holy temple, the Lord, his throne is in heaven* (v. 4). He goes on to explain what he means. *His eyes behold the poor*: from heaven and from your temple you survey the poor person unsupported by such help.[2] (65) *His gaze examines the sons of men*: he makes a distinction in what has to be done both for what he suffers unjustly and for what he does justly. *The Lord examines the righteous and the godless* (v. 5): he knows each person's behavior. *He who loves unrighteousness hates his own soul*: since you, O God, have such an attitude to those guilty of such things, the person complicit in injustice is probably unaware of hating himself.

What in fact happens to such people? *Because on sinners he will rain down snares, fire, and sulphur, and a blast of a storm the portion of their drinking cup* (v. 6): from above, from your high places, you dispatch on them various punishments in which they are ensnared and consumed as though by fire. Now, by *blast of a storm* he refers to a force propelling them down to Hades: It is their *portion*, he says, it is their lot (by *drinking cup* here referring to death itself, as the Lord also says, "Father, if it be possible, let this cup pass me by,"[3] that is, death and the cross). For these reasons God deals thus with the ungodly and unjust. He goes on, in fact, *Because the Lord is righteous and loved righteous deeds; he saw uprightness before his eyes* (v. 7): being righteous and upright, he does not refrain (66) from giving this impression to those not displaying such an attitude.

---

[2] The text read by Theodoret and apparently by Theodore speaks of "the world" where Diodore's has "the poor," which is that cited also by Chrysostom, who then proceeds to speak of the Lord "looking attentively on the whole world" (a phrase reminiscent also of 2 Chr 16:9).

[3] Matt 26:39.

Psalm 12

The twelfth psalm bears the title, "To the end, on the eighth. A psalm of David." By "eighth" the Hebrews normally refer to what we now call the Lord's Day: since the cycle of the week is contained in seven days, they refer to the day after the seventh as both eighth and first.[1] So the title indicates that some good came David's way on the first day, which was after the sabbath. It has been suggested from many examples, however, that the titles are not factual, and for our part we feel we are wasting our time on the process of coming up with absurd interpretations. Lest the reader be ignorant of this, however, we shall follow this same process as far as we can.

Now, the true theme of the psalm is as follows. Blessed David utters this psalm on his own part, finding fault with those who, while pretending friendship with him, traduce him to Saul: many people under the guise of friendship but courting the favor of the one in power tried to trap blessed David into saying things so as to have the opportunity to traduce him and thus curry favor with the other. He therefore accuses such people, on the one hand making a general accusation in view of the seemingly harmless conversation, while hinting at such peoples specifically: he does not accuse all human beings, especially since it was not absolutely impossible for him (67) to have a real friend, having Jonathan and perhaps someone like him, remember.[2] In line with the theme I mentioned, however, he hints at some people while also uttering sentiments of a general nature.

Save me, Lord, because there is no holy person left (v. 1). *Holy* here means sincere and carefully adhering to the norms of friendship. *Because truth is esteemed little among the sons of men. Truth is esteemed little* means, Truth has perished and disappeared from human beings, the majority now choosing and loving falsehood by currying favor with the one in power. *Everyone spoke lies to their neighbor* (v. 2). *Lies* means things harmful and full of pretense, which (he says) he speaks to me (the meaning of *to their neighbor*) so that they might seize upon my words and represent them to the

---

[1] This term representing the Hebrew *sheminith*, which modern commentators think may be a musical notation, Diodore discussed at its occurrence on Ps 6, allowing a reference to days of the week, but disallowing other exotic interpretations.

[2] Cf. 1 Sam 18:1–4.

king. Hence he goes on, *Lying lips in the heart and evil spoken in the heart*: plotting one thing *in the heart*, they propose another on their lips, like flattery and compliments; while saying such things, in reality they have a heart full of wickedness.

The Lord will destroy all deceitful lips (v. 3): have done (68) with this kind of thing, he is saying, or rather, Let such people even fall foul of God's righteous verdict, which gets rid of such people. *Boasting tongue.* He calls the tongue not speaking what is right *boasting*: it was a mark of arrogance to bypass the position of the righteous man and to stir up and provoke Saul against him. *Those who say, We shall give free rein to our tongue* (v. 4): whoever have this overconfidence in harming people with their tongue and believing God does not survey human affairs, devoting themselves completely to speaking and hatching evil. Hence he goes on, *Our lips are our own. Who is our master?* as if the words were theirs: just as if there were no one to make judgments on what is said and done, so they devote themselves completely to doing evil with their tongue and with their lips, and take pride in it.

So what is the response? *For the sake of the hardship of the poor and the groaning of the needy I shall now arise, says the Lord* (v. 5). But on account of the hardship and weakness caused by the slanderers, and because of the groaning of those suffering such things, God promised to rise up, seek out and avenge righteousness, and publicly and without exception punish the pretenders and boasters. For this reason he goes on, in fact, *I shall place them in safety, I shall speak frankly with them.* So he promises to give heed to the righteous person and (69) punish the wrongdoers, and to save good people being slandered, not secretly or furtively, but openly and boldly.

At this point, then, David in person goes on, *The Lord's sayings are pure sayings* (v. 6): of such a kind, then, are God's sayings, of such a kind are his promises and of such a kind his commands; I know them to be true, and I do not lie (the sense of *pure*, his meaning being, He will really do it). *Silver tested in the furnace, proven in the ground, purified seven times.* Since he said, The Lord's sayings are pure and unmixed with falsehood, he goes on, As silver brought into contact with fire is found to be purified of every defilement, so also such commands of God emerge sincere and unaffected by falsehood. The phrase *seven times* means repeatedly, his meaning being that it is exceedingly pure and untainted with falsehood.

Having said as much by way of inspired composition, at this

point he goes on in the style of prayer. *You, Lord, will protect us, and defend us from this generation and forever* (v. 7). *This generation* means the pretenders, the liars, the slanderers, referring to all of this kind as their *generation*. *Do the godless roam around? You prospered sons of men in your loftiness* (v. 8). The clause *Do the godless roam around?* is to be read as a question with the meaning, If you wanted (70) to *preserve and protect us from this generation*, even if the godless and demons and agitators surround us, even if they besiege us and cut us off, you will render us superior with your help. Hence his saying *in your loftiness*, since you are superior to all, and with the help you show us you render us superior to the scheming of those surrounding us. The verb *prospered*, in fact, means will prosper, the tense being changed to give the meaning, You will be very attentive to us: just as neglect brings diminishment, so attention brings increase. *The sons of men* means ourselves when slandered and subjected to a dire fate. In short, then, the sense here is, When you care for us, even if we are abandoned among those guilty of hostility and scheming, we emerge superior on account of the care of the Most High.

Psalm 13

"To the end. A psalm of David." "To the end" means concerning future events; but this is not factual, either.[1] The psalm's theme, in fact, is clear: it is uttered on the part of David himself when he suffered the effects of the sin with Bathsheba. On falling foul of every harsh, grievous, and painful incident on that account, remember, he then identified the sin as the cause, especially on hearing that "the Lord has taken away your sin."[2] (71) You see, while he received the gift as coming from a loving lord, he thought it behooved him not to forget the sin, but instead to advance in virtue with the degree of determination he required to be preserved from committing such a sin against so good a lord. But on being caught up in the events involving Absalom in particular, he believed the outcome was God's abandoning him, and realized the sin was most of all to blame. He therefore asks God to be completely reconciled

---

[1] The phrase (thought by modern commentators to be a direction to musicians) has occurred several times already. Diodore contests its accuracy as an index of events to come, unlike Theodoret. In Ps 19 Diodore will see the phrase referring to David's old age.

[2] Nathan's words to David in 2 Sam 12:13.

to him and not forsake him, but lift the weight of misfortune that was proving too heavy for the strength of the sufferer.

How long, Lord? will you forget me forever? how long will you turn your face away from me? (v. 1). He says it in this fashion as though in the case of an angry master unable to bring himself even to look on his wayward slave. *How long shall I hold counsels in my soul, pangs in my heart day and night?* (v. 2). If you were reconciled to me, he is saying, you would free me from pondering and suspecting the cause of the punishments, namely, the sins which bring me no little pain in my pondering. *How long will my foe be exalted over me?* So cut short the inroads of the trouble, bring to a halt the foe lording it over me to such an extent, and be reconciled to me.

Look at me, hearken to me, Lord my God. Give light to my eyes lest I sleep in death (v. 3). By *death* he means as though in death: Since the misfortunes and the tribulations render the sun, which (72) is a source of pleasure to everyone, dim and faint to me, he is saying, free me from the misfortune so that I may see good things as they naturally are and not as the tribulations represent them. *In case my foe should ever say, I prevailed over him*: not even the one hostile to me and pursuing me thinks this comes to me from you, instead attributing everything to his own power. *Those distressing me will rejoice if I falter. Falter* means lose the kingship: Even the foes will rejoice, he is saying, unaware that what is happening is retribution for sin, and will instead attribute it to their own strength.

But I hoped for your mercy (v. 5): but even with their taking such an attitude to me, I shall not despair of your loving-kindness (*I hoped* meaning, I shall not cease hoping, the tense being changed). Hence he goes on *My heart will rejoice in your salvation*, that is, in the safety provided me by you. *I shall sing to the Lord my benefactor, and shall celebrate in song the name of the Lord Most High* (v. 6): when things turn out this way, and safety is given me against the odds, I shall not cease singing the praises of the benefactor all my life or celebrating his love in song. (73)

Psalm 14

"To the end. A psalm of David." Here once again "To the end" means, The contents of this psalm will come to pass in later times. The theme refers to Sennacherib at the time when he sent the Rabshakeh to prevail upon the inhabitants of Jerusalem, make war on them, take them captive, and make them slaves of the king of the

Assyrians, namely Sennacherib. This Rabshakeh, then, was from the Jews (so the story goes), and on going over to Sennacherib he surpassed everyone in godlessness, as his very words indicate, "Do not let Hezekiah deceive you into thinking your God will save you. The other gods did not save their nations: are you thinking your God will save you?"[1]

Since he was carried away and uttered such blasphemies, therefore, he was right to say, *The fool has said in his heart, There is no God* (v. 1). He hints at this same Rabshakeh and all his company as believing that either God does not exist or does not look after his own. Now, it is worth marveling at the grace given to David of foretelling so many years before not only the events but also people's ways of thinking at that time. *The fool said in his heart, There is no God.* So what is the result of this? (74) *They became corrupt and loathsome in their pursuits*: beginning with their view that God does not exist they gave themselves to every loathsome and evil pursuit and every practice that was no good; he goes on, in fact, *There is no one who does good, there is not even one.* Blessed Paul in the letter to the Romans understood this as said in general of all human beings. While taking it from the divine Scripture as supporting his own words, however, he did not actually undermine the psalm's particular theme, it being a literary characteristic to apply what is said in reference to particular cases as having general and unspecified reference.[2]

He goes on, then, *The Lord looked down from heaven on the sons of men to see if there is anyone who is intelligent or seeks after God* (v. 2): in this way all the enemy advancing on us with the Rabshakeh were bereft of all godliness and truth, the result being that even God himself looked carefully down from heaven and studied whether any of their number had a care for virtue or righteousness, and did not find one. Hence he proceeds, *All went astray and at the same time proved useless* (v. 3), while at the same time finding everyone involved in vile deeds. *There is no one who does good, not even one.*

He proceeds to explain what they are perpetrating.[3] *Their throat*

---

[1] Cf. 2 Kgs 18:30, 33; Isa 36:18, 20.

[2] Diodore is remarking on Paul's approach in Rom 3:9–12 in citing most of vv. 1–3 of the psalm to make a general reflection on humankind after dealing separately with Gentiles and Jews respectively.

[3] At this point some forms of the LXX (Diodore's text but not Theodoret's) include a lengthy coda to v. 3 drawn from Paul's catena of Psalm verses (5:10;

is an open grave, that is, They are loud-mouthed, uttering things deserving of death. (75) *With their tongues they acted deceitfully*: they utter words full of guile, intent on drawing their listeners to death. He is hinting, in fact, at the words of the Rabshakeh in particular with which he spoke to "those positioned on the wall" of the city, "Listen to me and be subject to the king of Babylon,[4] so that each of you may live happily under his vine and under his fig tree"—which was trickery and malice. *The venom of asps is under their lips*: their words are no different from the venom of an asp, a very harmful animal. *Their mouth is full of cursing and bitterness*: thus their mouth and words are filled with numerous infamies. *Their feet swift to shed blood*, that is, they are murderous and swift to take life. *Destruction and hardship in their paths*: all their behavior is full of hardship and damage. *The way of peace they have not known*: they were not interested in being familiar with peaceful and benign behavior, nor did they intend to be. He summarizes what is responsible for all this in the words, *There is no fear of God before their eyes*: all this causes them to make a point of not having the fear of God before their eyes and not thinking (76) that everyone will be required to give an account of their way of life and their pursuits.

Will they have no knowledge, all those who commit lawlessness, who eat up my people like a meal of bread? (v. 4). The phrase *Will they have no knowledge* is to be read as statement and reply, or as confirmation, the meaning being, Such people will never learn from experience what a harsh thing it is to do wrong to the Lord's people, so bitter are they toward us as to wish to treat us like a meal of bread.[5] *They did not invoke the Lord. There they were gripped with fear where there was no fear* (v. 5): since they are ready to swallow us raw, then, and do not have the Lord before their eyes, fear will overtake them from a quarter whence they do not expect it (foretelling both the punishment inflicted on them and the assault by the angel).[6] Now, he asks, what is the reason why this happens to them? *Because God accompanies the generation of the righteous*: so that God

---

140:3; 10:7; 36:1) and Isaiah 59:7–8 at Rom 3:14–18 following his citation of this psalm's opening. Theodore, predictably, follows Diodore's text; Chrysostom's is not extant.

[4] Sennacherib, of course, is king of Assyria; but the Antiochenes use Babylon and Assyria interchangeably.

[5] All the Antiochenes find this verse problematic (as do modern commentators), and make suggestions as to how it should be read or "declaimed" (Theodoret's suggestion).

[6] Cf. 2 Kgs 19:35; Isa 37:36.

may show that he cares for those devoted to righteousness. *You confounded the intention of the poor one, but the Lord is his hope* (v. 6). By *intention of the poor* here he refers to the intention of Hezekiah, calling him *poor* for his attitude, not for his external possessions, regal and wealthy as he was. So he is saying, Since you discounted Hezekiah (77) for not even daring to lift a weapon against you, and having recourse only to prayer, you are in a position to know that by hoping in God he does what is deserving not of shame but of understanding and restoration.

He adds the following, *Who will give from Sion the salvation of Israel? When the Lord averts the captivity of his people, Jacob will rejoice and Israel be glad* (v. 7): it thus behooved both Hezekiah to hope in God and God himself to help him and all his people. After all, who else was able to bring the captivity to an end, return the people to their own ways and bring joy and happiness to the whole community if not God himself alone, who is capable of everything?

PSALM 15

The fifteenth psalm also has the same theme: with the Israelites freed from the enemies' attack through the king's virtue and piety, blessed David, having recourse to wisdom, brings such encouragement and benefit to the people. He sees fit to ask God who are those ever freed from the enemy and from every recurring difficulty, and who will enjoy uninterrupted possession of Jerusalem. Having asked this in his own person, as it were, he presents God replying on his own account that only those people devoted to virtue and piety like Hezekiah and all of his company. Exhortation is sufficient, you see, when the one exhorting from close by and on his own account can offer the example of what is said. So by way of introduction David poses the question (78), *Lord, who will abide in your dwelling, or who will dwell on your holy mountain?* (v. 1). In other words, Who will escape falling victim to captivity, perils from enemies, or any other hardship?

Then in what follows, as though God were replying, he goes on to say, Who else if not a person like this? *He who walks blamelessly and performs righteousness* (v. 2): whoever is interested in the way of life of the faultless and attends to righteousness as far as possible. *Speaking truth in his heart.* Then by way of commentary on what *truth* is, *He did not deceive with his tongue, nor do evil to his fellow, nor incur a reproach in the case of his neighbor* (v. 3): whoever did harm neither to foreigner nor to family so as to be reproached for not even sparing kith and kin (*neighbor* often being used for the person linked by kinship).[1]

In his eyes every evildoer is despised, whereas he honors those who fear the Lord (v. 4): whoever abhors the wicked, even if they are very rich, while *honoring those who fear the Lord*, even if they are very lowly and poor, will live in honor and respect. There is therefore need to consider how in the apparent reply of God complete instruction in virtue emerges, the intention being for a person firstly to attend to piety and righteousness, then to keep one's distance from all wicked behavior, and after this not to admire the deportment of the rich if piety does not accompany wealth. On the other hand, one should have especial regard for the (79) poor provided they did not have a change of heart for the worse as a result of poverty and instead continued to be devoted to a godly way of life. He wants such a person not to have recourse to oaths, but if at some time forced to take one, not to swear falsely; he goes on, in fact, *He makes an oath to his neighbor without breaking it.* He next teaches that such a person should not be greedy or given to usury, saying in fact, *He did not lend his money at interest* (v. 5). His further wish is that such a person should also be careful about upright behavior in giving judgment and should not be partial to bribes, his further remark being, *Or take bribes against the innocent,* that is, He did not accept bribes to give an adverse verdict against the innocent and condemn him.

His comment on all this as though coming equally from God, *He who does this will never be moved.*

Psalm 16

"An inscription for David." An inscription means the engraving of words on a pillar concerning people's beneficence; this is all he put into the title. Now, the theme is as follows: he speaks on the part of the whole people when God rescued them from their neighbors; Moabites, Ammonites, Amalekites, and Ishmaelites were constantly attacking. So since he unexpectedly rescued the Israelites and invested the foreigners (80) with retribution, the psalm is in thanks-

---

[1] The (extant) Antiochenes find this final clause ambiguous, Theodoret with the Hebrew seeing the righteous person responsible for the taunt, Diodore (and with him, typically, Theodore) object of the taunt.

giving as though written on a pillar—hence the title "Inscription" given to it. In its content it resembles the ninth psalm.

Protect me, Lord, for in you have I hoped (v. 1). *Protect* means You protected, a change of tense occurring. So he is saying, You protected me for hoping in you and for placing all my hope in you. He goes on, in fact, *I said to the Lord, You are my Lord* (v. 2). *I said* means, in fact, I determined to acknowledge you alone as God, and hence I was helped. *Because you have no need of goods from me*: I did well to conclude that I have need of you in everything, whereas you need me for nothing, except my gratitude, and even this does you no good, but only me when I am grateful.

So what is the upshot of this? *The Lord has shown his wonders to the holy ones in his land* (v. 3). By *holy ones* Scripture means not only those dedicated to God, but also those in some respect conspicuous for other things. So *He has shown his wonders to the holy ones in his land* means, He gave evidence of wonders in each land of the neighbors to the mighty and warlike or also to those eminent in some way, punishing them remarkably (the meaning of *He has shown his wonders*, that is, he gave evidence of marvels). *Because all his wishes are in them*: all I longed to see I saw in them, (81) that is, I was fully satisfied with the various forms their punishment took.

Their weaknesses were multiplied, later they accelerated (v. 4): the neighbors got no benefit from their own gods (by *their weaknesses* referring to their gods, applying the term on the basis of fact). That is, since in time of war their gods did not help them, he called them *their weaknesses*; so his meaning is, *Their weaknesses were multiplied*, that is, even if they invoked many gods in battle, they still proved weak despite them. The phrase *later they accelerated* means, far from a delay in their being weakened, their loss proved immediate. *I shall not assemble their assemblies of blood, nor make mention of their names on my lips*. He means, For this reason we never met with them nor assembled together on account of their being idolatrous and murderous, despite their claiming kinship with us on the basis of descent from Esau, Hagar, Ishmael, and the like. On the contrary, we kept ourselves apart from their assembly on account of their lust for blood and idols, whereas we embraced peace in our God as bidden. We have no intention of remembering them, nor broadcasting their works and deeds on our lips; instead, we even abhor naming them (the meaning of *nor make mention of* (82) *their names on my lips*, that is, we did not even mention them, just as before also we did not even meet with them).

The Lord is part of my inheritance and my cup (v. 5): God and his commands were always my portion and lot (*inheritance, cup,* and portion meaning the same thing). *You are the one to restore my inheritance to me*: for this reason I did not fail in my purpose, since you always personally preserved my land, which from the very outset you measured with a cord, as it were, and gave us through the mighty men preceding us (meaning Joshua son of Nun and Caleb son of Jephunneh).[1] It was sufficient for me, and far from grasping at anything more, I tailored my appetite to the place assigned me, entertaining no greed like them (the meaning of the following verse). *Cords fell out for me among the finest; my inheritance, after all, is the finest for me* (v. 6): what fell to my lot like portions measured out by the fathers with a cord I took possession of and was content with.

I shall bless the Lord who gave me wisdom (v. 7): this was also a gift from you, O God, for me; the law given us from you (83) made us wise, not desirous of more but of abiding with the righteous. *Even until night my entrails brought me to my senses*: your laws I kept ever in mind (the sense of *entrails*) even throughout the night, when I spent my time meditating on them and kept them in my heart. *I had the Lord in sight ever before me* (v. 8): as if you, O God, kept guard and watch on my thoughts, so I was afraid to form any wrong plan. *Because he is on my right hand lest I be moved*: and as if you were standing at my right hand, so I pondered and kept your laws in mind, fearful of straying or departing from you.

Hence my heart rejoiced and my tongue was glad (v. 9): so I did not fail in my purpose; for this reason I continued living always in happiness, adding victory to victory and linking thanksgiving to other previous thanksgiving in my very heart and in my mouth (the meaning of *my tongue*). *Further, my flesh will rest in hope. My flesh* means myself: With these hopes, then, he is saying, I shall dwell in the land without fear of removal. *Because you will not abandon my soul in Hades, nor will you allow your holy one to see corruption* (v. 10): you will never allow the one dedicated to you to be consigned to decay, nor be admitted to Hades. On the contrary, you will keep them in the enjoyment of pleasant things and in good actions. (84)

You made known to me paths of life (v. 11). *You made known to me* means, You provided me with deeds that are the source of life. *With your presence you will fill me with joy.* The phrase *With your presence*

---

[1] Cf. Num 16:6, 8, 16.

means From your presence: Even after this, he is saying, I shall be filled with complete joy at your coming. He says as much, in fact, *With delight at your right hand forever*: By *at your right hand* he means with your help: Granted your help, he is saying, we shall be in perpetual delight and joy and satisfaction. Now, it should be noted that blessed Peter in the Acts of the Apostles took these words as applied to the Lord, the verse *You will not abandon my soul in Hades, nor will you allow your holy one to see corruption*. He did not, however, take the words as though he were undermining their factual basis, but as more applicable to the Lord than to those of whom they were said, especially since it was also in the case of the Lord that the outcome of the events more appropriately brought out these words than in the case of those who live for a while but later are consigned to death—the Israelites themselves, I mean. Nothing therefore prevents either the factual basis being preserved or these words being understood of the Lord.[2] (85)

Psalm 17

Blessed David prayed this seventeenth psalm when being pursued by Saul. The title suggests the same thing, reading as follows, "A prayer of David." *Hearken, O Lord, to my righteousness, attend to my pleading* (v. 1). *My righteousness* here means righteous request, in my view: it was mentioned before as well that *righteousness* means righteous request.[1] *Give ear to my prayer in lips that are not deceitful*: you will find my petition and prayer coming sincerely from a pure heart, not with the purpose of harming my pursuer nor treating him deceitfully, but of being freed of harm from him. *Let my judgment proceed from your countenance* (v. 2), that is, show me your righteousness (*my judgment* meaning, Judge in my favor and show me your righteousness). *Let my eyes see uprightness*: as you have the custom of judging things with a just eye, so now as well turn examiner of what I am enduring from Saul and what he inflicts on me unjustly.

You tested my heart, you came to me in vision by night, you examined me by fire and no wrong was found in me (v. 3): why is it now that

---

[2] Acts 2:29–32; cf. Paul at 13:35–37.

[1] Cf. Diodore's comment on Ps 4:2, where like Chrysostom and Theodoret he avoided the implication of the phrase that would have David claiming righteousness for himself.

I say, (86) Test and judge? Especially since even before I make the request, my predicament does not escape you, nor are you ignorant of all the designs in my heart that I experience in the night and ponder by day, that I am caught up in these tribulations to which you exposed me (the meaning of *you examined me by fire*) though I mean no injustice or evil to the one wronging me in this way. *There was no way my mouth spoke of people's doings*: on the contrary, I stop myself even putting into words the deeds and actions done to me by Saul and his company. Why am I doing all this? For no other reason than fearing you and ever taking to heart your commands. He goes on, in fact, *On account of the words from your lips I have kept to difficult paths* (v. 4). By *the words from your lips* he means your commands and laws: It is because of them, he is saying, that I endure every hardship and difficulty.

Perfect my steps in your tracks lest my steps be shaken (v. 5): but since what is inflicted by Saul is more pressing than judgment of me, and I need help to achieve my goal, help and support me lest I lose my way (the meaning of *lest my steps be shaken*). *I cried out and you hearkened to me, O God* (v. 6). There has been a change of tense in *you hearkened*, the meaning being, (87) Hearken to me when I cry, O God. Hence he goes on, *Incline your ear to me, and hearken to my words. Let your mercies be objects of wonder, since you save those who hope in you* (vv. 6–7). *Let your mercies be objects of wonder* means, Cause your loving-kindness to be admired by everyone, since it so remarkably saves those who hope in you. *From the adversaries at your right hand*. He did well to refer to Saul and his company as *the adversaries at your right hand*: it was his decision to anoint David to rule, whereas they on the contrary actually warred against the anointed. Consequently, he called his foes opponents of God's *right hand*.

Protect me, Lord, as the apple of your eye (v. 8): for your part, apply greater surveillance and greater protection to me, Lord, and as you secured the apple of the eye with many coverings, so also ring me around with greater assistance. *Shelter me in the shelter of your wings*. He is speaking in figurative fashion, using the metaphor of birds keeping their young safe with their wings. He highlights the extremity of the adversaries' scheming by mention of the greater assistance: he would not have requested such great security and assistance unless the hardship and scheming against him were extreme. *From the gaze of the ungodly who afflict me* (v. 9): those trying to bring such hardship upon me. (88) Now, I mentioned above that he is censuring Saul and those in his company, whom he also calls ungodly for setting no store by godliness.

He then describes the magnitude of the disasters to the extent possible. *My foes surrounded my soul*: they encircled me on all sides. *They hemmed in their fatness* (v. 10). *Fatness* means the joy and prosperity of life, giving the sense, They abused their own prosperity (the meaning of *They hemmed in*). So they abused prosperity and influence, and thus encircled me on all sides to the point of death. *Their mouth uttered arrogance*: they even employ boasts to proclaim the great things they do to me so as to hush up the experience of sufferings. *They cast me out and at that moment encircled me* (v. 11): having expelled me from my ancestral land, they still did not stop pursuing me, even extending their pursuit to a foreign land. *They set their eyes to bring me to the ground*: their whole purpose and intention is as follows, for me to be expelled from my ancestral land, Saul thinking to circumvent God's decree by which he decreed that I should be king by driving me out of the country of Judah completely (*bring me to the ground* (89) thus meaning, bring me down and hunt me out to another land). Then, to indicate also in figurative fashion the might of the pursuers, he went on, *They came upon me like a lion ready for the prey, like a lion cub lurking in ambush* (v. 12). *Lion* and *lion cub* mean the same: They are ready for hunting and scheming against me like a lion or its cub.

So what to do? *Rise up, Lord, anticipate them, and trip them up* (v. 13): since they are so powerful, swift and fleet of foot in evildoing, anticipate them with your help and check their course like someone tripping up or getting in the way, so that the pursuers will fall while the pursued finds relief. *Rescue my soul from the ungodly, your sword from foes of your hand.* There is some elliptical expression in these verses that causes obscurity, his meaning being,[2] Rescue my soul from the ungodly sword of the foes of your hand. In other words, just as above he said that his adversaries were opponents at God's hand, so here too he refers to his foes, the ungodly, as foes of God's right hand in opposing God's right hand, since in accord with it he intended David to be king. *Lord, sow confusion in the ranks of those who live in this way so as to wipe them out from the earth* (v. 14): what I therefore (90) ask of you, Lord, is this: you have the power to wipe out people from the earth in death, and not wipe

---

[2] Diodore finds difficulty in the reading of his text, where "sword" is in the genitive, as Aquila also reads it, whereas the LXX generally reads an accusative, like Theodoret, and Theodore is aware also of a dative.

them out but extend their life. So do not keep the punishment for them till that time, since they will be consumed by death; rather, punish them while alive, confusing their plans and making them advance on one another, whereas at the moment they are concerted in action against me. And since I do not know how to ask for manifest punishment of them, whereas you are aware, having as you do hidden treasuries of wisdom, inflict on them the punishments you best know.

Hence he goes on, *Let their belly be filled with your hidden things.* By *your hidden things* he means, Fill them with punishments that are invisible, of which you have knowledge but I do not. *Their belly* is his circumlocution for Them. *Let them be filled* means Fill, a change of tense occurring—hence his saying *their belly*, to suggest both them and those born of them; he proceeds, in fact, *Their sons were sated, they left their remnants to their infants.* Again a change of tense occurs with *were sated*, past for future, his meaning being, Satiate them with the hidden punishments known only to you—them and their sons and their descendants (the meaning of *they left their remnants to their infants* in the sense of, And (91) their sons also will bequeath the punishments to those born of them). *I, on the contrary, shall appear in righteousness in your sight* (v. 15): so that I may thus enjoy your righteousness (*I shall appear* meaning, I may have the pleasure). *I shall be satisfied in the appearance of your glory to me*: and I your son may be filled with every enjoyment and happiness when I see this inflicted on them.

Psalm 18

"To the end. For David, the servant of the Lord, what he said to the Lord, the words of this song, on the day the Lord rescued him from the hand of all his foes and from the hand of Saul. And he said." This psalm has a title consistent with the theme, as can be found also in the Kings.[1] Blessed David uttered it in thanksgiving, in fact, toward the end of his life when reminding himself of all the favors he had been granted by God throughout his life. It is typical of pious people, you see, to keep constantly in mind God's kindnesses done to them, and especially (92) at the time of death it seems right to them to number them, both out of gratitude and also

---

[1] Cf. 2 Sam 22.

to teach those coming later how great is God's providence and loving-kindness toward those hoping in him.

I shall love you, Lord, my strength. The Lord is my steadfastness, my refuge and my rescuer (vv. 1–2). The phrase *I shall love* does not mean, I shall love you from this point on since you always provided me with many things; rather, the tense has been changed, and the meaning is, My love and affection for you my master was always right and proper. I felt benevolence and longing for God, in fact, for he proved to be everything to me in time of need—strength in war, steadfastness in endurance, refuge in misfortune, rescuer from all the schemers. So while even the opening of the psalm sufficed as a perfect hymn of praise, anyone with love for God repeatedly adopts the same sentiments as an intense form of thanksgiving when occupied in recalling God's graces. In a range of texts, in fact, he seems to recite and go over the same sentiments in the process of recalling every event from childhood to old age in which God provided him with help and support.

Hence he goes on, *My God is my helper, and I shall hope in him*: he always proved a help to me, since I hope in him and never in anyone else. *My protector, horn of my salvation, my defender*, from (93) the metaphor of those brandishing shields and arrows and rescuing captives, while by *horn* he means strength. So his meaning is, He provided me with strength and support beyond a shield. *In praise I shall call upon the Lord and shall be saved from my foes* (v. 3). By *I shall be saved* he means *I was saved*. So he says *In praise I shall call upon him*: rightly I recall God in hymns and songs of praise, since he always proved my help.

Having made his introduction to this point, from now on he recounts more descriptively how many dangers he encountered and how God against the odds rendered him always superior to the schemers. He also recounts the dangers in a very figurative manner, as also the help of God, the greater the difficulties, the greater the loving-kindness rescuing him from such awful dangers. So his description goes this way, *Death's pangs encircled me, and torrents of lawlessness threw me into confusion; pangs of Hades surrounded me* (vv. 4–5). He calls the sudden and violent intrigues *torrents*, and the tribulations drawing him to death *death's pangs*. *Death's snares caught me unawares*. Since he said above, They seized me, here he said, They stole a march on me, referring to the extremity of the difficulties.

And after that? *In my tribulation I called upon the Lord, and cried out to my God* (v. 6). He is either hinting specifically at the situation with Saul or (94) is referring generally to all the tribulations; there is no difference in the interpretation except that he introduces an attitude of thanksgiving in recounting the misfortunes besetting him and the favors from God. So he goes on, *The Lord heard my voice from his holy temple, my cry before him will reach his ears.* By *will reach* he means has reached, the sense being, He hearkened.

What was the effect of this? *The earth was moved and began trembling, and the foundations of the hills were shaken and were moved, because God was enraged with them* (v. 7): the effect of God's hearkening and being moved to wrath was that everything together was reduced to alarm and confusion, their common master being enraged. *In his wrath smoke arose, and fire will flame from his face* (v. 8): the wrath of God could be seen resembling fire from which smoke issued forth; it also had the effect of indicating the intensity of the wrath—so *will flame* means flamed. Then, to continue the figure of the fire and smoke, he goes on, *Coals were kindled by him. He bent down the heavens and descended* (vv. 8–9). Although above he had said, I was heard *from his holy temple*, now he went on, *He bent down the heavens and descended*, to bring out that he was the one dwelling in the temple and appearing from the sky. Then, since he had said, (95) *He bent down the heavens and descended* (all of this happening invisibly without anyone seeing him descending for assistance to David), he suggests as much in the words, *Dark clouds were under his feet*, that is, invisibility: all this was done by him invisibly, whereas in tangible fashion I was the beneficiary of the assistance. *He rode on cherubs and flew* (v. 10), indicating the rapidity of his coming and the assistance. *He flew on wings of winds.*

Since he had said that this happened invisibly, he goes on in turn, *He set darkness as his concealment* (v. 11), that is, he set it in motion invisibly. And since he had said *He set darkness as his concealment*, he went on, *His tent around him*. Having mentioned the darkness and the invisibility in reference to human beings' inability to see God, in reference to God himself he said *His tent around him*, meaning that he was enveloped in light of his own as though in his own tent. Next, since he had said *He bent down the heavens and descended*, he then presents the coming in terms of events visible to human beings by way of confirmation of God's activity. *Waters of darkness in clouds of air. In the distant splendor before him the clouds pass by, hail* (96) *and coals of fire. The Lord thundered from heaven* (vv. 11–13): then in coming to my aid he came with thunder. *The*

Most High uttered his sound: he thundered as if to suggest he was uttering of his own accord a loud and impressive sound.

He next proceeds to say what he did, having come to wage war. *He fired arrows and scattered them* (v. 14). He presents him as a general come to the aid of his own man, mentioning as *arrows* all the missiles indiscriminately—hail, coals, things that are naturally used as missiles. *He multiplied his lightning flashes and alarmed them*: along with the missiles he dispatched also lightning flashes to prevent the enemies' looking closely at me. *The fountains of the waters appeared, and the foundations of the world were revealed* (v. 15): in fear of the one appearing and the missiles and lightning flashes, the earth bared itself in all directions so as even to reveal its hidden secrets, springs, and anything else hidden in its depths. *At your rebuke, Lord*. The exclamatory remark emphasized nicely that creation had no one else to dread in this way except the author of creation himself. *At the blast of the breath of your rage*. He linked *the breath of rage* with the rebuke, as if to (97) bring out that it was no simple rebuke.

What happened after the terrorizing of the enemy and the shaking of creation? *He sent down from on high and took me; he drew me out of the flood of waters* (v. 16), by *flood of waters* meaning the waves of the enemy and the misfortunes. *He will deliver me from the powerful foes and from those who hate me, because they were too strong for me* (v. 17), *will deliver* meaning delivered: He freed me from the very powerful and strong foe. *They forestalled me on the day of my misfortune* (v. 18): these foes not only pressed upon me in the time of misfortune, but also took the step of shutting off any way to safety, as it were. *The Lord became my support and brought me out into a wide space* (vv. 18–19): but my God not only rendered me superior to the enemy, but also established me in a wide space, that is, in prosperous circumstances. *He will rescue me because he wanted me*. There is a change in tense, the meaning being, He rescued me, since it seemed good to him also to save me. *He will rescue me from my powerful foes*: hence he rescued me from the very strong foes.

The Lord will repay me for my righteousness, (98) *and for the purity of my hands he will repay me* (v. 20): as he realized that while I do them no wrong, they are keen to do away with me, he exercised his characteristic righteousness in repaying me with good things and them with evil in return for their wickedness. Far from giving witness here to a completely blameless life, note, he is stating that by comparison with the schemers he had cleaner hands and was more righteous in not initiating the war but defending himself. *Because I kept the ways of the Lord* (v. 21): he saw me keeping his laws and choosing not to wrong anyone. *And did not forsake my God for impiety*: he saw me concerned for piety. *Because all his judgments are before me, and his decrees have not failed me* (v. 22): his gaze found me attentive as far as possible to righteousness in response to his commands and judgments. *I shall be guiltless before him* (v. 23): he saw me blameless to the extent possible in observance of his laws. *I shall keep myself from my lawlessness*: because I kept myself from every transgression (even if the tense has been changed in the verses, and he uses future (99) for past, the movement of thought still suggests this). *The Lord will repay me for my righteousness* (v. 24): for this reason, then, that I was not intent on wronging the schemers, the Lord repaid me for this choice of mine. *And for the purity of my hands before his eyes*: just as he saw me keeping my hands from the blood of the schemers, he in turn dealt with me.

With a holy one you will be holy, and with an innocent man you will be innocent (v. 25): it is his habit to treat people appropriately, helping those devoted to him and protecting those choosing not to do wrong in the face of wrong. While thus dealing with the holy ones devoted to him, then, how do you treat the wayward? *And with the crooked you will turn about* (v. 26): the wayward and those unwilling to obey your commands you invest with punishment and loss of direction. He then proceeds to say, *And with a chosen one you will be chosen*: those who completely choose the better you in turn choose so as to protect them from every trouble.[2] Then, to bring out that not only does he act this way in the case of each individual, but also (100) proves to be like this with ordinary things, he shifts from an individual's point of view to a general point of view in the words, *Then you will save a lowly people and you will lower the eyes of the haughty* (v. 27): you deal thus also with the peoples; you protect those observing moderation and not turning to war, but invest with humiliation those who are haughty and bent upon doing wrong.

Because you will light my lamp, Lord my God, you will shed light on my darkness (v. 28): you also treated me in accordance with this attitude of mine, everywhere revealing to me my duty and rescuing me from misfortunes. By *darkness* he refers to the tribulations, as by

---

[2] Diodore or his text reverses the order of the two parts of this verse. An Antiochene is unlikely to find in this verse in its LXX form an element of predestination.

lamp and *light* to assistance and support. Hence he proceeds, *Because in you I shall be rescued from temptation, and by my God I shall vault a wall* (v. 29), by *in you* meaning through you. You freed me from every temptation, he is saying, and if ever insuperable disasters confronted me like a wall, you caused me to rise above them with your help. *O my God, his way is faultless* (v. 30): these are the actions of my God, pure and faultless in helping the struggling and in humbling the arrogant. (101) *The sayings of the Lord are proved by fire.* He says the same thing, meaning, Such commands of my God are pure and devoid of any fault, as silver in the furnace is rid of dross. Then in general terms, *He is the protector of all who hope in him.*

Next, as though forthrightness also now arises from the assistance, he goes on, *For who is God except the Lord? and who is God but our God?* (v. 31). Who proves to be God, he is saying, so attentive to us and righteous to the adversaries? *The God who girded me with strength* (v. 32): this God imparts power to me. *And made my path flawless*: and kept me safe. *He furnished me with feet like a deer's and set me on the heights* (v. 33). On the one hand, he said *girded me with power* in reference to conquering; but if ever there was need to flee human difficulties, as it were, he is saying, he made me fleet of foot like the deer and superior to the schemers. (102) *Training my hands for war* (v. 34): he also made me effective in the event of having to strike the enemy. *He set my arms as a bronze bow*. Since in the previous clause he mentioned accuracy in aiming, in this part of the verse he refers also to strength, saying, He made me accurate if ever I released a bolt, and as strong as if I had arms of bronze. *You gave me protection of my safety* (v. 35): in everything you gave me help to be freed from the foe. *And your right hand supported me*: as if aided by your right hand, so did I dominate the enemy. *Your instruction guided me to the end, and your instruction itself will teach me.* By *instruction* he meant learning from the law. In everything, he is saying, you show favor to me: firstly, in giving laws by which I learned my duty; then, in learning from the laws how I should not do wrong, and abstaining from it. Instead, you provided sufficient help to avoid my being harmed by such goodness.

You gave my steps room under me, and my footprints were not weakened (v. 36): if ever there was need to pass by and be freed from the schemers, you made me fleet of foot, strong and durable. (103) *I shall pursue my foes and lay hold of them* (v. 37): if there was need to pursue the foe and prevail over them, again your powerful help.

I shall not desist until they fail: I did not cease pursuing them until I prevailed over them. *I shall cause them distress, and they will not succeed in standing firm* (v. 38): so far have I pressured them that they can find no way to stand firm or to flee. *They will fall under my feet*: of necessity they were in subjection under my feet. *You girded me with strength for war* (v. 39): you made me so strong in battle. *You put all those rebelling against me under my feet*: if anyone rose up against me, you made them vulnerable and subject to me. *You made my foes turn their back on me* (v. 40): everywhere you put my adversaries to flight (*you made them turn their back on me* meaning, You allowed me to aim at the back). *And those who hated me you destroyed*: you invested my foes generally with punishment. (104) *They cried out, and there was no one to save them; to the Lord, and he did not hearken to them* (v. 41). Since he had said he invested them with punishment, he means the foreigners in particular, the sense being, Under pressure from you, the true God, they looked to their own gods for help and found none, and rightfully were in all sorts of trouble (in the clause *They cried out, and there was no one to save them; to the Lord, and he did not hearken to them*, the term *Lord* means the God of the nations, his meaning being, Since their gods were nothing and they gained no help by calling upon them, what of me, who trusted in you?). *I shall beat them as fine as dust before the wind* (v. 42). He is referring to the foes being insubstantial. *I shall grind them like dirt of the streets*: I trampled them like someone treading and grinding dirt on the street.

Deliver me from opposition from the people (v. 43). Again the tense has changed, the meaning being, You it was who caused me to prevail over the people in opposition and at war (referring to the foreigners). *You will appoint me as head of the nations*: having appointed me ruler of the foreigners. Hence he goes on, *A people whom I did not know served me*: thus the foreign nations (105) served and were obedient. *On their ears' hearing they hearkened to me* (v. 44), that is, They proved responsive, subservient, and subject. *Foreign sons were false to me*. Since he had said above that the nations *served me*, the phrase *were false to me* means that they did so unwillingly: They served us and through us our God, doing so first through fear, and later doing so also with affection, turning fear into affection, the experience of true religion thus getting the better of their unwillingness. *Foreign sons grew old and went limping from their paths* (v. 45): in time (the meaning of *they grew old*) such people forsook their own superstition on discovering the error of polytheism, and were converted to our ways on learning the force of the true religion.

The Lord lives! Blessed be God (v. 46): for this I sing hymns to the living God and judge him worthy of being praised. *Let the God of my salvation be exalted*: I exalt him for (106) ever giving me against the odds the grounds of salvation. *The God who gives me vengeance and subdued peoples under me* (v. 47): this God who always provided me with complete vengeance and subjected the nations to me. *My rescuer from my wrathful foes* (v. 48): he it is who often rescued me even from my own, if at times they gave vent to baseless anger against me (referring to his own people, like those in Saul's company at first, and later those in Absalom's company). Hence he goes on, *From those rebelling against me you will raise me up*: you rescued me from all those rebelling against me, you lifted me above their intrigue. *From an unrighteous man rescue me*: he rescued me also from an unrighteous man (probably hinting at Ahithophel, Shimei, or some other lawless person who rebelled against him).

Hence I shall confess to you among nations, Lord (v. 49). *Among nations* here includes many current ones, whether Israelites or also the nations beyond. In all cases, he is saying, I shall give thanks for the good things of which you have always given evidence to me. (107) *And I shall sing to your name*: I shall recite your name in hymns. *Magnifying the deliverances of the king* (v. 50): you are the one who demonstrated the surprising and marvelous deliverances[3] to me. *And showing mercy to his anointed*: it is you who ever displayed great loving-kindness to him whom you anointed, myself, David, you who still generously promise to exercise it also to all my successors. Hence he goes on, *To David and his offspring forever*. Since by the Holy Spirit he understood that God's promises were not confined to him alone, but would pass also to his offspring, so he spoke in this way here with particular reference to Christ's life. The outcome, in fact, showed that *David's offspring*, blessing and sanctifying the nations, referred to no one other than the Lord of all. The blessing affected the offspring without restriction, after all, and following David, remember, there were many famous descendants of his in each generation (Christ himself thought to be the one proven to be famous and great)—firstly Solomon, then Uzziah, then Hezekiah, then Josiah—yet none emerged as more precisely realizing the force of the promise than Christ alone, and after him

---

[3] NRSV "triumphs," Dahood "victories," LXX σωτηρίαι.

there was no one, nor is there anyone to whom the blessing of the promises would be thought to refer. After all, with Judah in captivity and the tribes (108) intermingled, and no clarity as to who was descended from whom, it is now obvious that the fulfillment of the promise rested with Jesus himself, to whom in this case as well both the prayer and the prophecy allude, *To David and his offspring forever*. I mean, those of the company of Hezekiah, even if they seemed to enjoy some grace from God, did not do so *forever*, death befalling each one with the result that they were not the subject of blessing *forever*.

Psalm 19

Of the psalms entitled "To the end. A psalm of David" some indicate that they were composed in his old age, some that they were composed in reference to future events, and so they have these titles. This nineteenth psalm is doctrinal: just as the fourth, also being doctrinal, censures those claiming that existing things do not benefit from providence, so too the present psalm levels an accusation against those who claim that things exist of themselves. The latter are worse than those saying they do not benefit from providence: those saying they do not benefit from providence do not go so far as to claim also that they exist of themselves, only that they were made by someone yet are not shown providence. Likewise of those denying providence there are many different kinds: some absolutely deny providence, others confine it to heaven, still others to the things of earth and the common lot of (109) humankind, not actually to each person individually altogether. Among the latter there emerges a variety of differences, but among those claiming independent existence the godlessness is one and the same without exception. The view obtains among all such people that existing things were made by no one, instead coming to be by themselves. Necessarily following on this is the view that these things also do not merit providence: with no admission of the creator, the provider is also not acknowledged by them, either.

Against such people, therefore, blessed David goes to some length in this psalm, censuring them in pointed fashion in the words, *The heavens tell of the glory of God* (v. 1). He did well to refer to all things alike in circumlocutory fashion as *glory of God* by mention of visible things instead of touching on God's creative activity, wisdom, and magnificence, since all these things contribute to the glory of God. *The firmament announces work of his hands.* Sometimes he speaks of heaven, sometimes of firmament, in keeping with blessed Moses, the latter saying, "In the beginning heaven and earth" were made, going on to say that on the second day, "And God said, Let a firmament be made in the midst of the water, and let there be a division between water and water," and he indicated the first was heaven and the other the firmament. It was called heaven in similar terms to the other, the visible one in likeness to the invisible to the extent of sharing its name with it, though not completely its nature as well.

Now, if David referred to heaven as *heavens*, this too is not unusual or out of keeping with Scripture, it being usual for it to speak of a single thing in the plural as many. Stating singular things as plural is a Hebrew idiom, especially in the case of heavenly things, either on account of their importance or also by another custom. Elsewhere he illustrates this more clearly by speaking in this case not in the plural but in the singular, "The heaven is the Lord's heaven," in the sense of dedicated, and he goes on, "but the earth he has given to human beings."[1] So his meaning here in the two clauses is that the upper heaven and the visible heaven declare a creator, organization, magnitude, wisdom, and orderliness. The phrase *announces work of his hands* means that the heavens were made by God's hands—an anthropomorphic expression.

Then, after mentioning the heavens, he goes on, *Day to day belches forth speech, and night to night proclaims knowledge* (v. 2): not only is it the heavens that declare by their orderliness that they were made, but also the sequence of days and nights in adhering to measures of a kind and not trespassing on one another or irritating one another, despite waning and waxing in keeping with due seasons, and likewise not exceeding their own order. Now, where there is order there is also proof of the one determining order, and there too denial of being self-made, (111) since what is not done by anyone cannot show order. All these visible things surely illustrate order. So he is saying, They announce some pattern and cry aloud the order of the orderer and the folly of the notion of being self-made (*belches*

---

[1] Ps 115.16, where unfortunately for Diodore's argument the terms again have a plural form in Hebrew, Dahood commenting, "Though the ancient versions such as the LXX . . . all understood the phrase *hassamayim samayim* as 'the heaven of heavens,' they doubtless would have been hard put to explain the syntax of the phrase."

forth and *proclaims* saying the same thing, a metaphor from what is uttered from the heart).

Then, after saying that day and night teach discerning people that they are ordered by God and that they give voice to this pattern, he goes on, *There is no speech nor word, their voices are not heard* (v. 3). *Their voices are not heard* refers to everything, his meaning being, The voices of days and nights are not such that they are heard only by some people, like the tongues of human beings: if Greeks, for example, they are understood by Greeks, not by barbarians; if barbarians, they are understood by barbarians, not by Greeks. The voices of visible creation are not like that; instead, they are equally clear to everyone, both Greeks and barbarians, giving everyone the one message, that they were made by someone and do not exist of themselves. To make the same thing clearer he goes on, *Their utterance went out to all the earth, to the bounds of the world their messages* (v. 4), by *their* meaning the creatures', the heavens' and the days'.

After mentioning them, therefore, he necessarily moves on to the sun, following the Mosaic sequence, as I said. (112) *In the sun he set up his tent*. So he is saying, This is the way he created the heavens and the nights and the days, and they supply knowledge of creation to all alike who look with understanding. The case of the sun, he is saying, offers also an extraordinary degree of wonder in that despite its size and massive dimensions he caused it to be moved by no one but to travel by itself and move itself (the meaning of *He set up his tent in it*, that is, He arranged for the sun to move itself, a mark of the extraordinary power of the creator). Then, after bringing out that the sun is marvelous not only for its size but also for its beauty, he goes on, *He emerges like a bridegroom from his chambers* (v. 5). While even the size sufficed for wonder, he went on to mention its beauty as well, bringing out the surpassing liberality of the creator: It is not only huge and beautiful, he is saying, but also meets urgent and demanding needs of life and good order.

What does he say, in fact? *He will rejoice like a giant to run the race. His emergence is from one end of heaven, and his course to the other end of heaven* (vv. 5–6). Since he had said that he completes a lengthy course, he indicated also the distance, saying that he travels from one end of heaven to the other in one day, which is a degree of speed incapable even of imagining. Now, he does well also to confute indirectly those who claim heaven is spherical and circular, a sphere and a circle having no beginnings and zenith, being self-contained and revolving around a center. Having mentioned the rate, then, he goes on to the need it meets. (113) *There is nothing concealed from its warmth*: the degree to which he meets needs and supplies heat and such life-giving energy escapes no one's notice, there being no existing thing which does not benefit from heat and the nourishing energy which it imparts to all earthly beings. In everything he shows admiration and praise for the sun so as to bring out the liberality of the creator: he mentioned its size, he mentioned its beauty, he mentioned its speed and after that the need it meets for existing things, namely, for nourishing energy and heat.

He then goes on in general terms, *The law of the Lord is faultless, correcting souls* (v. 7). *The law of the Lord* means that discerned in nature: what the written law does by teaching its intentions to those with a knowledge of writing the law in nature does by teaching those with an understanding eye that there is a creator of visible realities. *The testimony of the Lord is reliable, giving wisdom to the simple*. Once again it says the same thing: just as in the case of the written law he refers also to the same law as testimony, ordinance, commandment, in terms of the same figure in the case of nature he employs the same words to show that as the written law makes simple people learned, so too the law in nature makes more religious those with a yen to be religious. *Giving wisdom to the simple* was well put to mean those with both the will and the capacity to learn, not those hostile and resistant to (114) the elect who practice religion and live a life of prudence. Having mentioned *the testimony of the Lord*, then, he goes on, *The ordinances of the Lord are right, gladdening the heart* (v. 8). He says the same thing also in what follows, *The commandment of the Lord is clear, giving light to the eyes*, that is, the command given us in nature to use our reason to find the creator, according to the text from wise Solomon, "From the greatness and the beauty of created things the creator is discerned by reasoning."[2]

After learning that there is a God who creates what exists, then, what must one do? *The fear of the Lord is pure, abiding forever* (v. 9): for the one who has learned that there is a God it is necessary also to fear him openly and always. *The decrees of the Lord are true, completely justified*: such a person—namely, the one fearing God, creator of all—knows that his verdicts are true, and it is impossible for the one transgressing them not to be called to account. *More*

---

[2] Wis 13:5.

desirable than heaps of gold and precious stones (v. 10): worthy of the love and respect of the devout beyond choice minerals. *And sweeter than honey or honeycomb*: this too is an index of the speaker's attitude: (115) the things that prompt him to be inclined to God and his commands also teach others how they should be inclined to them. Hence he goes on, *Your servant in fact keeps them* (v. 11), that is, just as they proved acceptable to me, so too they were judged to be both desirable and sweet. *Abundant the repayment for keeping them*: and not without benefit to the one keeping them, bringing many fine rewards.

Having to this point shown how the devout person should be disposed to God and his creation, at this point he proceeds to try to teach what a person should observe after such devotion, namely, that the devout person should be careful also not to commit sin in human affairs, perfect virtue being devotion to God and righteous behavior to people. So having given instruction in regard to devotion, at this point he proceeds to speak of the sins in respect of human beings and puts people on the alert so as to realize what is an involuntary sin and what voluntary, and how they differ from each other, and further into how many types involuntary sin is divided. He employs an admirable division, firstly dividing sin into two, voluntary and involuntary. After this he divides the involuntary sin into three, since for example we fall when compelled, or through weakness, or when misled; or we do something when an incident occurs that is more influential than good intentions, or we prove too weak to overcome the power of lust and fall into sin, or in many cases we make a judgment with the best of intentions but by some deception we are inveigled into doing the opposite. (116)

Blessed David did well to survey the whole human condition and make this distinction between sins, beginning at this point, *Who will understand faults?* (v. 12), namely, this lesson on sins. Who will be so understanding as to see and be on guard and know the difference between voluntary and involuntary faults? So having said *Who will understand faults?* he immediately proceeds to the voluntary fault in the words, *Purify me from my hidden ones. Spare your servant from external influences* (vv. 12–13). By *hidden ones* he refers to the situation with lust in which we are overcome, and by *external influences* to what befalls us unexpectedly from without, normally called accidental by the uninitiated—or rather, to put it more plainly, what befalls us by way of temptation and an onset of the devil, as for example what happened in the case of the martyrs, when all of a sudden persecution came upon them in a time of tranquillity, then they fell under the power of the authorities, then they were subjected to torture and often, though having good intentions, they succumbed to the great number of tortures and fell into the involuntary sin of denial. What was not of their doing, therefore, but originated and befell us from without he calls *external influences*.

He proceeds to say the same thing more clearly, *If they do not gain dominion over me, then I shall be faultless*, that is, if you strip away the inclinations of lust besetting me furtively and pressures coming from outside that lead me to (117) sin, and they do not gain dominion over me, you will find me with an upright mind-set. Hence he goes on, *And I shall be purified from serious sin*: I will be found guiltless of a voluntary fall, that is, of a serious sin. It was, in fact, for this reason that the sin that happened voluntarily he called *serious*, since an involuntary fall, even if grave, deserves pardon, whereas the voluntary one, even if slight, involves condemnation. A bad action of ours that is voluntary, you see, even if of the slightest, is condemned more on the basis of the mind-set of the one making the choice, whereas the action of ours that is not voluntary but is the result of pressure coming from outside perhaps merits pardon of the loving judge, who judges our actions on the basis of what comes from us, not of what is not from us when we are forced by chance from another source.

Having said *And I shall be purified from serious sin*, then, he goes on, *My mouth's utterances will meet with favor, and my heart's intention is completely in your presence* (v. 14). *With favor* means to your satisfaction: You will find my mind-set, he is saying, always attentive to duty and always desirous of good. If the sins besetting me from outside you do not prevent from happening, or you pardon them when they happen, then you will find the movements of my will are worthy of a religious man.

Having to this point conducted also his treatment of sins, he sets the seal on it all with a prayer, going on, (118) *Lord, my helper and my redeemer*: on your part, then, Lord, help me in this disposition when I make the right choices, and redeem me in cases when I opt to fall.

Psalm 20

The twentieth and twenty-first psalms have the same theme, foretelling the future—to do with Hezekiah, I mean. In some way the title also suggests as much, "To the end. A psalm of David," that is, about future events. They differ from each other in this way, however, that while the twentieth is recited with the people still in need and Hezekiah benefiting from loving-kindness from God when the Assyrian—Sennacherib, I mean—advanced on him and sent the Rabshakeh to taunt and belittle him, the populace, and the city, the twenty-first is a triumphal hymn on the people's part for Hezekiah's having won the bloodless victory when the angel was sent and slew 185,000 Assyrians.[1]

Now, the actual beginning of the twentieth psalm also suggests that the people are in need, saying, *The Lord hear you in a day of tribulation!* (v. 1). Blessed David (119) used the actual words which Hezekiah and those in his company spoke at the time so as to bring out that the power of grace mentions not only the events but also the actual dispositions of those destined to suffer later and the actual words, the force of inspiration reaching as far even as the future events. So when Hezekiah and those in his company sent to Isaiah, they used these words, "This very day is a day of tribulation and taunting," and "Birth pangs have come, but lack the strength to deliver." So let a prayer be raised for us, it says, to the Lord God.[2] Since those in the company of Hezekiah were on the point of saying from the depths of their heart, "A day of tribulation, taunting, and rebuke has come," therefore, David prophesies as though on the people's part in the words, *The Lord hear you in a day of tribulation.*

He then goes on, *The name of the God of Jacob protect you!* The name means the one mocked by the Assyrians: since the Assyrians claimed, Which god rescued his own so that your God should in turn rescue you? saying this in mockery of the awesome name,[3] he therefore responds *The name of the God of Jacob protect you*, that is, the name mocked by them. *Send help from the holy place* (v. 2), *holy place* meaning the temple. Hence he goes on, *Support you from Sion! May the Lord remember all your sacrifice, and your holocaust enrich me* (v. 3): may he now (120) call to mind your zeal for the sacrifices and consider well your burnt offerings.

May the Lord grant you your heart's desire, and implement your every purpose (v. 4). What else did Hezekiah's purpose involve than the toppling of the enemy and the victory of his own? *We shall*

---

[1] Cf. 2 Kgs 18–19; Isa 36–37.
[2] Cf. 2 Kgs 19:2–4; Isa 37:2–4.
[3] Cf. 2 Kgs 18:33–35; Isa 36:18–20.

rejoice in your salvation, and be magnified in the name of the Lord our God (v. 5): when this happens, we shall all enjoy happiness, glory, and magnificence, thanks to our God. *The Lord fulfill all the requests of your heart. Now I know that the Lord saved his anointed* (vv. 5–6), that is, I shall know (the tense being changed). *He will hear him from his holy heaven*: I shall know for a fact that he saved his anointed and hearkened to him. *In sovereignties the salvation of his right hand*: and I shall know it (by *his right hand* referring to his assistance). So I shall know and experience, he is saying, that his God gave evidence of power for his salvation (referring to it, as I said, by *his right hand*).

Some rely on chariots, some on horses, whereas we shall call upon the name of the Lord our God (v. 7): since the Assyrians trust in numbers, horses and weapons, make clear, Lord, that we have better assistance—hope in you. (121) *They were entangled and fell, while we got up and stood straight* (v. 8): when this happened, it was inevitable that while some fell and perished, we stood firm and were saved. *Lord, save the king; hear us on the day we call upon you* (v. 9). Having begun with a prayer, he concluded with a prayer. The phrase *on the day we call upon you* indicated that these events were due to happen later.

Psalm 21

Such, then, is the twentieth psalm. The twenty-first in turn, as though the victory had already been attained, presents the populace celebrating and singing God's praises as follows. *Lord, in your power the king will be glad* (v. 1), that is, the king was glad (with further change in tense). *And will rejoice exceedingly in your salvation*, that is, rejoiced. Hence he goes on, *You have given him his heart's desire* (v. 2). He indicates in this that the previous clauses also involved a change in tense, future for past. *And you did not deprive him of the request of his lips*, (122) that is, you provided him with all he requested.

Because you anticipated him with blessings of goodness (v. 3): why say, You gave all he asked? You gave him more than he asked, in your generosity exceeding the petitioner's appetites. Then in an even more figurative fashion he proceeds, *You set on his head a crown of precious stones*, a metaphor from the great conquerors being crowned with some splendid wreath, which he uses to give an inspired account also of the events after the victory as though these, too, had already happened. You see, since the charism has no difficulty seeing future events, instead regarding them as already past, in different ways he mentions future events as already happened, as also Isaiah, "He was led like a sheep to slaughter,"[1] that is, He will be led. So he goes on, *He asked life of you, and you gave him it* (v. 4). To bring out that the victory went to Hezekiah's head, and he was then chastised by illness and petitioned God, he confessed and God granted him a further fifteen years of life, he accordingly says *He asked life of you, and you gave him it*. It was also to bring out that not only did he rid him immediately of illness, but he also extended his later life, granting him fifteen years after the illness. In fact, he goes on, *length of days for age upon age*, by *age* referring to his past life, and by (123) *age upon age* to the later life of fifteen years.[2]

Thanks to your salvation his glory is wonderful (v. 5): you also made him famous for the rescue from the Assyrians against the odds. *You will endow him with glory and magnificence*, that is, You endowed him (a further change of tense occurring). *Because you will give him blessing forever* (v. 6), that is, you caused him also to be constantly praised for future generations: wherever the report of all the happenings reaches, there consequently Hezekiah will also be the subject of hymns of praise for attaining salvation against the odds. *You will gladden him with joy with your presence*, the phrase *with your presence* meaning from your presence, referring by God's *presence* to his appearance and assistance. So his meaning is, You gladdened him and filled him with joy by appearing to him and helping him. Then he also adds the reason, *Because the king hopes in the Lord* (v. 7): since he personally hoped in the Lord, it was right for him to attain what he attained. *And by mercy of the Most High he will not be moved*: through the loving-kindness of you, the Most High, he was not moved or lost his way; instead, he stood firm in his remarkable security.

What, in fact, happened? (124) *Let your hand be found on all your foes* (v. 8). *Let your hand be found* means, It was found, namely, your action and retribution, firm against all your foes. He did well to speak of the people's foes as God's foes: those taunting the people taunted God by saying, Surely your God will not rescue you from our hands?[3] Then he goes on, saying the same thing, *May your right*

---

[1] Isa 53:7.
[2] Cf. 2 Kgs 20:6.
[3] Cf. 2 Kgs 18:35.

hand find all those who hate you, that is, your right hand (in other words, strong help) found (that is, fixed upon) all those who hate you. How, in fact, did you do away with them? *Because you will set them like a baking pan of fire at the time of your appearance* (v. 9): you made them resemble a baking pan of fire; by appearing to them in retribution you scorched them as though in a baking pan of fire.

The Lord in his wrath will confound them, and fire will consume them, and rightly so: since you are Lord of all and were angry with them, consequently you also confounded them and set them alight as though by fire. *You will destroy their fruit from the earth and their offspring from the human race* (v. 10): you so wiped them out as to leave no offspring, as if to say, along with their possessions and (125) all their kindred you wiped them out. For what reason? *Because they directed evils against you* (v. 11): since they uttered blasphemous remarks against you, it was right for them to be subjected to such punishments.

He then also recalls in detail the Assyrians' blasphemy so as to heighten the glory of the one who conquered, going on, *They devised plans which could not succeed in practice*, that is, they could not be implemented. What in fact did they intend? To dispose of the king, set fire to the city, capture the populace; but their plan could not be carried out when your help for us unexpectedly appeared. *Because you will put them to flight; in your remnants you will prepare their countenance* (v. 12). In these clauses a change of speakers is involved: instead of saying, In their remnants you will prepare your countenance, he said the opposite, this obscurity obviously consequent upon the translation;[4] the sense of the clauses, on the contrary, is as I say. *You will put them to flight* means, You turned some of them into fugitives: Sennacherib and those in his company learned of the unexpected destruction of the 185,000, and took to flight; so the phrase You put them to flight means, You destroyed some and turned the survivors into fugitives. Far from sparing even them, you hardened your countenance even against the survivors themselves, the phrase *You will prepare your countenance* meaning, You hardened it, in the sense that you did not overlook even the survivors (126) and fugitives until you slew them as well. This in fact was what happened: the Assyrian fled to his own city,

---

[4] The verse contains more than one hapax legomenon, sending modern commentators to Ugaritic for light. For his part Diodore makes alterations to his text in the light of what history tells him of Sennacherib's fate (2 Kgs 19:36–37).

and on going in to worship when he thought he was in safety, he was assassinated by his own sons.

Be exalted, Lord, in your power (v. 13): exalted though you are, then, you are shown to be more exalted through your power and in outdoing all the arrogant, as by inflicting the blow on them from on high. For this reason we shall not cease singing your praises always. He goes on, in fact, *We shall celebrate and sing of your sovereignties.*

PSALM 22

"To the end. On support at dawn. A psalm of David." By "support at dawn" the title probably refers to rapid support and immediate help.[1] The psalm is composed from the viewpoint of David when pursued by Absalom, God permitting him to fall foul of such trials on account of the sin with Bathsheba. Now, similarities in facts emerged also in the case of Christ the Lord, especially in the passion, (127) such that some commentators thought from this that the psalm is uttered on the part of the Lord. But it is not applicable to the Lord: David is seen to be both mentioning his own sins and attributing the sufferings to the sins, something in no way applicable to Christ. The partial resemblances in the sufferings do not completely displace the psalm's theme: it is possible both for the factual basis to be preserved and the resemblance to occur as well, with neither displacing the other.

For a start, then, some commentators thought the opening and the rest apply to the Lord since the verse in the text, *O God my God, attend to me: why have you abandoned me?* was spoken by the Lord;[2] but it is not possible that the rest is recited on the part of the Lord. It goes on, in fact, *The words of my failings are far from saving me.* David's meaning is this: Lord, be reconciled to me and do not abandon me any further; instead, attend to me, even if my faults put me far from being saved by you (the phrase *the words of my failings* meaning the failings themselves). Nevertheless, be faithful to yourself, do not cast an eye on the magnitude of the sin but on the magnitude of your loving-kindness. Then the following also still more clearly applies to David than to the Lord—namely? *O God, I shall cry to you by day, and you will not hearken to me, by night, and*

---

[1] The phrase is probably another musical cue, "The Deer of the Dawn," and at any rate has been mistranslated by the LXX, who saw *'eyalut*, "support," in *'ayyelet*, "deer."

[2] Cf. Matt 27:46; Mark 15:34.

not to my folly (v. 2): cast your eye on this, Lord, that (128) both by day and by night I cry aloud to you, and when not heard I am led to entertain foolish thoughts—not that I claim you have no providence for human affairs, knowing the reason why I am not heard, the cause being sin. How does this or the rest of the psalm apply to Christ?

You, on the contrary, the praise of Israel, dwell in the holy place (v. 3). What of this, then? was not Christ holy? It applies to David: since he had said, Both by day and by night I call upon you, and when not heard I am led to entertain foolish thoughts, he goes on as though consoling himself, I am convinced that *You dwell in the holy place* and you quickly hearken, so that your not hearing me at present comes not from your neglect but from my sin. Of the fact that you quickly help those dedicated to you and all the holy ones, and support them, whereas you allow those in sin to be neglected, I have proof in advance. Namely? *Our fathers hoped in you, they hoped and you rescued them. To you they cried out and were saved, they hoped in you and were not disappointed* (vv. 4–5): this is the way, then, with all the holy ones; why is it that I am not heard?

He goes on, *But I am a worm, not a human being, reproached by human beings and scorned by the people* (v. 6). *Scorned by the people* was well put: since with God's permission (129) the people chose Absalom as king and imagined him to be so, he says, I am a mockery to the people. And not only this: I am reduced to such a state that *at the sight of me they all turned up their nose at me* (v. 7). He is referring in particular to those in the company of Shimei, when they insulted him as he left, saying, "Off you go, man of blood, off you go, man of iniquity; the blood you shed the Lord brought upon your own head."[3] He recalls also others who probably mocked him at that time and said what foes normally say. So after saying *At the sight of me they all turned up their nose at me*, he goes on, *They muttered under their breath and shook their head.* What did they say? *He hoped in the Lord, let him rescue him, let him save him because he wants him* (v. 8). These words, too, were applied to the Lord;[4] and, as I said, nothing prevents both the psalm's theme being preserved and the resemblances very precisely to the Lord emerging. What of David, then? While they take this attitude to me, speak this way and

---

[3] Cf. 2 Sam 16:5–8.
[4] Cf. Matt 27:39–44.

make these taunts, I am convinced the opposite is true of your lordship toward me. Namely? That from the very outset you continued to show the same providence to me as in making me. Why, in fact? (130)

Because you are the one who drew me out of the womb, my hope from my mother's breasts. On you I was cast from the womb, from my mother's womb you are my God (vv. 9–10). He did well to focus his attention on providence in general, asking, How is it you are not showing providence to me now when I am pursued and wronged after being the object of your overall providence before having any dealings with people? Who is the one who shaped me in the womb, who the one who brought me from the womb, who the one who nourished me at maternal breasts and brought me to this stage of life? Having anticipated my needs and provided me with such benefits when I contributed nothing, then, will you now cut me adrift when I both perceive your kindness and am able to give thanks? What, then? *Do not keep your distance from me, because tribulation is nigh, because there is no one to help me* (v. 11): as you provided all these benefits on your own initiative, therefore, now too, when they all advance against me with intrigues and you are the only one left for my salvation, lend help. *There is no one to help me* was well put: everyone belonged to Absalom's party.

He then mentions both their desperation and their frenzy against him so as to move God further to lend him support. *Many young bulls surrounded me* (v. 12), as if to say, the might of his subjects. *Fat bulls encircled me,* as if to say, the leaders and rulers. *They opened their mouth at me like a lion striking and roaring* (v. 13), that is, (131) both the subjects and the rulers came gaping at me to swallow me like a lion its prey. So what was the result of this? *All my bones were poured out and scattered like water* (v. 14): at this threat and promise of theirs all my power flowed away and disappeared like water. *My heart was melted like wax in the midst of my belly.* He mentions what is typical of people worried and distressed: since all worry affects the heart, he did well to add *My heart was melted like wax,* my mind having no stability or composure or sound hope; instead, under pressure from the threats and depressing expectations my thoughts dissolved like wax. Next, as happens also with those in distress, *My strength was dried up like a potsherd* (v. 15): all my condition left me, depression reducing me to great dryness. *My tongue has stuck to my throat.* This, too, is typical of people dehydrated and incapable of speaking. *You brought me down to the dust of death*, that is, as if to the dust of death: You allowed me to suffer at their hands to such an extent, he is saying, as to be no different from those already buried and mingled with the dust.

Then, having mentioned in the foregoing the enemies' power and (132) control by reference to lions and bulls, he goes on to mention at this point their effrontery as well, proceeding thus, *Because many dogs surrounded me* (v. 16), that is, like audacious dogs as well. *A mob of evildoers encircled me*: in short, a band of wicked people and a mob of evildoers encircled me. What did they do? *They dug my hands and feet, they numbered all my bones* (vv. 16–17). I mentioned that the resemblance emerged more properly in the Lord's case to the extent of its being possible to see the nails driven into his hands and feet. David, on the other hand, says of himself *They dug my hands and my feet, they numbered all my bones* in the sense, They scrutinized my every action and all my capacity, and submitted my life to examination (the meaning of *they numbered all my bones*). This did not happen in the Lord's case: even if the first clause *They dug my hands and my feet* applies, the second does not, *They numbered all my bones*; we are told they did not break a bone of his, according to Scripture. So the fact that they scrutinized my total capacity and my every action and subjected them to examination applies to David.[5]

He mentions also those taking possession of the palace and going through everything. *Whereas for their part they stared and peered at me*: in short, whatever they wanted to see of me (133) they saw, and saw in detail (the meaning of *they stared and peered at me*). Then, following upon his saying, They scrutinized my complete condition and subjected it to examination, he goes on, *They divided my garments among them, and on my clothing they cast lots* (v. 18), that is, they parceled out everything of mine. Now, this was fulfilled more properly in the case of the Lord to the extent of lots being cast to divide his very clothes. But it is not in opposition to the psalm's theme: it is possible, as I said, for the resemblance to emerge in greater detail in that case and for it to happen here in actual fact.

Hence the sequel applies more properly to David. *But you, Lord, do not keep your help at a distance from me; have an eye to my support* (v. 19). And the fact that the sequel does not apply to Christ,

---

[5] Diodore pits the citation by all the Evangelists of vv. 16–17 against John's citation (19:36) of Exod 12:46 to the effect that none of Jesus' bones was broken, and so in his view ἱστορία is not respected in the case of Jesus, only David.

either, is clear from this; he goes on, in fact, *Rescue my soul from a sword, my single possession from the grasp of a dog* (v. 20). Being rescued from a sword was applicable to David, but was not applicable to the Lord; since the passion proceeded with his permission, he was not set upon with a sword. Now, by *dog* here once again he refers to Absalom and Ahithophel, and by *my single possession* to my soul alone. Then, to highlight the wickedness of the schemers, he goes on, (134) *Save me from a lion's mouth and my lowliness from unicorns' horns* (v. 21). A lion is a strong animal, and a unicorn—so they claim—stronger; so to suggest figuratively the foes' strength, he thus introduced these animals.

When this happens, what will occur? *I shall tell of your name to my brothers, I shall sing to you in the midst of the assembly* (v. 22): I shall gather together those who are now fleeing with me, make a great assembly of them and sing your praises by recounting the events of the unexpected rescue at your hands. *You who fear the Lord, praise him; all the descendants of Jacob, glorify him* (v. 23): and so it will then be possible for me also to say that all you who fear God keep him forever in hymns of praise, since he it is who against the odds saves those who hope in him. *Let all the descendants of Israel stand in awe of him.* This, too, is connected with the above: I shall cry aloud in the midst of the assembly, he is saying, that everyone should both fear him and sing his praises. Why? *Because he did not despise or abhor the prayer of the poor* (v. 24). By *the poor* he means himself. He indicates that all who know him should fear him because he does not reject or despise the prayer of the poor. *Nor turn his face from me; when I cried to him, he hearkened to me*: (135) far from turning his face from me, he even readily hearkened to my request in real need.

From you comes my praise (v. 25): the very action of praising you also comes from you; since you came to my aid unexpectedly, you provided me with the occasion of singing your praises. *I shall confess to you in the great assembly*: in the thronged assembly I shall both confess and give thanks to you. And not only this: *My vows I shall pay before all who fear him*: if I make a vow, I shall fulfill it completely before many witnesses. *The poor eat and will be filled, and those who seek him out will praise the Lord* (v. 26): and so all who hope in you and obey you (meaning these poor people) have occasion for joy in my situation. *Their hearts will live forever*, that is, they will constantly have joy of heart. Not only that: as well, those hearing of us from afar, how our situation was of concern to you, will themselves also acknowledge their duty, persuaded that the one who is so interested in their affairs is the true God. Hence he proceeds, *All the ends of the earth will remember, and will be converted to the Lord, and all the clans of the nations will bow down before him* (v. 27): when those not belonging (136) to our nation know the extent of his providence for your situation, they in turn will be converted to you. *Because kingship is the Lord's, and he rules the nations* (v. 28): they will also confess that you alone are king and lord of all.

All the prosperous of the earth ate and adored him (v. 29). *They ate* means They eat (the tense has been changed): since he had said above *The poor will be filled*, also *the prosperous of the earth*—that is, the affluent and the wealthy—will have the same experience. *All who go down to the earth will be prostrate before him*. He means, Every mortal will adore you (the meaning of *those who go down to the earth*). *My soul will live for him, and my descendants will serve him* (vv. 29–30): thus even those at a distance from us will give thanks, but more so I and my descendants the more that we enjoy his favor. And since he had said *my descendants* (the future generation was understood), he goes on, *The generation to come will be reported to the Lord*: both the later generations and these will report your glory, and because you judged justly in our favor, they will recount it with thanksgiving, and those in turn to those after them. Hence he goes on, (137) *And they will report his righteousness to the people to be born, whom the Lord made* (v. 31), that is, whom the Lord will make: As long as he for his part does not cease creating generations, he is saying, so long our descendants who receive his kindness will not cease recounting to later ages and broadcasting his praise.

Psalm 23

This psalm is by those returning from Babylon: since on their release by King Cyrus they took possession of their own places with great satisfaction, blessed David consequently foretells this, too. So on the part of the very ones returning he says, *The Lord shepherds me, and nothing will be wanting to me* (v. 1). *Shepherds* was well put, as if in the case of wandering sheep. *He settled me in a green place* (v. 2). He maintained the image: since by sheep he referred to the people, he called their satisfaction *green place*. *Near restful water he nurtured me*, as if to say, near water (describing a place that is green and irrigated, suggesting in everything their satisfaction). *He corrected my soul; he guided me in paths of righteousness* (v. 3). Since they

(138) were on the point of taking possession of Jerusalem, where the laws and the way of life according to the law obtained once again, he consequently suggested, It was in the interests of our soul and all the rest to live and conduct our lives from now on in keeping with the law. *For his name's sake*: he did not do all this because we are worthy; instead, he granted everything for his own sake.

For even if I travel in the midst of death's darkness, I shall fear no evil, because you are with me (v. 4): so from this assistance we gained sound hope even for the future, so that if I reach the very gates of death, I shall once again call on God's help. *Your rod and your staff comforted me.* By *rod* he refers to kingship, and by *staff* to strength. So his meaning is, Your powerful reign, which brought this consolation, proved my salvation.

You laid a table for me in opposition to those distressing me (v. 5). By *table* here he refers once again to satisfaction, whereas the phrase *those distressing me* means those scheming even involuntarily: it was not by chance the Babylonians plotted their death, but the Lord proved more powerful and released them from captivity. *You anointed my head with oil.* (139) He lists what follows in the case of the rich and famous: after feasting they normally anoint their heads with fragrant oil. *Your cup inebriates me like finest wine*: you brought me to a state of happiness in such a way as if mixing a cup of contentment, refilling it and intoxicating me. *Your mercy will closely follow me all the days of my life* (v. 6): hence I hope that from now on your loving-kindness will not forsake me, but will guide and care for me to the end. *So that I may dwell in the house of the Lord for length of days*: you will provide me also with this, to suffer no exclusion from the holy temple and the good things in it.

Psalm 24

Logically, the twenty-fourth psalm should precede the twenty-third, encouraging as it does those taken off to Babylon, while the twenty-third is by those who had returned. But, as was remarked also at the beginning, the psalms do not occur in order, instead being assembled as they were discovered. Blessed David, then, aware that the captives found very difficult the removal from their own places and from the temple, consoled them from a distance and taught them in these words, *The earth is the Lord's and its fullness, the world and all who dwell in it* (v. 1), that is, (140) Do not let Babylon depress you: if you attend to virtue, you will find God there, too, especially as everything is his, and "in his hands are the ends of the earth."[1] *He founded it on seas, and established it on rivers* (v. 2), that is, All the earth is his, and God is everywhere. He directs attention, note, to the power of God as if saying, How can he not be everywhere who thus put it between waters, some in marshes, some in rivers and in many other places, and maintains its being? The phrase *on seas*, in fact, means not that the land is placed on water but that there is a combination of both, and each keeps its own being by the power of the one who made it this way.

Having said this for their consolation and brought out God's power, in what follows he causes them to give attention to virtue, seeming to ask God, Who will return again from Babylon, recover their own possessions and be among their friends? As if asking God a question, he goes on, *Who will ascend the Lord's mountain, and who will stand in his holy place?* (v. 3). Having put the question, he introduces God replying as follows, *He who is innocent in hand and pure in heart* (v. 4), that is, the one keeping himself from impiety and sin. He goes on, in fact, *He who has not received his soul in vanity*, (141) that is, whoever does not give his soul to the pleasures of this world and the festivals of the idols. Then another thing, too, *And has not sworn deceitfully to his neighbor*. He included the whole catalog of vices in these two clauses: not fixing one's eyes on impiety or on harm of one's brother is the mark of one who abstains from wickedness, on the one hand, and is ready for the practice of virtue, on the other.

He goes on, *Such a person will receive blessing from the Lord and mercy from God his savior* (v. 5): such a person will be accorded goodness and loving-kindness from God. Then what follows, *This is the generation of those seeking the Lord, seeking the face of the God of Jacob* (v. 6). The phrase *This is the generation* means, Those abstaining from evil and practicing virtue are the ones seeking the Lord: just as he speaks of *generation* in the case of the wicked according to the statement, "You, Lord, will protect us, and defend us from this generation forever"[2] in the sense of such people, so too here he used *this generation* in the sense of the good.

He next describes also the joy of those returning, using the words those entering Jerusalem after a long time would have used. *Lift up gates, your rulers; be lifted up, eternal gates, and the king of*

---

[1] Ps 95:4.
[2] Ps 12:7.

glory will enter (v. 7). As though God were leading them, canceling (142) the captivity, making the captives victorious and entering a splendid city with a display of trophies, the populace are bidden, *Lift up gates, your rulers.* He calls *eternal* the gates closed for a long time. Then, since such verses had to be recited antiphonally, one group responds in the form of a question, *Who is this king of glory?* (v. 8). The other group answers in turn, *A Lord mighty and powerful, a Lord powerful in war.* Other people naturally also take up the same motifs, saying, *Lift up gates, your rulers* (v. 9): so let it happen. *Be lifted up, eternal gates, and the king of glory will enter.* In turn those who asked the first question ask again, *Who is this king of glory?* (v. 10). They are thus right in replying from the evidence of the events, all crying aloud, *The Lord of hosts, he is the king of glory.*

Now, it should be noted that some commentators take this in reference to Christ the Lord and his ascension into heaven. For our part, however, we claim both that those adopting this interpretation offer a helpful interpretation, and that we allow it while not undermining the historical basis. (143)

Psalm 25

This twenty-fifth psalm also is composed from the point of view of the people begging to be freed from the captivity in Babylon. Now, let no one be surprised if the general run of psalms prove to have the same theme; rather, let everyone be astonished at the fact that in adopting the same theme blessed David varied his expression, with the result both that the Israelites give themselves to the same ideas and that with a change of expression they do not tire of the frequency. Hence he recites some of the psalms by way of encouragement of those about to be made captive, and recites others as though from those already there and begging to be freed, and some as though they have returned and have recovered prosperity. Again, there is a difference in the latter, with his reciting some of the psalms as though from persons among them practicing virtue, and some on the part of the whole people, like this twenty-fifth psalm and the following twenty-sixth.

You see, while this one is recited on the part of the whole people asking to be redeemed from captivity, the twenty-sixth is on the part of those among them practicing virtue and imploring on account of the actual practice of virtue to be freed from the troubles besetting them. Such people—I mean those exercising virtue—blessed David presents begging confidently so as also to urge everyone in the people to practice the same virtue so as to enjoy the same confidence.

To you, Lord, I lifted up my soul, O my God, in you I trusted, may I not be put to shame forever (vv. 1–2). He presents the Israelites benefiting from the captivity (144) and no longer attending to idols, but now placing all their hope in God, having learned from experience that this is better than before. *And may my foes not ridicule me*, by *foes* meaning the Babylonians. *Let all those who wait for you in fact not be put to shame* (v. 3). They learned from experience how much care those enjoy who have acquired hope in you. *May those who break the law for no reason be confounded*: turn shame upon the transgressors, Lord, and not upon us, who have done no wrong (the meaning of *for no reason*).

Make your ways known to me, Lord, and teach me your paths (v. 4). *Make known* and *teach* me through events, his meaning being, Bring me enjoyment from your action, that is, bring me back to my own place. Hence he goes on, *Guide me in your truth, and teach me that you are the God who is my savior* (v. 5). *In your truth* means, Give me an experience of your honest verdict, through which you had me take possession of my own place. *I waited for you all day long*: waiting for such a verdict constantly (the meaning of *all day long*), I have no difficulty with the sufferings. (145)

Be mindful of your compassion, Lord, and your mercies, because they are from the beginning (v. 6). He assembles reasonable grounds for asking to be freed from captivity: firstly, he says, because you decided and are reliable; then, because you are naturally merciful and compassionate and do not require to be asked for this, being ever faithful to yourself. *Do not call to mind my youthful sin and ignorance; remember me in your mercy* (v. 7). By *youthful sin* he refers to the people's sins in Egypt, where they committed idolatry, remember. So now, he is saying, remember not those sins but your loving-kindness, by which even then you were kind to them in their ignorance and had mercy on them of your own accord even without being asked; and so now, too, exercise such care and loving-kindness for your own sake. Hence he goes on, *For the sake of your goodness, Lord*.

And not only this, he is saying, but the fact that you are naturally like that, as was said. He goes on, in fact, *Good and upright is the Lord* (v. 8). He did well to combine goodness and uprightness: since the objection is made, How is it, if he is naturally loving and merciful, that he allowed some people to be subjected to punishments? he added *and upright* to bring out that justice accompanies goodness. He goes on, in fact, *Hence he will legislate for sinners in the way*: for this reason, that justice also is an attribute of his, (146) *he will legislate for sinners in the way*, that is, he will correct sinners so as to bring them to uprightness. In regard to sinners, he is saying, he gives evidence of justice, whereas in regard to others it is goodness. Hence he continues, *He will guide the gentle in judgment, he will teach the gentle his ways* (v. 9). Again by *teach* he means cause to enjoy, using words in place of deeds. *All the ways of the Lord are mercy and truth for those who seek out his covenant and his testimonies* (v. 10): nevertheless, whether someone is punished or enjoys happy outcomes, they find everything happening to their own benefit, provided the mind is set on God and does not waver.

For your name's sake, Lord, have mercy for my sin, for it is grave (v. 11): since this is the way you are, then, Lord, now out of your loving-kindness overlook my failings both old and new. *Who is the person who fears the Lord? He will legislate for him in the path he has chosen* (v. 12): I am convinced that if from the beginning I had chosen and preserved godliness, you would altogether have established me in good things and not allowed me to experience the present distress; no one who gives priority to godliness would fail to be established in good things. Hence he also phrased the question *Who is the person?* to bring out that no person who opted for (147) godliness failed to enjoy good things, and he well said *He will legislate for him in the path he has chosen*. Just as each one personally opted and chose, he is saying, so too God, being kind and just, confirmed such a person in what he had chosen.

His soul will repose in good things (v. 13), the soul of such a person, that is. *And his descendants will inherit the earth*: blessing will pass to his descendants as well. *The strength of the Lord is in favor of those who fear him* (v. 14): God will also be the might of such people. *And he will reveal his covenant to them*: all God's lawgiving has this in view, bringing good people to enjoy what they have chosen (the meaning of *will reveal to them*, that is, establish them in enjoyment of what they have chosen). *My eyes are always turned to the Lord, because he is the one who will pluck my feet from the snare* (v. 15): so now I placed all my hope in God, convinced that he will redeem me from captivity.

Have regard for me and have mercy on me, because I am alone and poor (v. 16). *Alone* means isolated, and *poor* destitute of every good.

(148) *The tribulations of my heart have been multiplied* (v. 17): I am overwhelmed with tribulations. *Rescue me from my difficulties*: spare me on account of the multitude of the trials. *See my humiliation and hardship, and forgive all my transgressions* (v. 18): be content, Lord, with the scourges inflicted on me, and remove me from the vengeance I endure on account of the multitude of my sins. *Note how my foes have been multiplied, and hated me with an unjust hatred* (v. 19). *See my humiliation*, he says, in being seriously weakened, and have regard for the arrogance of those hating me in their afflicting me with such punishments, though never wronged by me. *Guard my soul and rescue me* (v. 20). He did well to make two requests: In Babylon keep me from being abused by them, and set me free. *Do not put me to shame, because I hoped in you*: it is right that I should not be put to shame, since I shall have no hope any longer in another. *Innocent and upright people stayed close to me because I waited for you, Lord* (v. 21): I shall be the clearest example of those practicing benignity and attending to righteousness (149) because I was not neglected by you; such people will be persuaded not to forsake you.

After saying this, he supplies a conclusion by again closing with a prayer. *Redeem Israel, O God, from all its tribulations* (v. 22).

Psalm 26

The theme of the twenty-sixth psalm was stated in the one before this, that it was composed from the viewpoint of those of their number who practice virtue and confidently call on God in the words, *Judge in my favor, Lord, because in my innocence I have kept to the straight and narrow* (v. 1). It should be noted that if ever *Judge in my favor* occurs with the dative, it means Give me a favorable verdict, as has often been remarked, whereas if he uses Judge me, or Judge them, with the accusative, it means Condemn them, while Judge in their favor, as has been remarked, means Give them a favorable verdict. So here *Judge in my favor, Lord*, means, Rule fairly between me and the Babylonians, because while I have treated them in all innocence, they have treated me with complete malice. *And by hoping in the Lord I shall not fail*: this too in reference to justice—that is, Conduct the trial of those opposed to me on the grounds that I do no harm even to the Babylonians, and did not desist from hoping in you.

Test me, Lord, and try me; use fire to test my entrails and heart

(v. 2). *Use fire to test my entrails,* (150) as if to say, my thoughts: Examine my thoughts to see if I am as I claim. *Because your mercy is ever before my eyes* (v. 3): because I never turned away from hoping in your loving-kindness. *I took delight in your truth*: hence I was eager to please *in your truth*, that is, you (by God's *truth* referring to God by a circumlocution).[1] *I did not sit with the council of futility, nor would I go in to join the lawless. I hated an assembly of evildoers, nor would I take my seat with the ungodly* (vv. 4–5). He put all this in his wish to bring out that they never had anything in common with the festivals of the idols or longed for the display of the ungodly, nor did Babylonian wealth attract their admiration. Instead, they had one interest, godliness and humility as a result of it.

I shall wash my hands among innocent people, and shall move around your altar, Lord (v. 6): on the one hand, I was a stranger to those festivals of the idols, and on the other I vowed to stay close to the innocent. *I shall wash my hands,* in fact, means sharing with the innocent: washing hands is taken in both senses in the divine Scripture, either sharing in a thing or not sharing, as Pilate "washed his hands," reluctant to share in the execution. (151) Here, on the contrary, the phrase *I shall wash my hands among innocent people* means, I shall share with innocent people so as with them to *move around your altar* and once again listen to the sacred voices.[2] He goes on, in fact, *So as to hear the voice of your praise and describe all your marvels* (v. 7). He means what was done in the temple in Jerusalem: nothing could be heard there other than hymns of divine praise and recitals of the favors God had done the people and all human beings.

Lord, I loved the decoration of your house and place of habitation of your glory (v. 8): with a view to justice note this fact as well, that this is my desire, and for it I have been pining. *Do not destroy my soul along with ungodly people, and my life with men of blood* (v. 9): so do not give me the same potion as the ungodly, or destroy me along with them. Then he lists also the vices of the Babylonians. *Whose hands are stained with iniquities* (v. 10), that is, they are ready for

---

[1] The LXX has induced Diodore to recognize an example of periphrasis here by reading the verb "to please" where our Hebrew has a similar form for the verb "to walk."

[2] The LXX's loose translation of the Hebrew "in innocence" induces Diodore this time to give an opposite sense to the familiar meaning of a phrase he documents from Matt 27:24 (and could have found recurring in Ps 73:13).

evildoing. *Their right hand was filled with bribes*: who traded justice for bribes, whereas we were not like that.

For my part, on the contrary, I kept to the straight and narrow (v. 11): but we displayed (152) complete innocence and gave evidence of utter abhorrence of evil. *Redeem me, Lord, and have mercy on me*: for this reason free me from the misfortunes. *My foot stood on level ground; in assemblies I shall bless you, Lord* (v. 12). Again *stood* occurs by a change in tense, the meaning being, May my foot stand on level ground so that I may bless your name in the midst of many.

Psalm 27

The twenty-seventh, twenty-eighth, twenty-ninth, and thirtieth psalms have the same theme, composed from the viewpoint of blessed Hezekiah and directed against the Assyrians. The inspired author David prophesied and adopted this theme on the other's part, using his very words in prophecy and displaying his feelings. The four have a certain change and difference from one another, which commentary on each psalm will mention: the twenty-seventh and twenty-ninth are triumphal odes on the destruction of the Assyrians alone, whereas the twenty-eighth and thirtieth make reference also to Hezekiah's illness and recovery. It is better, however, to take up commentary on the text itself. (153)

The Lord is my light and my salvation: whom shall I fear? (v. 1). A cry befitting triumphant warriors, mentioning also the one responsible for the victory. *Light and salvation* was well put: tribulation caused the Israelites to live in darkness, as it were, whereas the Lord's support proved a light and help to them. *The Lord is the protector of my life: whom should I dread?* The phrase *whom should I dread?* is said by way of admiration: What will be found so powerful in intrigue, he is saying, as God is powerful in helping? *When evildoers pressed upon me to devour my flesh, those who distressed me and my foes themselves fainted and fell* (v. 2). Having referred to the victory in the introduction, he states these two clauses by way of narrative; lest he seem to be giving thanks needlessly, he introduces as well the reason for thanksgiving in the words, When some enemies assembled against me who were so fierce and unrelenting as even to take a piece of me, as it were, then in particular I clearly sensed God's help, with their fall and our conquest. So what is the result now? *If a fortress were constructed against me, my heart would not fear; if war broke out against me, I would still hope in it* (v. 3), by *in it* meaning in help, of which I already had experience, and on account of which I dread no other battle array. So I dread nothing with such help affording me shelter. (154)

One thing I asked of the Lord, this shall I seek (v. 4), *one thing* meaning grace and beneficence. What was it? *To dwell in the house of the Lord all the days of my life.* A pious soul, that of blessed Hezekiah, showed that he thanks God most of all for not severing connections with the temple and with piety. Now, this was his principal request; the one concerning his salvation was second. *To behold the charm of the Lord and visit his holy temple*: you granted me this further request, Lord: having saved me and made me superior to the enemy, you granted me also the place in which I might utter sentiments of thanksgiving. *Because he hid me in his tabernacle on the day of my troubles* (v. 5): from his temple (the meaning of *in his tabernacle*) I had shelter and help. *He kept me in hiding in his tabernacle.* By *in hiding* he means as if in hiding: Though conducting many searches for me, he is saying, the enemy did not find me, thanks to God's sheltering me. *He set me high on a rock.* Again he omits the phrase "as if," his meaning being, You set me high as if on a rock. You see, since the multitude of the Assyrians advanced on him like waves, and a rock in particular naturally resists the waves, he used the example of the rock to imply, He made me superior to a huge multitude, (155) his purpose being for the waves to suggest the uprisings of the enemy.

And now, see, he lifted my head above my foes (v. 6). It follows the same train of thought, although the phrase *And now see* is a slovenly translation from the Hebrew, the meaning being, See, even now he made me superior to the foe (the sense of *my head*). So he goes on to explain what the one in receipt of such great gifts would do. *I circled about and sacrificed in his tabernacle a sacrifice of praise and acclaim.* There has been a change of tense in *circled and sacrificed*, past being used for future. He means, I shall circle and sacrifice *in his tabernacle a sacrifice of praise and acclaim.* Now, *acclaim* is a triumphal sound; but at the same time he also brought out that God takes more satisfaction in the praise in these sacrifices than in the slaughter of animals. *I shall praise and sing to the Lord.* Notice that here he restored the tense by saying *I shall praise.*

Then also in the following, *Hearken, Lord, to the cry that I utter* (v. 7): after sacrificing and directing the praise and thanksgiving song to God, I shall in turn also make suitable requests; the one who is grateful for what you have given is all the more ready to receive also future things. *Have mercy on me, and hearken to me*: in your loving-kindness hearken to my words. (156) *My heart said to you, I shall seek the Lord* (v. 8). He did well to say *my heart* with the purpose of bringing out that the request did not only reach to words but also proceeded from the very depths of the heart. *My face sought you out*, that is, I shall seek your face, Lord, *face* similarly meaning you and support from you. *Do not avert your face from me, and do not turn away in anger from your servant* (v. 9): what is it that I am asking? For you not to keep silent if ever I sin as a human being, or dismiss without concern my situation, leaving me unschooled in better ways. Instead, correct and reform me in a loving way. *Be my helper, do not dismiss me*: instead, be my helper and do not cast me off (the meaning of *do not dismiss me*), that is, do not put me beyond your care. Hence he goes on, *Do not abandon me, O God my savior*: see, you proved it in practice at the time. What, in fact? *That my father and my mother abandoned me, whereas the Lord accepted me* (v. 10): though disaster pressed upon me at the time along with the assault of so many enemies, neither my father nor my mother was of any help; but you for your part emerged as my helper in place of all.

Guide me in your way by law, Lord, and lead me in the right path (v. 11): so do not cease bestowing a like (157) care in the future (*Guide me by law* meaning Instruct me), whence it follows that I should improve and correct my attitude. *On account of my foes do not hand me over to the souls of those harassing me* (vv. 11–12): you do two things at the same time, making me better and not giving the foe an occasion for taunting or for thinking that they will be able to harm me against your will. *Because unjust witnesses rose up against me*. He means the Assyrians, calling them *unjust witnesses* for speaking falsely of him without reason and saying that he receives no help from God. *And injustice gave false testimony against itself*: but the falsehood came undone of itself, since I was seen to be accorded help from God, and the falsehood was seen to be dissipated by itself.

I believe that I shall see the goodness of the Lord in the land of the living (v. 13): I did not cease believing that I shall see the good things of God in Jerusalem (referring to it as *land of the living*), nor shall I cease. *Wait for the Lord* (v. 14): I said this to myself in the time of tribulation. (158) *Play the man, let your heart be strengthened, and wait for the Lord*: I gave myself the advice not to lose heart but to suffer nobly and await help from you; I also received it and give thanks for it.

Psalm 28

The twenty-eighth psalm, as was remarked, makes mention both of the illness and the recovery of Hezekiah himself: when the victory went to his head, human as he was, illness chastised him.[1] But he was also freed from it, and he gives thanks for both. *I shall cry out to you, Lord, do not keep silence with me, O my God* (v. 1). Since after the victory he had thought his own virtue responsible for the victory, with a change of heart he admits the truth. *I shall cry aloud to you, Lord*: I shall attribute the fact of the victory not to my virtue but to you, the God who proved its source for me. The phrase *Do not keep silence with me* means, Do not forsake me any more, now that I have come to a better frame of mind. *Lest in your silence with me I become like those going down to the pit*: if by chance you now turn away from me, I shall be no different from the dead (the meaning of *those going down to the pit*), as you made clear at this time by distancing yourself from me for a while and allowing me to be near to death. (159) *Hearken, Lord, to the voice of my entreaty when I entreat you* (v. 2).[2]

Then he mentions the voices he raised in his illness and uttered when reduced to a state of need. *When I lift my hands to your holy temple, do not drag me away with sinners, and with workers of iniquity do not destroy me* (vv. 2–3). Here he seems to be censuring in particular those at the time of his illness who exhibited the hostility they had for him at one time; the general run of his subjects thought he would really die, and at that time gave evidence of the ill-feeling they had kept hidden, a pious king being a burden to those with inclinations to impiety. Hence he proceeds, *Those who talk peace with their neighbors, but in whose hearts is evil*: people giving evidence of cordiality on their lips conceal wickedness deep down. *Repay them, Lord, according to their works, and according to the wickedness of their exploits repay them* (v. 4). Then, to lend emphasis, he says the same thing, *For the works of their hands repay them*: bring their

---

[1] Cf. 2 Kgs 20; Isa 38.
[2] This, the reading of the Paris manuscript, recommends itself ahead of the Coislinianus manuscript, cited by Olivier, in view of Diodore's following remark, Theodoret's text (Theodore not extant), and other forms of the LXX.

wickedness upon themselves; may they not get the better of me, who am guiltless of wrongdoing.

Because they did not understand the works of the Lord and the works of his hands (v. 5): such people were not prepared to consider that it is by you that I am chastised, and that the illness was motivated by benefit (160) to my soul, not by real anger. Nor were they prepared to understand that the one granting the victory over the Assyrians would not have exercised severe wrath against me, only moderate correction for my betterment. *You will destroy them and not build them up*: so for this reason make them weak, and let them never be lifted to the heights in their practice of evil.

Blessed be the Lord because he hearkened to the sound of my petition (v. 6): may they get their just deserts. For my part, on the contrary, I shall not cease singing the praises of the one responsible both for the victory and for the recovery of health. *The Lord is my helper and my protector* (v. 7): he is and was. *Because my heart hoped in him, and I was helped and my flesh grew strong again*: I knew that there was no one else in whom I had hope in any danger and was consistently granted help. *My flesh grew strong again* was well put: since illness wasted the flesh and reduced it to nothing, God's help caused it to grow strong again and flourish. *I shall willingly confess to him*: so I bring willingness to my thanking him.

The Lord is the strength of his people, and protection of the salvations[3] *of his anointed* (v. 8): he it is who saves both kings and (161) peoples as he wishes and when he wishes to confirm their way of life in blessing. He goes on, in fact, *Save your people, Lord, bless your inheritance, shepherd them, and raise them up forever* (v. 9). *Raise them up* means elevate and glorify; the term *forever* indicates the insatiable desire of the one praying.

Psalm 29

The twenty-ninth is a triumphal psalm, making no mention of illness, and recited only in thanksgiving for what happened to the Assyrians. In the introduction, for example, Hezekiah bids his subjects sacrifice with great eagerness to the one keeping the city and the temple unharmed and unscathed. *Bring to the Lord, sons of God* (v. 1). By *sons of God* he refers to those in receipt of great care from

---

[3] Cf. note 3 to Ps 18. This time, where Hebrew and LXX are as in Ps 18, and where Dahood suggests a royal plural in the sense of "Savior," Diodore's paraphrase gets the sense.

God and saved against the odds, God sparing them as if they were sons. *Bring to the Lord sons of rams,* that is, newborn rams.¹ *Bring to the Lord glory and honor*: in addition to the sacrifices (162) utter things worthy of glory and honor in regard to him. *Bring to the Lord glory for his name* (v. 2): the more you render God's name glorious through your gratitude, the more you will have it as a guarantee of secure help.

Having to this point given instructions for the ritual of sacrifices and praise-giving, he now mentions as well the reasons for which he bids sacrifices be offered. What, he asks, did he do in the case of the Assyrians? Then he gives a description by proclaiming the events themselves, our need being to recognize it as very figurative: the figures heighten the events with the purpose of rendering the beneficiaries of the assistance more grateful by the loftiness and grandeur of the language. *Voice of the Lord on the waters, the God of glory thundered, the Lord on many waters* (v. 3). By *waters* he refers to the vast numbers of the Assyrians, his meaning therefore being, He routed such a vast number by his voice alone, with no need of weapons, no need of any other military equipment; instead, like a skillful general he required only his voice to get the better of the enemy. Hence in place of saying that he gave a decision, he said *He thundered* to bring out the magnificence of the declaration. And in case you should think that his voice was simply that, a futile and ineffectual voice, he goes on, *Voice of the Lord in power* (v. 4). And not only that: *Voice of the Lord in majesty,* (163) that is, in splendor and in the actual demonstration of events.

He then moves to the figure, proceeding, *Voice of the Lord shattering cedars* (v. 5). Having referred above to the Assyrians by *waters,* he once again calls them *cedars,* bringing out their vast number by mention of waters and their lofty and arrogant attitude by the cedar. Hence he continues, *And the Lord will shatter the cedars of Lebanon.* Since the cedars of Lebanon are taller than all others, he compared the Assyrians to the cedars of Lebanon, and added that the Lord shattered them by his voice alone. *He will beat them to powder like the shoot of Lebanon* (v. 6). By *shoot of Lebanon* he refers to the suckers which vinedressers normally speak of; by "planting" they mean putting in the small trees.² So since he had

---

¹ Diodore does not detect in "rams" the LXX's confusion of two similar Hebrew forms.

² The Hebrew here speaks of a calf, and the LXX's μόσχος reflects it. But perhaps because "calf of Lebanon" (an unhappy version of the LXX) is not

referred to the Assyrians as *cedars of Lebanon* and said that the Lord smashed them, in his wish to suggest figuratively the ease he went on to say that he smashed them (namely, the great cedars) like suckers recently transplanted. While this, then, he is saying, was the impression he gave of himself in regard to the enemy, what did he do in our regard, his own people? *And the beloved like a son of unicorns*: we are the *beloved* people, myself and my subjects; we became as fearsome to the enemy as this fearsome animal is to the other animals, which it surpasses in strength, the unicorn being said to be the strongest animal.³ (164)

Having spoken also about the Israelite people, he shifts his attention in turn to the enemy in the words, *Voice of the Lord who flashes a split of flame* (v. 7). He says this in figurative fashion as well: he referred above to the Assyrians by *waters* on account of their vast numbers, then by *cedars* on account of their loftiness, whereas now he calls them *flame* for consuming everything they encounter. So he means, God's voice both split this flame and dimmed it. *Voice of the Lord who shakes the wilderness, the Lord will shake the wilderness of Kadesh* (v. 8). By *wilderness* he refers to the rescued city, calling it a *wilderness* from the Assyrians' hopes of making it so. He thus goes on in this way to speak of the *Lord shaking* in the sense of trampling upon the Assyrians when they were bent on turning the whole place into a wilderness, the sense being that the place the Assyrians thought to call a wilderness God shook in destroying those entertaining this hope, and in turn he strengthened the place. He calls the holy place *Kadesh*, which in Syriac is normally Kaddeis, referring to the same holy place.

He then continues, *Voice of the Lord furnishing deer* (v. 9). One would be surprised at the degree to which blessed David maintains a sequence of figurative references—firstly, in referring to them as *waters* for their vast number, then in calling them *plants* at the time of their being smashed, then later (165) *flame* on account of their disappearance, whereas when he then wiped most of them out at the bidding of the angel and the survivors fled, he now calls them *deer*, this poor creature also being very prone to take flight. So his meaning is, He caused the Assyrians to take flight like deer. *It will bring*

---

transparent in meaning, Diodore opts for another meaning for the form μόσχος, "young plant," as having some connection with "cedars of Lebanon." Theodore will follow his lead, whereas Theodoret stays with "calf," though unable to relate the calf (of gold on Horeb) to Lebanon.

³ The LXX is responsible for the appearance of the mythical unicorn.

woods to light. It is a figurative expression, his meaning being that just as in the wood so many deer are often present as not to allow the ground to be visible, whereas when they flee the wood comes to light, so the city and the sanctuary were not visible when the Assyrians were ensconced there, but at their slaughter and flight the charm of the city then came to light and was visible. Hence he goes on, *And in his temple everyone says Glory*: just as with the recovery of the temple and the city it is now possible for the inhabitants to enter the house again and glorify the savior.

He then proceeds, *The Lord dwells in the flood, the Lord will be enthroned as king forever* (v. 10). Once again by *flood* he refers to the same holy place and the city: since the enemy in their vast numbers threatened to bring on the places a *flood*, as it were, the place that was expected to be flooded therefore offers glory to God, is occupied, and has God enthroned in it and reigning forever. Next, as is customary with him, (166) he concludes his treatment with the blessing of the people, going on to say, *The Lord will give strength to his people, the Lord will bless his people with peace* (v. 11).

Psalm 30

The thirtieth psalm, as was mentioned before as well, makes reference both to Hezekiah's cure from illness and his victory over the Assyrians. Firstly, however, it mentions the illness in the words, *I shall extol you, Lord, because you have supported me, and have not let my foes rejoice over me* (v. 1). The phrase *I shall extol you* means, Let me say lofty things of you, because you took an interest in me, cured me of illness, and brought to an end my foes' exultation (the godless clearly not rejoicing in the life of the pious king).[1] *Lord my God, I cried to you, and you healed me* (v. 2). This can be found more clearly expressed in Isaiah: the prophet Isaiah was sent to Hezekiah and said to him as if from God, "Set your house in order: you are about to die." He turned about and wept bitterly in the words, "Remember, Lord, I walked before you in the way of righteousness." Once again the prophet was sent to him with the words, "I have heard your prayer and seen your tears; lo, I give you fifteen more years of life."[2] So blessed David makes the same inspired remark (167) on his own part, *Lord my God, I cried to you, and you*

---

[1] The term "clearly" in this final explanatory comment indicates that Diodore sets no store by the reference in the title to (re)dedication of the temple.
[2] Isa 38:1–3.

healed me. Lord, you brought my soul up from Hades, you saved me from the ranks of those going down into the pit (v. 3). Again he is referring to death.

What to do, then? *Sing to the Lord, you his holy ones, confess to the memory of his holiness* (v. 4). He is referring to all those piously inclined to him, calling them *holy ones* as dedicated to God: All who practice piety toward me, he is saying, and make the same choice of God and protector, take occasion for hymns in praise of God with a theme to do with me, and exploit the occasion generously. Why *to the memory of his holiness? Because there is wrath in his anger and life in his will* (v. 6). He did well to associate *life* and *will*, and *wrath* and *anger*, bringing out that the will for life is his, whereas it is necessity and need on our part that leads to the expression of wrath. He next mentions the event itself and the situation of the enemy. *There will be weeping in the evening, but in the morning joy.* This is in fact the way things turned out: by making many threats in the evening the Assyrians reduced the Israelites to grieving, but with the appearance of the angel and slaughter of the Assyrians break of day revealed the corpses and brought joy to the Israelites (the meaning of (168) *There will be weeping in the evening, but in the morning joy*).

It was not logical for me, Hezekiah is saying, to be puffed up in my thinking, believing my virtue responsible for the winning of the victory, as a result of which I was chastised. Confessing this attitude of his, he goes on, *As for me, however, I said in my prosperity, I shall not be moved forever* (v. 6): when I received such a favor, I believed I would remain unchanged in the enjoyment of good things. *Lord, by your will you provided power in my beauty* (v. 7): I did not admit that it is your choice to make me famous and cause my kingship to be seemly (the meaning of *in my beauty*, referring to his kingship as *beauty*). Since I did not give this a thought, what happened? *But you turned your face away, and I was disturbed*: for a while as a result of such an attitude of mine you averted your face, everything of mine that was famous and admirable you reduced to tatters, to instability and danger.

So what will happen from now on? *I shall cry to you, Lord, and make my petition to my God* (v. 8): from now on I acknowledge the one responsible and shall not be reluctant to admit that all the good things I have are from you. This expression *I shall cry to you, Lord, and make my petition to my God* Scripture is in the habit of using; such an expression is not an interchange of persons, nor in fact is he speaking of the Lord and God as different, unless one were to suspect that with inspired vision (169) he is hinting at the Father and the Son. He next cites as well the plausible reasons he gave at the time of petition and thus received loving-kindness. What, in fact, did he say at the time? *What good is there in my blood, in my going down to destruction? Surely dust will not confess to you or proclaim your truth?* (v. 9). I said this while ill, that if I die, the possibility of thanksgiving is also removed from me, whereas if I gain help, I shall be grateful, the actual favor not allowing me to be silent, but prompting me to constant hymn-singing and confession of the one responsible.

God heeded these praises. *The Lord heard and had mercy on me, the Lord became my helper. You turned my lamentation into joy for me* (vv. 10–11): the grief I expected to have and the lamentation I was fearing would happen in my case God chose to turn into joy and happiness for me. *You rent my sackcloth and clad me in joy*: the course of the illness and that of the war came together: when the enemy advanced, I put on sackcloth (as actually happened),[3] but with the advent of victory the sackcloth was rent and I was clothed in joy. *So that my glory might sing to you and I might feel no compunction* (v. 12): for this reason, then, all my kingdom and your honor will be devoted to thanking God, and I shall not repent of this attitude, as I repented in the former case when I thought my virtue was responsible (170) for the victory (the phrase *I might feel no compunction* meaning, I shall not repent of the present purpose as in the former case). He goes on, *Lord my God, I shall confess to you forever*. And in Isaiah he said in the song, "I shall not cease praising you with a harp all the days of my life."[4] He said the same thing here, *Lord my God, I shall confess to you forever*.

This is the commentary and the actual content of these four psalms. The psalms' titles, on the other hand, are quite ridiculous, and you would be unable to control yourself if you considered the superficiality of the titles.[5] I mean, first of all, the title of the twenty-seventh psalm reads, "A psalm of David, before he was anointed." Now, what person with sense would suppose that David composed a psalm before his anointing? After all, there is firstly the fact that his youth was untried and untested in regard to composing

[3] Cf. 2 Kgs 19:1.
[4] Isa 38:20.
[5] Already in his preface Diodore dismissed the titles as anything more than the result of guesswork by the compilers of the Psalter in the time of Ezra when it had been lost in the exile.

psalms. If, however, you concede the stripling was also clever, how did he write without the grace of the Spirit? I mean, even if he wrote before the illumination of the Spirit, anointing would have been unnecessary, Samuel's journey unnecessary, even the grace itself would have been destined to be unnecessary. What they intended in writing the titles for this psalm, however, I for one have no idea, nor I believe did those who wrote them understand.

The twenty-eighth psalm, on other hand, bears the title, "A psalm for David," where the connection with ignorance is not tight: they claim when it says "of David," the psalm was composed by him, whereas when "for David," it was composed in reference to him by someone else.[6] (171) But while they did not put a title on the one referring to him, obviously not being able to prove it, neither do we know who was the one in receipt of such a charism if not David alone; whereas others were also accorded inspiration, no other was accorded rhythmical melody along with inspiration. Now, those called singers or psalm singers by the divine Scripture did not personally compose the psalms: they only performed them orally or to musical instruments; the psalms they received from David. So much for the twenty-eighth psalm.

The twenty-ninth psalm bears the title, "A psalm for David, of a tabernacle procession." The title is suggesting, in my view, that the psalm was composed in connection with the procession of the Feast of Tabernacles: they held the feast called Tabernacles for seven days, and it indicates that it was composed for the festal procession. So what connection do the words have with the title? It seems to make no mention of tent or tabernacle, especially as there was still no temple or city of theirs when they first pitched tents. Instead, at all points the psalm mentions victory over the enemy, who were of the harshest. Now, from the time they had the city they experienced nothing harsher than the Assyrians.

The thirtieth psalm in turn bears this title, "To the end. A psalm for singing at the consecration of the house. For David." The title indicates that with the intention of consecrating the temple (172) to be built he wrote ahead of time a psalm befitting the consecration. The fact that the words are out of keeping with this theme, however, even one of little understanding will realize: what

---

[6] In taking issue with the approach of those who find the phrase in the genitive in Pss 27 and 28, e.g., and in the dative in Pss 29 and 30, Diodore does not check with the Hebrew to see if there is a basis for the difference in the LXX (there is not). So he falls to logic.

connection with the consecration of the temple has the verse, "You rent my sackcloth and clad me in joy," or the verse, "Lord, you brought my soul up from Hades," or the verse, "You saved me from the ranks of those going down into the pit"? It is obvious instead that, as was said, what was composed by blessed David long before the events apply to Hezekiah, such being the charism of inspiration, looking ahead to events from a distance and teaching people ahead of time that God is not uninterested in humankind, and it is appropriate for people who receive help to give thanks in general to the one who brought salvation.

Psalm 31

The thirty-first psalm, having to do with Babylon, lies between those with a theme about Hezekiah. Immediately after it, of course, the thirty-second, thirty-third, and thirty-fourth have the same theme about Hezekiah as prior to it did the twenty-seventh, twenty-eighth, twenty-ninth, and thirtieth. Now, the reason for this, as was said in the introduction to the Psalms, is that instead of being assembled in order, the Psalms were compiled as they were found: the book was lost at the time of the captivity, found scattered on return and put together in this form on being found. (173) So it happened that three or four on the same theme were discovered, and likewise the reverse, one often found in the middle on a different theme from those on the similar topic, such as this one found in the middle of psalms on the theme of Hezekiah, as was remarked, though having to do with Babylon.

Now, this thirty-first psalm likewise has a title in no way related to the previous psalm, being entitled "To the end. A psalm for David, of perplexity." What did "perplexity" mean to the person who gave the title? That person would have had a better idea; but in my view it implies the actual astonishment of the author at God's surprising actions.[1] While this is what the title means, then, the psalm is clearly full of petitioning. A petition for gifts, however, is very different from astonishment once favors have already been given: the person who is yet to receive makes a petition, whereas the one who has received a lot is astonished. As we said, however, it is recited on the part of the people while in Babylon, begging and

---

[1] Theodoret maintains that the form of the LXX in the Hexapla did not contain this term ἐκστάσεως, only some ἀντίγραφα. Unlike Diodore, he traces it to v. 22, and looks for a likely speaker.

imploring God to be released from the fate of captivity and to return to their own places and enter the holy temple and the city, itself also holy.

In you, Lord, I hoped; let me not be forever ashamed (v. 1). Here too he presented the Israelites as showing benefit from the misfortunes: the sentiment, I now hope in you, is the mark of someone admitting that before this they set little store by God, but were instructed by the misfortunes not to put hope in anybody other than the one capable of saving. Hence he went on, *Let me not be forever ashamed*, meaning, Let me not be abandoned forever: having reformed my ways I have a claim on receiving loving-kindness. Hence he goes on, (174) *In your righteousness rescue me and snatch me away*. By *righteousness* here he referred to loving-kindness in the way of which we have spoken: it was right for the person who mended his ways to be granted loving-kindness as well. *Incline your ear to me, speedily snatch me away* (v. 2). He means *snatch me away* from captivity and the Babylonians oppressing us. *Become a protector God for me, and as a house of refuge to save me*. When he cannot cite a greater example, he cites a lesser one: it is not so much the house that saves the fugitive as God, yet he cites the lesser example to bring out that should God ever want an example, this is the way he saves.

Because you are my might and my refuge, and for your name's sake you will guide me and nourish me (v. 3), *might* meaning my strength and power lest I be undone. With the same help, he is thus saying, he also brought me back. *You will draw me out of this snare which they have hidden for me* (v. 4), by *snare* referring to the captivity. *Because you are my protector, Lord*: you always protected me, as in battle the stronger protect the weaker. He is referring to the ancient struggles against Egypt and against the Canaanites and all the following ones. *Into your hands I shall commit my spirit* (v. 5): so now that many disasters all at once beset me and I find no other adequate assistance, I commit my soul to you, only you being capable of snatching me from these troubles.[2] *You redeemed me, Lord God of truth*. There has been a change of tense with *redeemed*, the meaning being, Redeem me, O God of truth.

You hated all those who paid constant attention to futile things (v. 6). Again by *You hated* he means Hate, and by *futile things* he means the Babylonians' wealth and idols and the enjoyment of the

---

[2] Diodore does not remind his readers of the occurrence of these words on the lips of Jesus in Luke 23:46 (as even Theodore will).

things the Babylonians clung to as having permanence and not passing away. *Whereas for my part I hoped in the Lord*: they put their hope in wealth, glory, and soft living, whereas I never forsook your assistance or the expectation of enjoying good things from you. Hence he says, *I shall be glad and rejoice in your mercy* (v. 7): so it is also fair that I should enjoy your loving-kindness and exchange the present distress for happiness on account of you. *Because you took note of my humiliation*: therefore *I shall be glad and rejoice because you took note of me* and helped me, meaning, In addition to this allow me to rejoice in the help and joy you provide. (176) *You saved my soul from distress*. It follows in the same line of thought: *I shall be glad that you saved my soul from distress. You have not confined me in the hands of foes* (v. 8). He says the same thing, I shall be established in joy if I receive this. *You set my feet in open spaces*: because you provided this as well (by *open spaces* referring to the independence of their way of life, and calling the enemies' yoke tribulation).

Hence he turns once again to petition in the words, *Have mercy on me, Lord, because I am in distress; anger has upset my eye* (v. 9). By *anger* he means not mine but yours—that is, Because by your anger my eye is upset, in the sense that my very vision is obscured, your anger not allowing me relief. *My soul and my stomach*: my stomach means my heart; by it he means, All my soul and my every thought are in utter turmoil and bewilderment. *My life is wasted with pain, and my years with groans* (v. 10): for a long time I had been hoping for return and did not secure it; after all of seventy years I attained relief. Hence he goes on, *My strength failed in poverty* (177). By *poverty* he refers to the lack of every good, not only money. *And my bones were disturbed*, that is, all my strength.

To all my foes I became a byword (v. 11). By *foes* he refers to the neighboring peoples: They were often given over to captivity, he is saying, but never for as long a period as ourselves. The fact that it is the neighboring peoples he calls *foes* he indicates by going on, *And to my neighbors and friends an awful fright*, by *fright* meaning, I became an ill-omen even to the very ones who had known me from the beginning and to my enemies. *Those who set eyes on me in public avoided me*: thus I appeared loathsome to every person on account of the misfortunes. *I was lost to the heart like a dead man* (v. 12), that is, I despaired in all my heart and all my mind, as dead people are despaired of. *I became like a vessel mislaid*, that is, useless, especially since useful things are searched for. *Because I heard the criticism of many huddling together* (v. 13). Again he says the same thing, I was vulnerable to everyone's mockery. *As they assembled together against me they plotted to take my life*: (178) every meeting of the Babylonians and every gathering of theirs had my destruction on the agenda.

But I hoped in you, Lord; I said, You are my God (v. 14): I did not abandon you, knowing that my helper is found superior to the schemers. *My lot is in your hands* (v. 15). He says *my lot* in the sense of all my relief and all my tribulation. Since everyone has times when they are distressed and times when they are also made happy, he means, *My lot*, the times allotted to me for being made glad and for being distressed, all these are *in your hands* and capable of being changed as you wish. Some commentators, on the other hand, claim that *lot* refers to possession of the land. Hence he goes on, *Rescue me from the hand of my foes and those pursuing me*: since *my lot* is *in your hands* and rescuing is easy for you, give evidence now as well of your loving-kindness. *Let your face shine upon your servant* (v. 16). Since it seemed as though God had turned away from them and was angry with them, he asks for reconciliation: Only have regard to me, he is saying, and it is sufficient for my salvation. Hence he continues, *Save me in your mercy. Lord, let me not be confounded, because I called upon you* (vv. 16–17): let the foe (179) have no grounds for taunting me with not being saved because I hoped in you alone. *Let the ungodly be put to shame and cast down to Hades*: instead, bring the shame upon the wrongdoers, who do not acknowledge you. *Let the lying lips become mute that speak iniquity against the righteous with arrogance and contempt* (v. 18): shut the mouths of those bent on mocking us with the claim that we gain no help from our God, the mouths that dare to utter such things against us in arrogance.

How great the extent of your goodness, Lord, which you have laid up for those who fear you (v. 19): grant us the return so that everyone may begin to say, Though rich in loving-kindness, you hid it in planning for our benefit, not in anger to our everlasting punishment. *You accomplished it for those who hope in you in the sight of human beings*: you stirred up your loving-kindness and gave evidence of it to us who hope in you, bringing such grace to the notice of all (the meaning of *in the sight of human beings*). *You will keep them in hiding in your presence*. There has been a change of tense with *You will keep them*, his meaning being, You kept such people *in hiding in your presence*, that is, caught up in tribulations, (180) misfortunes, and snares, you kept them in hiding with your support and help with the result that no hardships approached them. *From the disturbance of people you will shelter them in a tabernacle away from contentious tongues.* Again there has been a change in tense, the meaning being, You sheltered them in a tabernacle (*in a tabernacle* meaning, as though in a tabernacle away from contentious tongues, and *contentious tongues* likewise meaning the same thing, the taunts of the Babylonians and the insults they hurled at them for idly hoping in God).

Blessed be the Lord, because he has mercifully shown his mercy to me in a city surrounded (v. 21). He means, as though in a city surrounded, by *a city surrounded* referring to the walled city. So he is saying, Everyone praises your name because you sheltered and guarded us with your help in such a way as if in a walled city. Let this happen to us from you, Lord; for my part I shall not cease mentioning it even in my relief from the misfortunes from which you have redeemed me, so grateful am I to my benefactor. Hence he continues, *I said in my perplexity, I am driven from the sight of your eyes* (v. 22). By *perplexity* he refers to the change in fortunes: When my situation changed, he is saying, and from prosperity I plunged into the misfortune of captivity, I despaired of my situation (saying this to highlight the help and indicate that it was particularly in the lack of resources that God supplied a loophole and hope of salvation). Hence he goes on, (181) *Hence you hearkened to the sound of my appeal when I cried out to you*: my despairing of my situation summoned you to my salvation.

Love the Lord, all you his holy ones, because the Lord looks for truth (v. 23): allow me to say this when I am granted the return so as forthrightly to urge on all who love you not to despair of their situation, aware that God is the one with a concern for truth and righteousness. Now, what do truth and righteousness mean? Giving respite to those distressed and chastised, on the one hand, and on the other punishing those who abuse prosperity. Hence he proceeds, *And he repays those who are guilty of extraordinary arrogance.* The word *extraordinary* goes with *repays* to make it inevitable: He repays extraordinarily those who are guilty of arrogance so as to bring out that God loathes this transgression more than every other sin. *Be bold, and let your heart grow strong, all you who hope in the Lord* (v. 24): this being the case, then, and this the outcome, let everyone with hope in God give evidence of boldness in possession of such hope, there being no chance of error for those who hope in him.

Psalm 32

The thirty-second, as was mentioned, (182) has a theme to do with Hezekiah, though it bears a title "For David, of understanding." The meaning is that understanding was given to David to recite it:[1] although David seems to be uttering the first part of the psalm on his own behalf, he has as his theme Hezekiah's being rid of illness as a result of his piety, of the Assyrians and the sin of the harsh war. He says, *Blessed are those whose iniquities are forgiven and whose sins are covered over* (v. 1). David says this in reference to Hezekiah by way of making a general statement to bring out that the one who is generous toward one person can also be generous to many if we hope in him. It was right for blessed Paul to cite this in reference to the faithful:[2] if the law was at that time in force, he is saying, inflicting punishment for every fault, and the time of generosity then arrived, what could later prevent the same God showing the same generosity to those who likewise believed? Having spoken in general terms in the two clauses, then, he now indicates also who it is the theme deals with, going on, *Blessed the man of whose sin the Lord takes no account and in whose mouth there is no deceit* (v. 2). He pronounces Hezekiah blessed, to whom (he says) God accorded forgiveness as though he had never uttered anything unfitting (*in whose mouth there is no deceit* meaning the one who did not think of sinning even in word).

He then mentions the thoughts that Hezekiah entertained at the time of the illness. *Because I kept silence, my bones grew old* (v. 3). Hezekiah confesses (183) his sin: When I stopped singing your praises and was silent on your favors, *my bones grew old*, that is, all my strength left me. *From my crying aloud all day long*. The phrase *From my crying aloud all day long* is unclear on account of the metaphor in the Hebrew, his meaning being, For this reason I kept calling out all day in my inability to bear the gravity of the illness. Hence he goes on, *Because day and night your hand was heavy upon me* (v. 4): the blow was severe that came upon me as though from such a hand, namely, God's. He then mentions also what was the cause of the illness. *I was reduced to distress with the thorn being fixed in me*: I was distressed with the sin fixed in me (by *thorn* here refer-

---

[1] The LXX's σύνεσις, "understanding," renders the Hebrew *maskil*, which modern commentators take to represent a type of psalm. Diodore is not inclined to take items on the titles as clues to liturgical genre.

[2] Rom 4:7–8.

ring to the sin, and calling it a *thorn* because it pricked him for a while and was then removed from him).

I made the sin known, and did not hide my lawlessness (v. 5): but just as I sinned and was punished, so I acknowledged it and was saved. *I said, To the Lord I shall confess my sin against myself, and you put away the impiety of my sin.* He wishes to bring out also the promptness of God's loving-kindness, saying, *I shall confess*, that is, I resolved to confess the fault to the Lord, (184) and your pardon anticipated my confession.

For this every holy person will pray at the right time (v. 6). By *for this* he means either the grace or the sin, his meaning being, Every holy person dedicated to God ought immediately pray for every sin and seek forgiveness. Hence he says *at the right time* to bring out that immediately after the sin is a fitting time for confession of the sin, since a sin that lingers is entrenched. What then happens after sins are pardoned? *Even in the rush of mighty waters they will not approach them.* The term *Even* here has no significance, being a Hebrew idiom. His meaning is, in fact, Such a person, on being granted pardon, even if in the midst of many calamities and stifled by them as though by waters, proves superior with God's help.[3] The comparison is actually unusual: how could many waters overwhelm someone without approaching him? Yet this unusual event occurs: calamities encircle one and God does not allow them to approach the one beset by them. *You are a refuge for me from the onset of tribulations* (v. 7). The person encountering misfortune says this. *My joy, rescue me from those surrounding me* (181), as if to say, the surrounding troubles.

I shall give you understanding and instruct you in the way you should travel (v. 8): this is what you say, O God, to the person dedicated to you, I shall make you follow the straight and narrow. *I shall fix my eyes on you*: I shall always keep any eye on your situation. For this reason, then, he exhorts all the others as well in the words, *Do not be like horse or mule that have no understanding* (v. 9): the person with understanding and reason perceives the sin, whereas the one without understanding does not perceive it, not wanting to. What happens, then, to those unwilling to perceive their sins? *Keep their jaws under tight muzzle and rein if they do not come near you*: all such people who do not have a change of attitude for the better are

---

[3] Diodore (and Theodore after him) believes the LXX's πλήν is an otiose reflection (of the Hebrew adverb *raq*), though he goes on in fact to illustrate its value.

inevitably converted by falling foul of illness or another trial or unexpected disaster, or when obliged by some such thing. *Many the scourges of the sinner* (v. 10): such punishments will not leave them untouched. *Whereas mercy will envelop those who hope in the Lord*: just as loving-kindness will not pass by the one who hopes in God.

What, then, is the purpose of the psalm? (186) *Rejoice in the Lord and be glad, you righteous ones, and boast, all you who are upright in heart* (v. 11): aware of this, then, all you who attend to virtue, be full of joy for the reason that God does not close a blind eye to those against us.

Psalm 33

The theme of the thirty-third concerns Hezekiah, though it bears the title "For David, without a title in the Hebrew."[1] Those that are untitled leave the readers free of uncertainty, being forced to grasp the theme from the actual words contained and not being led astray on the basis of a title with a conjectured relation to the contents. This psalm, too, therefore, as was remarked, was spoken by blessed David from the viewpoint of Hezekiah on the victory against the Assyrians.

Rejoice in the Lord, you righteous ones; praise becomes the upright (v. 1). He calls the Israelites *righteous* by comparison with the Assyrians, and likewise the same people *upright*. So he urges such people to sing God's praises for the unexpected events worked in their favor. *Confess to the Lord with a lyre, sing to him with a ten-stringed harp* (v. 2). Having said above that they ought sing God's praises, he went further to say here (187) they ought do so with musical instruments. *Sing him a new song* (v. 3): for a new and unexpected victory they ought offer a new song and hymn. *Sing well to him with full voice*. The term *well* means with understanding, with

---

[1] Theodoret, too, implies that his form of the LXX carried some such rubric as this denying the existence of a title, though other forms carry the brief "For David" known to Diodore, who sees the absence of a title giving him ("the readers," he claims) leeway in divining the psalm's ἱστορία instead of leaving it as a hymn to the creator God. Almost as though he had Diodore open before him, Weiser warns that "it can hardly be assumed that the psalm served to commemorate a great act of deliverance whereby Yahweh saved the nation from the threat of some peril, such as the miraculous deliverance of Jerusalem from the siege of Sennacherib (701 BC); the hymn is couched in too general terms to suit such a purpose" (*Psalms*, 289).

appreciation of the hymns; and *with full voice* means precisely a sound of triumph.

Because the word of the Lord is upright, and all his works in faithfulness (v. 4). By *word* here he means the verdict against the Assyrians, the fact that it proved to be firm. And rightly so: since all his works are firm, he is saying, necessarily his verdict also proved to be so. *The Lord loves mercy and judgment* (v. 5): this is typical of God, both to show loving-kindness and to judge—to show loving-kindness for those who hope in him, and to condemn those who trust in themselves. *The earth is full of the Lord's mercy.* At this point he develops his treatment in a more general fashion, his meaning being, It is not surprising if he gave evidence of such an attitude in regard to our race and those dedicated to him when he actually gave evidence also of strength and goodness from the very beginning in regard to the whole world, bringing things to exist from nonbeing, on the one hand, and on the other assigning to everything that is made a providence suited to it when made.

Hence he goes on, (188) *By the word of the Lord the heavens were established, and by the breath of his mouth all their power* (v. 6). Once again here by *the word* he means the verdict: in his wish to magnify the verdict against the Assyrians as strong, mighty, and firm, he goes on to say that this verdict at some time brought the heavens from nonbeing to being. The phrase *and by his breath* means by his power; and *all their power* means all their righteousness. After speaking of things in heaven, he goes on to treat also of things on earth. *Collecting the waters of the sea like a flask, putting the deeps in storehouses* (v. 7). By the phrase *Collecting like a flask* he means that he collected the sea as if in a flask: as a flask holds what is put in it, so God's verdict and command keep the sea on all sides from pouring out and spreading over the earth. In the phrase *putting the deeps in storehouses* he calls *storehouses* not only what is hidden but also what is unconsumed, his meaning being that he also keeps the deeps of the sea in storehouses, as it were, lest they gush up and flood the land.

Having spoken very descriptively in a general fashion, therefore, he again resumes his line of thought in the words, *Let all the earth fear the Lord* (v. 8): it is right, then, for all the inhabitants of the earth (189) to fear and thus all the more admire and reverence him. *And let all the inhabitants of the world tremble before him.* The term *tremble* means the same thing, that is, fear. *Because he spoke, and they were made; he commanded, and they were created* (v. 9): he it is who produced everything with a word.

The Lord frustrates nations' plans (v. 10): God himself, who brings everything from nonbeing to being, is the one who also frustrates the plans of the Assyrians, who intend both to slay the king and also to enslave the people and sack the city. But even as they planned this, he appointed them an angel to slay their hordes and frustrate their plans. Hence he goes on, *He sets aside people's thoughts*, by *people's* meaning again the Assyrians' themselves. *He sets aside rulers' plans*, by *rulers'* meaning their own leaders'. *But the plan of the Lord abides forever, thoughts of his heart from age to age* (v. 11). He says *thoughts* in human fashion: since in the case of the Assyrians he used *thoughts* to refer to the enemies' assaults, here also (190) in the case of God by *thought* he likewise indicates after a fashion that the victory had been achieved, not that God plans things but, as remarked, he expresses it in a rather human fashion. *Happy the nation whose God is the Lord* (v. 12). By comparison with the Assyrians he now declares blessed the Israelites as recipients of unexpected help. *The people he chose as his own inheritance*. He says the same thing.

From heaven the Lord looked down, he saw all the sons of men (v. 13): being by nature more elevated than all, from that height he surveys and judges human affairs. *From his ready abode* (v. 14). By *ready* Scripture refers to permanence and stability, as when it says, "Your throne ready from of old," that is, stable and permanent. On the basis of his permanent abode he considers him permanent and unchanging: just as he indicates the weakness of human beings on the basis of their dwelling, as in the case of Job when he says, "He leaves those dwelling in houses of clay,"[2] to imply the weakness of human beings from their dwellings, so too in the case of God from the permanence of his dwelling he referred to the immobile and unchanging nature of God as though occupying it forever. *He looked on all the inhabitants of the earth*: he looked on in the process of judging, of passing judgment on the Assyrians who were attacking and the Israelites who were being attacked. (191) *He forms their hearts individually, he understands all their deeds* (v. 15): he is the God who understands the Assyrians' thoughts and renders them futile.

Next, as though ridiculing the vast numbers of the Assyrians, their cavalry, and the weapons that were no good to them, he goes

---

[2] Ps 93:2; Job 4:19.

on, *A king is not saved by great power* (v. 16), hinting at Sennacherib. *And a giant will not be saved by the greatness of its strength.* By *giant* here he refers to warlike valor and skill. *Worthless a horse for safety, it will not be saved by the greatness of its power* (v. 17). Since the Assyrians gloried particularly in the number of their horses, saying, We shall give you horses if you are able to provide riders,³ and against the odds they were destroyed, he naturally says that vast numbers of horses are of no use in war without God's influence: *It will not be saved by the greatness of its power.*

Lo, the eyes of the Lord are on those who fear him, who hope in his mercy (v. 18): all who have hope in him achieve a crushing victory. (192) *To rescue their souls from death and sustain them in famine* (v. 19). He means that he saves those who hope in him by rescuing their souls from death. The phrase *and sustain them in famine* means their overall plight: since the Israelites themselves with the onset of the enemy were reduced to lack of all necessities, and against the odds had a favorable change in fortune, he suggests as much by saying *and sustain them in famine. Our soul waits for the Lord* (v. 20): we ought therefore with all our strength wait upon God, our never-failing helper, and not trust in anyone else. Why? *Because he is our helper and protector.* And not only this, but the rest: *Because our heart will rejoice in him, and we hoped in his holy name* (v. 21).

And as is customary with him, he sets the seal on his inspired work with a prayer, saying, *May your mercy be shown to us, Lord, as we have hoped in you* (v. 22).

Psalm 34

"For David, when he altered his appearance in the presence of Abimelech, and he dismissed him, and he got away." (193) Some commentators interpreted the thirty-fourth psalm according to the title, and in bringing some slight persuasiveness to their commentary they gave the impression of departing to no great degree from the truth.¹ Our claim is, therefore, that such an interpretation is not

³ Cf. Isa 36:8.

¹ The facts (ἀλήθεια) referred to in the psalm title involve an incident in David's life recounted in 1 Sam 21 (whether the visit to Nob, where Ahimelech was priest, or to Gath, where he was dismissed as a fool by King Achish—whose Semitic name may have been Abimelech, Dahood, *Psalms*, 1:205, opines). Whether or not confused about the priest's name (as Mark was at 2:26) or the person involved, Diodore at any rate prefers to see Hezekiah in focus.

without help or value to the readers, but a theme to do with Hezekiah is closer to the truth; this psalm resembles the ones before it, as the actual text reveals more clearly; for example, the verse *An angel of the Lord will encamp around those who fear him and will rescue them* (v. 7) applies more properly to the situation of Hezekiah than to the time when David "altered his appearance" and Abimelech "dismissed him." While here, in fact, David's own cleverness and artfulness seem rather to be portrayed in such a way that Abimelech did not recognize the real issue, it is in the case of Hezekiah's situation that the coming of the angel in person, the slaughter of the Assyrians, and the unexpected rescue of the Israelites bring the interpretation to bear more properly on the psalm. You would, however, grasp the truer sense from verse-by-verse commentary.

I shall bless the Lord at every moment (v. 1). *In every moment* was well put: tribulation from the enemy was inflicted, and I did not desist from blessing; once again God's support and the unexpected victory came to the fore, he is saying, and of necessity I was under an obligation to offer thanksgiving. So it is right for him to say *I shall bless the Lord at every moment*, both at the moment of tribulation and at the moment of happiness. And to express the same thing more clearly, he goes on, (194) *Praise of him always in my mouth*. Why? *In the Lord will my soul be commended* (v. 2), that is, since in the Lord's eyes my soul appeared deserving of honor, and he did not hand me over to the enemy. *Let the gentle hear and be glad*. By *gentle* he refers to those experiencing help from God: people's compliance and piety he refers to as gentleness, as the divine Scripture does in most cases, such as the expression, "Remember David and all his gentleness,"[2] that is, his compliance and obedience to you. So he means, All who have the same sentiments of piety and compliance as myself can hear about my situation and can become more pious, concluding that it is not in vain that gentleness is their pursuit. Hence he goes on, *Magnify the Lord with me, and let us exalt his name together* (v. 3): so come now, let all who with me are gentle and pious recount marvelous things of God to do with the unexpected salvation.

---

[2] Against the biblical evidence (except for this citation, Ps 132:1), it would seem, David becomes proverbial for his gentleness, πραότης, by Chrysostom for one. Unfortunately, the LXX is reading "gentleness" in a form differently vocalized in our Hebrew to mean "hardship" or "triumphs"—more to the point for the David we know.

Why? *I sought out the Lord, and he heeded me, and from the midst of all my tribulations he rescued me* (v. 4): Let all of us who practice piety glorify him, because I called upon him in a time of tribulation and (195) did not fail to receive his loving-kindness. Then also by way of exhortation, *Approach him and be enlightened, and your faces will not blush* (v. 5): so let no one on the basis of my situation despair of God's support (by *enlightenment* referring here to his coming that provides help in good time). *This poor man cried out, and the Lord hearkened to him, and saved him from all his tribulations* (v. 6): say this of me, *this poor man* (by *poor man* Hezekiah referring to himself as being deprived of all human help in time of war). So say (he means) that the one who was in need of everything and given up as lost by people implored God in a moment of tribulation, and the Lord hearkened to him and saved him against the odds.

He next explains also the manner of the rescue. *An angel of the Lord will encamp around those who fear him, and will rescue them* (v. 7): by the angel's intervention he rendered those fearing him superior to the enemy, while annihilating them. *Taste and see that the Lord is good* (v. 8): if you do not believe what happened to me, try for yourself and thus have no need of urging to hope in God. Hence he proceeds, *Blessed is the man who hopes in him*: the one who has experience of God's care inevitably persuades himself to have hope, and from this becomes blessed as I myself now am. (196) *Fear the Lord, all you his holy ones, because those who fear him want for nothing* (v. 9): it is not possible for the one who fears God and hopes in him to fail. *Wealthy people felt poverty and hunger, whereas those seeking out the Lord will not suffer lessening of any good* (v. 10). It is an expression of likelihood and possibility: It is no more possible, he is saying, for those hoping in God to suffer lessening of any good than for the very rich to be reduced to poverty.

Come, children, listen to me, I shall teach you fear of the Lord (v. 11). The exhortation was applicable to Hezekiah after the experience of God's help, as a result of which he recommends the others as well to a like piety. What, then, is he recommending? *Who is the person who chooses life, who loves to see good days?* (v. 12). So what would one do who desires life and enjoyment of good things? Such a one should have a care for virtue. Hence he proceeds, *Keep your tongue from evil, and your lips from speaking guile* (v. 13): firstly, such a one should also be on guard against the sin of the tongue, this being a simple matter more than others. And what else? *Turn away from evil and do good* (v. 14): after being on guard against the sin of the tongue, (197) you must shun every vice and cling to every good, this being perfect virtue. *Seek peace and go after it*, that is, let such a one also be peaceable (*go after it* meaning pursue it, that is, put peace into action so as to be peaceable to all and not inflame conflict with everyone by lusting after others' possessions).

What will be the result for such a one? *The eyes of the Lord are on the righteous, and his ears open to their appeal* (v. 15): God also looks closely at such a one, pleased with his choices and, if ever he finds himself in need of imploring God, gives him a prompt hearing. Now, Hezekiah was worthy of belief in saying this on the basis of his attention to a good life and on the basis of his asking and obtaining God's ready response. So much for the righteous, then; but what of the person of indifferent life and lax piety? *But the face of the Lord is on evildoers* (v. 16). Here he used *face* in the sense of retribution: just as in the case of the righteous above he made mention of scrutiny and attention, so here in the case of the sinner he used God's *face* for his wrath and retribution. Hence he goes on, (198) *To destroy remembrance of them from the land.*

Having stated how God treats the sinners, too, he once more resumes his treatment of the righteous in the words,[3] *The righteous cried aloud and the Lord hearkened to them, he rescued them from all their tribulations* (v. 17). *The righteous cried aloud* means we ourselves; it has been often mentioned that by comparison with the Babylonians they call themselves righteous for doing nothing wrong to the Assyrians but rather being wronged by them. He confirms this very point in the words, *The Lord is near to the contrite of heart, and he will save the humble in spirit* (v. 18). There is a contradiction in this: how is it that the righteous are often exposed to trials, even though enjoying such care from God? Hence he goes on, *Many are the tribulations of the righteous, and from them all the Lord will rescue them* (v. 19): Pay attention, not to their being exposed to many trials, but rather their being freed from them all with God's help. I remarked already that in saying this, Hezekiah was worthy of belief in citing facts as witness of what was said.

The Lord protects all their bones, not one of them will be broken (v. 20), that is, he will preserve all their strength, the phrase (199) *all their bones* meaning, God accords all their affairs his providence. While such is true of those who hope in God, he is saying, what of

---

[3] This feature of the psalm that Diodore perceives—its lack of consistent movement—arises from its acrostic character, something lost in translation, of course.

the wicked? *Wickedness means death for sinners, and those who hate the righteous will come to grief* (v. 21). Here he hints once again at the Assyrians, providing an example from close at hand; he highlighted the many thousands of Assyrians brought down without bloodshed. To round off the whole thanksgiving, he goes on, *The Lord will redeem the souls of his servants, and all who hope in him will not come to grief* (v. 23), *will not come to grief* meaning will not fail in their purpose.

Psalm 35

The thirty-fifth psalm is recited from the viewpoint of Jeremiah, as the text itself demonstrates: if you compare the actual text of his inspired work and that of the psalm, they would be found completely similar, the result being that there is no possibility of their being applicable to any other person. The title only implies that it was composed by David, reading of it suggesting no one else. From the outset, then, he appears as someone complaining about those wronging him and praying against the godless who abuse him. While the psalm possibly gives the impression of a curse, it is completely a piece of prophecy: the author foretells in the form of a prayer what the godless were destined to suffer. (200) Many such forms are found in the divine Scripture: Jacob gave the impression of cursing Simeon and Levi in the words, "I shall divide them in Jacob, and scatter them in Israel."[1] While the form was that of a curse, the prophecy was seen to be realized in fact: they were divided into the twelve tribes after Levites were appointed, and especially the descendants of Levi, who were recognized rather as a blessing of the people than as a curse of the tribe.

Thus, here, too, Jeremiah prophesies in the form of a prayer the troubles due to overtake the ungodly. *Judge, Lord, those who wrong me, war against those who war against me* (v. 1). In the same breath he gives evidence of the piety of his attitude in recommending judgment to God and indicates the extremity of the troubles he suffered by mention of the help he seeks from God; he would not have

---

[1] Gen 49:7. Diodore has shown himself appreciative of various genres represented in the text of the Psalms. Gerhard von Rad remarks on the Genesis passage, "It is interesting that our saying and ch. 34 consider *Levi* to be a tribe like Simeon and the others; they apparently do not yet know it in its exceptional position as a tribe of priests" (*Genesis: A Commentary* [trans. John H. Marks; OTL; Philadelphia: Westminster, 1961], 419). Is that the corrective Diodore is supplying?

sought great help if he had not been extremely tried. Hence he goes on, *Take up large shield and shield and arise to help me* (v. 2). A *shield* is a kind of large shield: by *large shield* they refer to the round one, and by *shield* to the square one.² So he means, Many weapons of yours are required and for you to arise and run to my help. In all this he indicated the ferocity of those attacking. Then in what follows, *Unsheathe a sword, and engage those pursuing me* (v. 3). By *Unsheathe a sword* he means Bare it: just as what is unsheathed from a jar is bared, so too the bared sword seems to be unsheathed—so by *Unsheathe* he meant Bare, (201) and by *engage those pursuing me* meet them and shut off their course, warding off their charge with a sword. *Say to my soul, I am your salvation.* By *Say* he means action: If you prevent the enemies' assault and frustrate their plan, you will in actual fact be saying to my soul, *I am your salvation*; and since you are the one who has care of my soul, I will be saved and they of this mentality will fail in their purpose.

Hence he proceeds, *Let those who seek my life be ashamed and fearful, let them be turned backward, and let those who devise evil for me be confounded* (v. 4), that is, those opposing your purpose; especially since you personally resolve that I be saved, whereas they in every way resist my intentions. *Let them be like dust before the wind* (v. 5), that is, let them become weak, vulnerable, and insecure, as dust is before the wind. *And an angel of the Lord distressing them*: let an angel also add to their weakness, that is, a force causing them to become weakened further. *Let their way be darkness and sliding, with an angel of the Lord pursing them* (v. 6), that is, let them be in the situation of people fleeing in darkness and on a slippery surface; let an angel also pursue them to prevent their (202) negotiating the slippery surface by moving at a leisurely pace. He hints at a complete collapse: the person who does not know where to run, then is on a slippery footing, and in addition to that is pursued by someone—what do they experience, with no help coming by eye or foot?

He then gives the reason as well. *Because they hid their destructive snare for me without cause* (v. 7). By *destructive snare* he refers to the occasion when the prophet meant to buy things for food, whereas his accusers misrepresented him as intending to flee to the enemy.³ *Rashly they reproached my soul*, that is, because they made false accusations against me. *Let a trap fall on him of which he is igno-*

---

² The terms in Diodore's text are, respectively, ὅπλον and θυρεός.
³ Cf. Jer 37:11–15.

rant; and let the prey he hid take them; in that trap they will fall (v. 8), that is, let them suffer what they tried to do to him.[4]

My soul will rejoice in the Lord, it will delight in his salvation (v. 9): in order that I may enjoy happiness by the escape from the intrigues. *All my bones will say, Lord, Lord, who is like you?* (v. 10). In other words, all my strength will sing God's praises. (203) *Rescuing the poor from the hand of those too strong for him and the needy from those despoiling him.* By *poor and needy* he refers to himself as being without help among human beings.

Then, to give a clearer comment on what he said above, *Because they hid their destructive snare from me without cause*, he adds at this point, *Unjust witnesses rose up against me, questioning me on matters I had no knowledge of* (v. 11): when I was making my way to the gate on other business, the schemers hatched an accusation of another kind and brought me almost to the point of being liable to punishment. *They repaid me evil for good* (v. 12): while I gave them good advice, namely, not to fight the Babylonians on account of the onset of divine wrath that would give strength to the Babylonians, they misrepresented me as speaking on behalf of the Babylonians—or, rather, the Assyrians—and not on behalf of the Israelites. *And claiming sterility for my soul.* He means, They took all possible pains to obliterate me from the land, thus *claiming sterility for my soul* (using *claiming* for the action)[5] with the result that memory of me was obliterated, not because the prophet was destined to have no children, but because childlessness was thought by the Jews to be utter obliteration.

On my part, by contrast, I wore sackcloth when they were causing trouble, and I humbled my soul with fasting (v. 13): instead of matching (204) scheme against scheme, or hostility against hostility, I added to my external plight an interior humbling by begging them even if they did not hearken. Hence he goes on, *My prayer will be directed to my lap*: even if my prayer proved unacceptable to God and was sent back to me on account of the unworthiness of what I prayed for, I nevertheless did everything on my part with the purpose of obeying God. And lest anyone think that he was simply praying for them, he goes on, *I was pleased as though for a neighbor,*

---

[4] The number of the pronouns in this verse varies in the different forms of the LXX; Theodore and Theodoret seem to retain the singular, against ἀκολουθία. The Hebrew is unclear.

[5] The word does not seem to appear in the text used by Theodore or Theodoret or in other forms of the LXX.

for our brother (v. 14): as though for kith and kin I zealously offered prayers to render their situation acceptable. And when I failed, what then? *I was humbled as though sorrowful and downcast.* It was a mark of perfect love to rejoice in their success and be sorrowful and downcast in their failure.

So if this was my attitude to them, what was theirs? *They gloated over me and gathered together; scourges were piled on me and I did not understand* (v. 15), *and I did not understand* meaning, for reasons I did not understand, his thought being that he was struck and scourged for reasons he was not understanding. *They were rent asunder and had no regrets*: (205) even though they proved to be at odds in their accusations; not telling the truth put them at odds with one another, and yet they were not sorry (the meaning of *they had no regrets*), instead persisting in confirming by their malice what they set their hand to later. *They made attempts on me, they sneered at me with sneers* (v. 16). By *sneers* he means King Zedekiah's frequently calling him and saying to him, Tell me truthfully if the Assyrians are taking the city, to which Jeremiah replied, They are taking it. Now, this was a piece of irony directed at those unwilling to hear the truth. But since the king then went so far as to swear an oath, he told the truth, that the Lord had given this city into the hands of the Assyrians.[6] After his telling the truth, they scoffed at him and shut him up in a dungeon, the meaning of *They made attempts on me, they sneered at me with sneers*: they made attempts on me, firstly, whether I told the truth or not; and when I did, they took to mocking me, and not only mocking me but also adding threats to it, betraying deep anger. He goes on, in fact, *They gnashed their teeth at me*: mocking did not go without anger, and both combined were directed at me.

He then proceeds, *Lord, when will you take note?* (v. 17). You survey everything, he is saying. *Restore my soul from their evildoing,* (206) *Restore* meaning Set free. He next brings out also the strength of the schemers, going on, *Rescue my solitary life from the lions,* by *solitary* meaning lonely, his meaning therefore being, my lonely soul. *I shall confess to you, Lord, in a great assembly, I shall praise you in a mighty people* (v. 18): the beneficiary of loving-kindness on many occasions, I shall give thanks (going on to say *in a mighty people,* that is, numerous and drawn from many sources).

Then he prays in turn to be freed from the schemers in the

---

[6] Cf. Jer 37–38. Diodore is struggling to get the psalm verse to reflect that portion of the Jeremiah narrative.

words, *Let those who hate me unjustly not rejoice over me, those hating me without cause and winking their eyes* (v. 19).⁷ At this point he accuses those speaking to him with dissimulation; hence he proceeds, *Because they spoke words of peace to me, but devised deceit in anger* (v. 20): though experiencing angry feelings toward me within, they gave the impression in their speech of being mild, but betrayed their anger by mocking me and communicating to one another in glances that my life was not worth saving.⁸ *They opened wide their mouths toward me* (v. 21), that is, they officially accused me, keeping no restraint on their mouth and letting their tongue loose. (207) *They said, Aha, Aha, our eyes saw it. Aha, Aha* is a cry of satisfaction, the meaning therefore being, All we longed to see happening to him we see, and we taunted him.

You have seen, Lord, do not be silent (v. 22): for your part, Lord, do not overlook it. *Lord, do not keep your distance from me*: since a vast number of enemies hem me in, do not keep your distance from me; you suffice as my only help in the face of countless schemers. *Awake, Lord, and attend to my judgment* (v. 23). *Awake*: since by his long-suffering he gives the impression of sleeping, as it were, he urges him to arise and deliver a verdict in his favor. *My God and my Lord, for the sake of my just cause*. This, too, is connected with *Awake. Judge in my favor, Lord, according to your righteousness* (v. 24). Here the phrase *Judge in my favor* means, Deliver me a verdict. It has often been remarked, remember, that when he says Judge them with the accusative, he means Condemn, whereas when he says Judge in my favor, he means, Deliver me a verdict. *Lord my God, and let my foes not gloat over me*: (208) judge in my favor lest my foes find occasion to gloat over me. *Let them not say in their hearts, Aha, Aha, in my soul* (v. 25), that is, let them not take the opportunity to give voice to a note of satisfaction against my soul.⁹ *Nor say, We swallowed him*, that is, Lest with no one to lend help they boast that I have come to grief.

On the contrary, *Let those who rejoice in my troubles be ashamed and afraid at the same time* (v. 26): let them rather fail in this awful purpose of theirs. *Let those who exalt themselves over me wear shame*

---

⁷ Citation of this verse by Jesus at the supper in John 15:25 passes without comment.

⁸ Our Hebrew contains a final phrase, "the oppressed in the land," which involves a *hapax legomenon* not registered in the LXX. Theodoret will be alerted to it by the alternative version of Symmachus. Diodore, on the other hand, not referring to such alternatives, passes on unawares.

⁹ Other forms of the LXX, even Antiochene, read "our soul."

and reproach. Exalting themselves is the term he applies to those saying of him that he is not a man of God and is not helped by him. Clothe them in shame, then, he is saying, by helping me and showing their intrigues to be unsuccessful. *Let those who wish justice for me rejoice and be glad* (v. 27): fill with happiness and joy all those devoted to piety along with me, *those who wish for justice* being all who long to see me attaining my just deserts, these being those of my company devoted to you their God. (209) *Let them say always, The Lord be magnified*: let the pious have the opportunity to make great utterances about you their Lord. *Those who wish his servant's peace.* He says the same as he said above. *My tongue will ponder your righteousness* (v. 28), that is, will give expression: I shall not cease recounting all the good things with which you provided me. *Your praise all day long*: I shall not cease proclaiming your praise in public.

Psalm 36

"To the end. For David, the servant of the Lord." This psalm was uttered from the viewpoint of David himself when Saul employed a range of wiles against him to do away with him. When, however, he was surprised in a cave, as it were, where the jar and the spear were taken from him, he called him "child" and gave the impression of professing friendship and praying for the one he could not at all bear to enter his presence.[1]

With an eye on his overall purpose, then, blessed David begins in these terms, *The law-breaker speaks within himself with a view to sinning* (v. 1). He says that this law-breaker Saul thinks that (210) he sins within himself—that is, he is not open, scheming in his mind but flattering in his words. Whence does this happen to him? *There is no fear of God before his eyes*: since he refused to keep the judgment of God at heart, and believes he does not survey people's intentions, hence he dissembles, believing that in this way he has escaped the attention of God as also of human beings. *Because he was not honest with himself* (v. 2), that is, before God: Hence, he is saying, even before God he devises trickery, with no fear of God before his eyes. *About the discovery and hatred of his lawlessness*: no

---

[1] Diodore seems to be conflating the two similar incidents from 1 Samuel where David takes a piece of Saul's cloak while he is in the cave in the wilderness of En Gedi (24) and where he takes the water jar and spear on the hill at Hachilah (26).

thought is given to the fact that God discovers his sin, and on finding it hates both him and it.

The words of his mouth were lawlessness and deceit (v. 3). He makes the same accusation: since he said to him repeatedly, "Is this your voice, David my child?"[2] but at heart entertained other thoughts, he goes on, *The words of his mouth were lawlessness and deceit*: it is not true friendship, but steps toward murder. *He had no wish to understand doing good*: nothing good of any kind in my regard was planned or intended. *In bed he plotted lawlessness* (v. 4): instead, both in action (211) and in repose he ponders ways of devising his slaughter. *He took every path that is not good*: every lawless action is attractive to him. *He did not abhor evil*: he has no hatred or hostility toward any vices.

Lord, your mercy is in heaven and your truth extends as far as the clouds (v. 5). Since at every point he accuses Saul as an awful schemer, he says, Make clear to him, Lord, your loving-kindness as loftier and superior (*in heaven* and *as far as the clouds* implying height, and *your mercy and your truth* meaning your true loving-kindness). After mentioning the heights of God's loving-kindness, he goes on to mention also the measure of righteousness, proceeding, *Your righteousness like God's mountains* (v. 6). It is surprising that while he cites the height of loving-kindness as immeasurable, in the case of righteousness there is something measurable (*God's* occurring as usual in the sense of yours, *your righteousness* being like your *mountains*). An objection now arises: how, then, if he is very loving, and attends also to justice to the extent measured by him, he allows the righteous to fall foul of such awful tribulations and trials? So he proceeds to deal with it. *Your judgments are like the great deep*: the pattern of your planning, by which you allow the righteous to fall foul of tribulations and pressures, despite your being incomparably loving and very righteous, (212) cannot be discovered by a human being, just as it is not possible to measure the deep.

In similar fashion Paul also embarks upon the discussion of the management of human affairs, and how God conducts human affairs, sometimes by investing righteous people in tribulations, sometimes by conceding riches in many cases to sinners, and the fact that at one time he allowed pagans to practice idolatry and chose Jews for the practice of true religion, and that some people he later abandoned on account of unbelief and made others his own on account of faith. After pondering all this he went on, "O the depth

---

[2] 1 Sam 24:17; 26:17.

of the riches and wisdom and knowledge of God, how unsearchable his judgments and inscrutable his ways!"[3] Hence David also pondered God's loving-kindness and his judgments concerning righteousness: he saw that while he in his piety suffers tribulations, Saul in his wickedness enjoys honor and wealth when practicing no piety, and at a loss he exclaimed, *Your judgments are like the great deep.*

Then, in his wish to comment on God's loving-kindness, he develops the same topic and shows to what degree it is extended, saying, *You will save human beings and cattle, Lord. How you extended your mercy, God!* (vv. 6–7): you extended your loving-kindness and mercy so as to care not only for human beings but also for cattle through human beings. Next, after mentioning that he cares for both human beings and cattle, he goes on, *The sons of men will hope in the shelter of your wings*: human beings, however, have an extra advantage in their reasoning to the extent that they fly up to you and are covered by your providence in the manner of wings. (213) And not only this: in true religion they have an advantage over all other living things. He proceeds, in fact, *They will be intoxicated with the rich fare of your house, and you will give them to drink of the flood of your delicacies* (v. 8). Here he refers to the teachings of religion, the knowledge of the laws, the hidden messages of the prophets, and everything else that gladdens the soul. *They will be intoxicated with the rich fare of your house* was well put, referring to the satisfaction coming from rational delicacies, *the rich fare of your house* being the teachings in the temple, and likewise *flood of your delicacies* being the abundance of satisfaction which those versed in the divine sayings and in piety obtain. Hence he continues, *Because with you is a fountain of life; in your light we shall see light* (v. 9): thanks to you it is possible for us both to live and to be enlightened unto piety: *In your light* we see you, as if to say, through piety leading to you we experience you.

Extend your mercy to those who know you, and your righteousness to the upright of heart (v. 10): but just as in giving evidence of loving-kindness and care for both cattle and human beings you provide something more to the human beings, the practice of piety, so likewise in the case of the human beings bring out a difference, providing more to those who are zealous in the practice of piety. *May the foot of arrogance not come my way, and a sinner's hand not move*

---

[3] Rom 11:33.

me (v. 11). *Foot* and *sinner's hand* are circumlocutions with the same meaning, the sinner: since we walk with our foot and (214) work with our hand, he means, Let no action of a sinner be acceptable to you. *All evildoers fell there* (v. 12). *There* means, It is fitting that the unrighteous and not the righteous fall foul of such actions (using place for person, *There* suggesting place). So, as was mentioned, he used place for person, his habit being to use place for person, as when he says, "There the path by which I shall show him my salvation," here likewise meaning action, using place for action. Elsewhere too, "Because there it was that the Lord ordained his blessing, life forever," that is, by such an action: since he had earlier said, "Behold, what a beautiful and charming thing it is for brethren to dwell together," he went on, "Because there it was that the Lord ordained his blessing,"[4] that is, by such an action, whence there is to be found love and the harmony of mutual affection. *They were thrust out, may they never stand*: it is fitting that the godless should fall foul of the actions of sinners, be thrust out by them and come to grief so as to have neither stability nor permanence.

Psalm 37

The thirty-seventh psalm is entitled, "A psalm for David"; it is one of the more moral psalms, those of a more universal nature, (215) even if applicable to Jews specifically. You see, since as was mentioned in the preface some of the moral psalms refer specifically to the Jews, like the fiftieth and eighty-second and others of the kind, while others admonish all human beings alike, this psalm has the appearance of being universal, even if perhaps seeming to refer specifically to Jews, as was said. It seems, in fact, to be of benefit to all human beings, the actual text bringing out its universal character.

Do not emulate evildoers, nor rival those committing iniquity (v. 1). Being human, we are all irked by the prosperity of the affluent, especially when they are dishonest. So from the outset he immediately gives this exhortation, Do not imitate evildoers, even if they are rich, nor law-breakers, even if from their wickedness they amass wealth. Why not? *Because they will quickly dry up like grass, and quickly fall like green foliage* (v. 2): though flourishing for a time, such people have a rapid end. He did well to compare them with

[4] Pss 50:23; 133:1, 3.

flowers: they also delight the eye for a time, but are unable to bear the heat and dry up at once.

So what should be done by such a person? *Hope in the Lord and do good* (v. 3). It has often been said that perfect virtue is avoiding evil and doing good. After giving the exhortation at this point (216) not to imitate the wicked, then, he urges them to pursue better things: For your part avoid declaring blessed the law-breakers, even if they are wealthy, place all your hope in God, and attend to righteousness with all your strength, this not being without benefit for you. Hence he goes on, *And inhabit the earth, and you will be fed on its riches*, the term *inhabit* meaning, God will make you wealthy in the land when you hope in him and attend to righteousness (using the imperative in place of the future). *Delight in the Lord, and he will grant you your heart's desire* (v. 4). Likewise *Delight* means, He will also cause you to enjoy the greatest delight and will bring to fruition all your desires.

Disclose your way to the Lord, hope in him, and he will act (v. 5). *Disclose* means, Be sincere in pursuing good, not pretending to be honest while being evil; instead, be good openly and as it were without disguise so that God may openly repay you with good. Hence he proceeds, *He will highlight your righteousness like a light* (v. 6), that is, openly as in the daylight he will reward you with the actual fruits of righteousness. And to bring out more clearly the sense of openly, he goes on, (217) *And your judgment like midday*: just as midday is the brightest moment of the whole day, so God will increase your good fortune in public and before everyone. This being the case, then, *Be subject to the Lord and beseech him* (v. 7): far from forsaking God, set your hopes on him and present your petitions to him, capable as he is of supplying good things.

Having to this point given proper advice, he once again resumes the same subject in the words, *Do not emulate the one who prospers in his way, with the human being who commits lawlessness*. He resumed the opening thought: This being the case, do not be surprised at the lawless person's prosperity. *Refrain from rage and desist from anger* (v. 8): do not be irked if this happens at some time. Why? *Do not emulate to the extent of doing evil*: do not let extreme irritation and being irked at such things cause you to imitate them, and yourself also come to be subject to the same punishment as they. Hence he proceeds, *Because the evildoers will be wiped out* (v. 9): this is the outcome of the evildoers' famous prosperity. (218) *Whereas those who wait on the Lord will inherit the land*. What he said above he repeats here:¹ All who are devoted to doing what pleases God securely occupy the land and enjoy the good things coming from it. So while in singing this psalm Jews thought the author is referring only to Palestine, the whole of humanity in singing it know the land and the good things coming from it are in common, the result being that of old it applied to Jews specifically and now to all human beings in common.

Yet a little while, and the sinner will not be around; you will look for his trace and not find it (v. 10): consider that point, too, how many of the wicked who experienced prosperity and gained a good reputation with many people were snatched suddenly away like a spider's web, with no trace of them left. *The gentle, on the other hand, will inherit the land, and will find delight in the abundance of peace* (v. 11). Here by *gentle* he refers to those doing God's will: They always acquire lasting goods, he is saying.² The result, then? The wicked not only grows rich but even plots against the righteous, God's permission causing both developments to go ahead; but let it not alarm you, God in his foreknowledge being aware of the fate of the wicked and seeing the righteous person's endurance. Hence he goes on, *The sinner will scrutinize the righteous one, and gnashes his teeth against him* (v. 12): frequently the wicked person (219) will be enraged at the righteous, and will plot and threaten with all his might. The upshot of this? *But the Lord will mock him because he foresees that his day will come* (v. 13): this is not God's view of such a person; God looks ahead to his fate and mocks his threats and his frenzy, aware as he is of the future. Hence in many cases when the wicked think they have got the better of the righteous, then it is that sudden ruin overtakes them when unexpected punishment is inflicted on them by God.

Hence he proceeds, *The sinners drew a sword and bent their bow to overthrow the poor and the needy, to slaughter the upright of heart* (v. 14): hence even if the wicked assault the righteous with a sword and prepare all their weaponry against them in the belief they have already got the better of them, what happens? *The sword will enter their own hearts, and their bows be broken* (v. 15): the wicked will fall victim to their own snares, be slain with their own swords and crushed by their weapons, and thus the righteous person will prove

---

¹ Again the psalm's acrostic character (in the Hebrew) is responsible for repetition.

² Citation of this verse in Matthew's Beatitudes (5:5) is not adverted to by Diodore.

superior to their intrigue. The result? *Better a little for the righteous than much wealth of sinners* (v. 16): for this reason, then, it should be realized that it is better (220) to be content with a little along with righteousness than to achieve great wealth along with lawlessness. *Because sinners' arms will be broken* (v. 17). By *arms* he refers again to all their power: just as above he had said that their weapons would be destroyed, so here as well he says their power will be consigned to ruin.

What, on the other hand, will happen to the righteous? *But the Lord upholds the righteous.* Symmachus says "supports them," implying the same thing.[3] *The Lord knows the ways of the blameless* (v. 18). *Knows* means makes his own, as in the first psalm, "Because the Lord knows the ways of the righteous,"[4] that is, makes them his own. *And their inheritance will last forever*: these people will also securely transmit their possessions to their descendants. *They will not be put to shame in bad times* (v. 19): even when difficult times come upon them, they will escape the difficulties by their righteousness and hope in God. *And they will have their fill in times of famine.* He means the same thing, though expressing it differently, referring to the time of misfortune as a time of *famine*, and correspondingly using the figure *they will have their fill* to imply that (221) such people will be freed of all wickedness.

Such being the case with the righteous, what of sinners? *Because sinners will perish, and the Lord's foes at the time of being glorified and exalted truly failed like smoke* (v. 20): those rejoicing in injustice and opposing God's commands, after being gleeful for a short time and thinking their life joyful, will be reduced to nothingness like smoke. So they should consider not the appearance of things but their outcome. *The sinner will borrow and not pay back, whereas the righteous has pity and gives* (v. 21). He means, There will be such a great change in fortunes that the one shortly before considered rich will come to such indigence as to borrow the necessities for nourishment and have no way of repaying, thus being caught up in the twofold problem of having no food and of begging in addition for what he consumed. The righteous person, by contrast,

---

[3] This is the first reference by Diodore to the alternative version of Symmachus (Aquila, contrary to the opinion of editor Olivier, having been cited on Ps 3:4), who will be cited only half a dozen times in the whole commentary, and only to confirm the commentator's interpretation (unlike Theodoret and Chrysostom, where variants are cited and compared with the LXX). Olivier puts the rarity down to Diodore's not having access to a copy of the Hexapla.

[4] Ps 1:6.

thought indigent and appearing pitiable to the general run of people, will be transformed into a person of wealth so as even to share with others. *Because those who bless him will inherit the land, whereas those who curse him will be wiped out* (v. 22): a person of this kind is placed in such a position of honor and prosperity that his own family are also held in regard and filled with many good things, while his foes suffer utter ruin.

Why does this happen? *A person's steps are guided by the Lord* (v. 23): since such a person (222) is guided by the Lord, all his doings will proceed successfully. Hence he goes on, *And he will take great delight in his ways.* The term *take delight* means be pleased, his meaning being, He will guide every action of such a person. *Whenever he falls, he will not be broken in pieces* (v. 24): if it happens that such a person is unsuccessful, as happens with human affairs, God does not permit it, instead renewing him once again. Hence he proceeds, *Because the Lord strengthens his hand,* that is, with his own hand God raises up such a person.

Then also he raises a point as though by discernment or introducing a supposition in the manner of Ecclesiastes.[5] For stronger confirmation of what is recommended or advised, remember, those so recommending claim to have seen so that those recommended would be persuaded that it was not idly or to no purpose that they make the recommendation, but from their own experience of the actual events. So he goes on in these terms, *I have been younger and am now grown old, and have not seen a righteous one abandoned nor his offspring looking for bread* (v. 25): I cite the experience I personally have had from youth to my present old age, that I have never seen a righteous person abandoned by God, and not only himself but even his offspring I have not seen reduced to want of any good (referring to all goodness by mention of *bread*). Instead, quite the opposite did I see. What was it like? (223) *All day long the righteous one shows mercy and lends money, and his offspring will bring a blessing* (v. 26): I saw a righteous person living in great prosperity and his family enjoying a like prosperity.

Turn away from evil and do good (v. 27): for this reason and in view of all I have foretold, you need to forsake evil and cling fast to good. And what is the effect of this? *And dwell forever:* so that you may dwell in the land and share unceasingly in its good things. *Because the Lord loves judgment* (v. 28): convinced that God has a

---

[5] Diodore shows familiarity with the style of Qoheleth: cf. 1:14; 2:11, 14, 24; 3:16; 4:1.

deep concern for justice. *And he will not abandon his holy ones*: he will never overlook his own. *Because they will be protected forever*: instead, he will guard them unceasingly. *But lawless people will be banished and offspring of ungodly people will be destroyed*: since he cares for justice, by the same token he both guards his holy ones and destroys transgressors. (224) *Righteous people, on the other hand, will inherit the earth and dwell in it forever* (v. 29).

Then, after speaking everywhere in terms of *righteous* and *holy* without saying what had to be done by such a person or the kind of person they should be, at this point he describes what kind of person it is that God guards and the sort of person they should be, in the words, *The mouth of the righteous will be concerned with wisdom, and his tongue will speak judgment* (v. 30): God guards the person of wise counsel and just judgment. And of what other attribute? *The law of his God is in his heart* (v. 31): the person with God's law and commandments always on his mind. *His steps will not be upset*: God will not allow such a person's steps to be upset, nor permit him to be turned away from good things, even if the sinner countless times schemes and attacks and employs all possible wiles to bring such a one undone. Hence he goes on, *The sinner scrutinizes the righteous one, and seeks to kill him. But the Lord will not abandon him into his hands* (vv. 32–33): even if the wicked person creates complete confusion and upset in order to do wrong to the righteous, God does not allow it, nor does he surrender him into lawless hands. *Nor does he condemn him when he is brought to judgment*: (225) God does not condemn him *when he is brought to judgment,* nor even when God conducts an interrogation of his affairs, aware of his good will and zeal.

Wait upon the Lord and keep his way, and he will exalt you to inherit the land (v. 34): for this reason, then, do not withdraw from God's commands; instead, be zealous in doing what pleases him. Thus God will also reward you by making you conspicuous for good things and affluent (the meaning of *inherit the land*). Then even more, *You will see his destruction of sinners*, by *will see* meaning *will observe*: You will have greater satisfaction, he is saying, in the misfortunes of the ungodly. Thus God will punish the wicked before your very eyes and take vengeance on your foes so that you will rejoice to see the vindication with your own eyes.

Next, he again raises a question hypothetically or by claiming in fact to have witnessed it, treating of the wicked just as he had of the good: as he had said of the good, *I have been younger and am now grown old, and have not seen a righteous one abandoned or his offspring looking for bread,* so too in the case of the godless and lawless he claims to have witnessed and been fully assured. Hence he goes on, (226) *I have seen the godless exalted and lifted up like the cedars of Lebanon. I passed by and, lo, he was no more; I searched for him, and no trace could be found* (vv. 35–36): I personally observed the lawless person wealthy, lifted up and elevated like the tall cedars, yet I saw also the overthrow of such a one; you made a slight change or reversal, as it were, and it proved impossible to know the place he occupied. What is the conclusion? *Preserve innocence and take note of uprightness* (v. 37): since this is the case, then, do not desist from upright behavior or from being blameless. *Because there is posterity for a peaceable person,* by *posterity* meaning descendants and heirs—in other words, such a person will be looked after so as to pass on happiness to children and heirs. *Transgressors, on the other hand, will be destroyed together* (v. 38): they will absolutely disappear along with children and descendants (the meaning of *together*). Hence, to make it clearer, he goes on, *The posterity of the godless will be destroyed*: not only will their descendants be consigned to destruction, but also anything else of theirs that is left.

Salvation of the righteous, by contrast, is with the Lord, and he is their protection in time of tribulation. The Lord will help them, rescue them, pluck them from sinners' clutches and save them, because they hoped in him (vv. 39–40). He did well to sum up all God's help at the (227) end of the psalm so as to bring out that the just will fall short of no good thing from God. He says, in fact, that such people will be saved by God, in time of misfortune he will protect them and rescue them from tribulation, in every affair and at every moment he helps them, and when foes rebel God supports them—in short, he accords them every help whenever they do not fail to hope in him.

Psalm 38

The thirty-eighth psalm resembles in its theme the sixth: just as that one is a confession of the sin with Bathsheba and a plea to God, so here too he begs to be freed from the misfortunes arising from Absalom's rebelling and bringing a range of tribulations upon him, at the same time confessing the sin and giving evidence at every point of the sincerity of repentance.

Lord, do not accuse me in your anger, nor chastise me in your wrath

(v. 1). He asks for the manner of chastisement to be changed, not that he is avoiding chastisement itself but begging that his suffering at God's hands may have the purpose not of vengeance but of reform. *Because your arrows have sunk into me* (v. 2), by *arrows* referring to the punishments. *And you have fastened your hand upon me.* He means that, just like people heaving and puffing and pressing down with their hands, (228) so are your punishments intolerable to me when your hand presses and pushes. *There is no healing in my flesh in the face of your wrath* (v. 3): hence I gain no relief from the fact that I am being punished as if you were angry with me and not correcting me.

He then straightway supplies the reason why he is suffering and makes his confession, and through this he was able to influence God to spare the one confessing his sin. *There is no peace in my bones in the face of my sins.* He meant, Your hand and your punishments are heavy, but my sins are the cause of them; it is not you who weigh me down with misfortunes—rather, I supply the occasion for the misfortunes. Reinforcing this very point, he says, *Because my iniquities reached beyond my head* (v. 4): the sins were too great to be pardoned; I committed such awful sins that the faults surpass the power of the one committing them. *They weighed me down like a heavy burden*: since this is the case, then, I cannot support the weight, since my sins are beyond the measure of my power.

He next hints also at the actual kind of sin. *My sores became putrid and rotten from my stupidity* (v. 5). By his *stupidity* he refers to the time of the illicit (229) desire: he clearly gave way to his feelings and surrendered himself to baser actions. So he says, After it is over, I believe the sores of my sin are burning and my fault smelling, with the result that on that account I am punished further. *I became miserable and downcast forever, I went about with a sad countenance all day long* (v. 6): even though you actually spared me, not inflicting instant punishment, Lord, yet the concern and thought of the sin committed reduced me to grave and overwhelming pangs and to be downcast and grief-stricken constantly. *Because my entrails are filled with mockery* (v. 7). He refers to the places around the loins, by mention of the loins suggesting lust. He speaks of *mockery* because, he says, those places (his description is rather solemn) became for me the occasion of many taunts and jibes. *And there is no healing in my flesh*: I got no relief from it. *I was afflicted and humbled to breaking point* (v. 8). He then expresses the intensity of this feeling. *I howled from the sighing of my heart*: the cry I uttered was not even human; instead, *I howled* like dogs dealt incurable blows.

What is the upshot of this? (230) *Lord, all my desire is before you, and my sighing was not hidden from you* (v. 9): you know what I desire, Lord, but I dare not mention it, the sin not allowing me to make such a petition; instead, it is sufficient for me to sigh to the one who knows what underlies the depth of the sighing. *My heart was disturbed, my strength left me* (v. 10). He cites the reason for his groaning to be freed from desire, namely, that he no longer has the strength and that his thoughts are confused, no longer perceiving what is to be done. And not only his thinking: what else? *And the light of my eyes, and it was not with me*: I do not even see light as I should; the darkness of misfortune does not allow me to perceive light properly.

My friends and my neighbors took up a position against me (v. 11): not only my son Absalom; rather, even if some people seemed to be my friends and kindred, they all acted the part of enemies to me. *And those close to me kept their distance*: even if some people seemed to be close on account of the favors done by me, at the time of the misfortune they deserted me and kept their distance. (231) *Those seeking my life were forced out* (v. 12): from this point on, as though there were no one available to help, those intent on doing away with my life brought every pressure to bear. *And those seeking my harm spoke empty words*: all intent on schemes against me told the greatest lies of me. *And plotted treacherous schemes all day long*: would that their words amounted to nothing and they did not combine their plots and various snares with calumnies.

For my part, however, like a deaf person I did not hear, and like a mute not opening his mouth (v. 13), that is, I did not open my mouth in reply to the calumnies coming from them, instead being seen to keep silence even in the face of the many accusations, aware that my humbling came from another quarter—namely, my sin. *I became like a person who does not hear and who has no censure in his mouth* (v. 14): so I kept silence for the most part, and though in a position to prove that they misrepresented me, I did not even do that, the sin burning my mouth. From then on I placed all my hope in you. *Because it is in you, Lord, that I hoped; you will hearken to me, Lord my God. Because I said, May my foes never rejoice over me;* (232) *when my foot slipped, they gloated over me* (vv. 15–16): while I made no reply to them, I put my hope in you, making the same request, that the enemy not gloat over me for long, nor that my reversal and change in fortunes prove a source of joy to those uttering boasts against me (*they gloated* referring to those gloating).

Because I am ready for the whips, and my distress is ever in my sight (v. 17): not that I asked to be spared the blows from you, Lord; instead, being fortified to accept them, I asked not to prove a source of joy to the foe (*ready* meaning fortified and firm). *Because I shall declare my lawlessness and ponder my sin* (v. 18): so I was strengthened to accept the scourges from you by knowing my sin was before my eyes, always destined to be in my thoughts and on my mind (the meaning of *declare* and *ponder*). *My foes, however, are alive and prevail over me; those who hate me unjustly are multiplied* (v. 20): while I was of this mind, enduring scourging from you and making no account of those calumniating me, they proved stronger and more numerous, *unjustly hating* me and reducing me to a stupor. *Those who repay me evil for good* (v. 20): in some cases (233) they were beneficiaries of mine. *They calumniated me since I followed after goodness*: since it happened that on many occasions when I was ruling I was moved by justice to impose a penalty on some people, now at the time of misfortune they abuse me (the sense of *calumniated*; he refers to abusing as calumniating). *Though I was beloved, they rejected me, loathed like a corpse*: the one they previously pretended to love and reverence as a benefactor for giving advice on their duty they now see in the role of a corpse that is cast out.[1]

Do not abandon me, Lord my God, nor keep far from me (v. 21): while they have this attitude to me, for your part on the contrary, Lord, do not leave me bereft of help. Hence he proceeds, *Come to my help, Lord of my salvation* (v. 22).

Psalm 39

This thirty-ninth psalm is also spoken on the part of David himself, even if the title runs, "To the end. Of Jeduthun, a song of David." It is likely that it was given by David to Jeduthun, a temple singer, for singing—though the (234) composition of the psalms was by David and no one else.[1] He recited this psalm when he was

---

[1] This third clause in v. 20 is missing in Hebrew and most forms of the LXX, but the Antiochenes read it in theirs.

[1] In his preface Diodore was not so insistent on Davidic authorship as he was on the provenance of the titles from other sources. Here he seems to change his position. Influenced probably by 1 Chr 16:41 on Jeduthun's liturgical role in

enduring all the intrigues on the part of Saul, the threats and pursuits, because in all these difficulties he showed long-suffering and sound values in expectation only of God's intervention.

I said, I shall guard my ways so as not to sin with my tongue (v. 1), *I said* having the sense, I determined, his meaning being, I determined within myself not to sin against my oppressor simply in action, but also not to say anything against him by word of mouth, especially since what is initially verbal abuse turns to physical abuse, and the person who is determined not to do physical harm ought not have recourse to verbal abuse. Hence he goes on, *I placed a guard on my mouth*: in particular I placed a tighter guard on my mouth, since it is easier than taking action. At what time (this being the important thing)? *When the sinner took up a position against me, I kept mute, was humiliated and made no mention of good deeds* (vv. 1–2). By *sinner* he refers to the person trying to wrong him with no justification. He now calls Saul *sinner*, therefore: the sinner's efforts to wrong him without cause are compared with his own determination to do no wrong. (235) So he is saying, When Saul was engaged in hatching all kinds of intrigues and calumnies against me without my appearing to hear of it, I was thus humbling myself and keeping silence, not choosing to avenge myself (the meaning of *good deeds*, since to the wronged person vengeance seems to be a good deed).

And my grief was renewed: though keeping silence and not taking vengeance, I had no peace of mind, instead being disturbed and upset like any man. Hence he proceeds, *My heart became hot within me, and in my meditation fire burned* (v. 3): instead, I was even inflamed with the consciousness of no wrong done by me, and the thought of the adversaries set alight my mind like a flame, and yet I put up with it. Now, he did well to proceed to express the event in terms of fire: heat always precedes flames, and hence he first said *became hot*, and then that a flame burst out in me.

I spoke with my tongue, Make known my end to me, Lord (vv. 3–4). He says only this: At that time when I did not presume to take vengeance and was distressed on that account, only then did I appeal to God to inform me of the end to the misfortunes, when they would cease. *And what is the number of my days so that I may know what is left to me*: and how much time I have to live so that I

David's time, he is now prepared to concede the likely authenticity of the title as specifying authorship and performance.

may calculate the extent of my sufferings and be rid of them (236), and attain some sound hope on the basis of some respite being left to me in my life. *Lo, you made my days handbreadths* (v. 5), by *handbreadths* meaning measured: since a *handbreadth* is so called as a measure, and he had said, Let me know also the end of the misfortunes and how much of my life is left, he logically went on to say, *You made my days handbreadths*—that is, far from assigning me an unlimited life span, you limited it by a certain measure according to your own knowledge. For my part, on the other hand, I know only this, that no matter how great the measure of life you set me, it is nothing by comparison with the Lord who lives forever. *And my existence is as nothing before you*: however much *my existence*, which has to do with living and the period it lasts, it is nothing in comparison with the one who lives forever, as was said.

Why, he asks, do I say my life is nothing? *Besides, everything is futility, every living person*: not even all the possessions amassed nor all humankind, if measured by their lifetime, from Adam to the last human being—not even this measure is anything in comparison with the measure of your life, Lord. *At any rate, a person goes about like a painting, of course* (v. 6). *Besides* and *of course* add nothing to the thought, being a slovenly translation from the Hebrew.[2] His meaning is, In comparison with your life (237) everything amounts to nothing, and the human being more so, being no different from a painting, which is cast aside in time. *Yet he is worried over nothing*: they nevertheless get tossed this way and that over riches and glory and power. Hence he goes on, *He stores up treasures, and does not know for whom he is collecting them*: and what is worse, he gets worn out in amassing money though having no heir and not knowing who will succeed to it, the result being that the actual collector incurs trouble and tedium while the profit goes to someone else, of whose identity in many cases he is ignorant.

And now what is my expectation? Is it not the Lord? My existence is from you (v. 7): for my part, I realize you are responsible both for my being and for my existing, and I await help from you, still not beaten black and blue by other people for such untoward desires. *From all my iniquities rescue me* (v. 8): it is you who are able to do this and free me from the misfortunes besetting me. *You gave me as an object of scorn to the fool.* He resumes what was said by him in the introduction, by *fool* referring to the person boasting and uttering

[2] Elsewhere Diodore dismisses as otiose the LXX's attempts to reproduce the Hebrew particle *akh-*, which in fact does "add to the thought."

loud threats with a poor conception of human nature, (238) and hinting at Saul and those of his company. While they taunted and threatened in this fashion, what of me? *I kept mute, I did not open my mouth, because you did it* (v. 9): for my part, I realized that this happens to me with your permission, and I waited longer in the knowledge that I would receive help from the same quarter from which comes also the allowance of my suffering. *Remove the scourge from me: I have fainted with the strength of your hand* (v. 10): for this reason, then, I beg of you also relief from the difficulties, since from you also comes the permission for me to suffer.

You chastised the human being with accusations of transgression (v. 11): admittedly, I realize that all your scourging proves to be for a person's correction and betterment; it is not as though you were indifferent to human beings in allowing them to suffer, instead preferring to improve their souls, as it were. Hence he goes on, *And wasted his soul like a spider's web*: thus you winnow it and purify it of its sins with the scourging. *Yet every human being is worried about a nothing*: but all those failing to understand this are fools in not realizing the reason for the permission, and so are alarmed and worried.[3]

Hearken to my prayer, Lord, and give your ear to my request (v. 12): for my part, on the contrary, (239) aware as I am of the reason, I beseech you to apply correction commensurate with my power lest the excess of sufferings prove my undoing and not a lesson for my betterment. *Do not hold your peace at my tears.* He then states the reason as well. *Because I am a stranger before you and a pilgrim like all my ancestors*: I shall not live long enough to match such awful punishment; rather, I must accept punishment commensurate with the limits of my life. Hence he goes on, *Give me relief so that I may catch my breath before departing and be no more* (v. 13): lighten my misfortunes, then, Lord, since death is at hand to snatch me away and bring me to my undoing, where correction will make no impact on me.

---

[3] Contrary to the opinion of Olivier, it would seem the "every" should appear in Diodore's text of this clause, as in other forms of the LXX.

Psalm 40

The fortieth psalm has a Babylonian theme. Blessed David's purpose is to show the Israelites benefiting greatly from the prolonged hardship, and the actual text makes the psalm clearer. It bears the title, "To the end. A psalm for David," that is, it aims at making a statement about future events, and begins thus: *I waited and waited on the Lord, and he attended to me* (v. 1). The repetition is a sign of emphasis, as when (240) Scripture says, "In my looking I have seen the abuse of my people in Egypt," that is, I looked hard and long, and, "In your knowledge you will know this,"[1] that is, Gain a precise knowledge. So he means, Since I waited earnestly on God, *he attended to me and hearkened to me* (reciting this psalm on the part of the people, who have returned from captivity). At the same time he also instructs all people to bear misfortune nobly and have a sound attitude to it, something that has good effects. *And he hearkened to my prayer.*

Tell us also what he brought you when he hearkened. *He drew me out of a pit of wretchedness and from a miry bog* (v. 2). *Out of a pit*, as if to say, as though out of a pit, and again *from a bog* as though from a miry bog, his intention being to indicate that the people in captivity were in such a condition as if in a very deep pit, one moreover that contained a great deal of matter from which the one falling in would find it very difficult to extricate himself. So he is saying, From such troubles God rescued me and restored me to his own. *He set my feet on a rock*. Again *on a rock* for as if on a rock, as if to say, He established me in security. *And guided my steps*: (241) he directed everything for me so that nothing should prove an obstacle to the return. *He put in my mouth a song, a new hymn to our God* (v. 3): he provided me also with the occasion of singing to him *a new hymn* (by *a new hymn* referring to this one directed to him unexpectedly). *Many will see and will fear, and will hope in the Lord*: I shall therefore from now on be an example also to others of those who ought fear the Lord. How and in what fashion? Because he emerged showing providence and protection for those who hope in him.

Then, by way of exhorting others, he goes on, *Blessed is the man whose hope is in the name of the Lord, whose eyes were not on futilities and deceitful frenzies* (v. 4): blessed in reality is whoever had God

---

[1] Exod 3:7; Gen 15:13.

alone as his hope and help, and did not sink to the level of the idols and the deception involved with them (calling it *futilities and deceitful frenzies*). *Many are the marvels you have performed, Lord my God, and in your thoughts there is no one to compare with you* (v. 5): just as even now you provide us who hope in you with many ineffable things that defy measuring (by God's *thoughts* referring to the immeasurable favors). *I proclaimed* (242) *and spoke of them, they were multiplied beyond counting*: although to the extent possible and as ability allowed I described many of them to many people, yet I was at a loss to describe them; words failed me on account of the surfeit of marvels (the meaning of *they were multiplied beyond counting*, as if to say, God's mercies and salvations abound, no matter how much you describe them and attempt to number them).

Sacrifice and offering you did not desire, but ears you fashioned for me (v. 6): and more marvelous and surprising, you did not want from me sacrifices to be offered by me, requiring of me instead only obedience (by *ears* meaning obedience). In other words, since it was impossible in captivity to sacrifice, and yet the law ordered prayers to be offered through sacrifices, he means, In your loving-kindness you surpassed even the law, not requiring sacrifices and being content only with obedience. Hence he continues, *Holocausts even for sin you did not look for*: since it was clear that sin was the cause of the captivity, in an extraordinary degree of loving-kindness you undid sin without requiring sacrifice. Now, this is very applicable to the case of Christ: since those belonging to Christ were destined not to offer sacrifice, and to replace it with obedience and (243) piety, and through such things be freed from sins, these words were rightly taken by Paul in reference to the divine plan involving Christ to the effect that it was possible even without sacrifices to attain forgiveness of sins.[2] *Then I said, Behold, I am coming* (v. 7). The phrase *Behold, I am coming* means, I obeyed: since he had said above, *Sacrifice you did not desire* but obedience, he says, Perceiving this I said, *Behold, I am coming*, that is, I obeyed, bringing obedience in place of sacrifice. *In the scroll of the book it is written of me. My wish was to do your will, O my God* (vv. 7–8). *In the scroll* means on the roll, his intention being to refer to the rolled text: the laws were written on rolls or books of skins. So he is saying, I practiced obedience and determined *to do your will* in such a way as if learning it from a book, my resolve being sufficient for me in place of the

---

[2] Heb 10:5–7.

reading aloud of words. Hence he goes on, *And your law is in my very innards,* as if to say, in my heart. So he means, With the law itself in my very heart, I was thus very zealous in doing what is pleasing to you.

I told the good news of righteousness in a great assembly (v. 9): for this reason, then, (244) even now that many have congregated and a thronged assembly gathered I shall proclaim your righteousness of which you gave evidence to us (*I told the good news* meaning, I shall tell the good news, and the sequel makes this clear). He goes on, in fact, *Lo, my lips I shall not forbid*: I shall not cease doing so, nor shall I close my mouth to prevent my announcing the good things you gave us. *Lord, you know my righteousness*: it fell to no one else to acknowledge that I had a rightful claim to return, you being the only one to know what is hidden (by rightful claim referring to the Babylonians, since they wronged the Israelites, not vice versa). *I did not conceal your righteousness in my heart* (v. 10): for this reason, then, I do not conceal the good things provided to me; instead, I shall publicize and bruit them abroad as far as I can. *I spoke of your truth and your salvation*: your truth and your salvation (meaning your truthful salvation) I did not hide but made clear to everyone. *I did not conceal your mercy and your truth from a numerous congregation*. He repeated the same thought in parallelism.

But as for you, Lord, do not keep your pity far from me (v. 11): for this reason, in your own case, Lord, (245) you did not withhold your pity from me (*do not keep* meaning did not keep). Hence he goes on, *Your mercy and your truth always assisted me*. Again *Your mercy and your truth* means, Your true loving-kindness *assisted* and helped me. He then recounts also the troubles from which God freed him with a view to augmenting the hymns of praise of the Lord. *Because evils beyond counting encompassed me, my transgressions laid hold of me, and I could not see* (v. 12): I was overwhelmed by so many misfortunes as a result of my transgressions that my head spun and I was unable even to gaze at the light. *They became more numerous than the hairs of my head*. Having mentioned above the severity of the misfortunes, at this point he hints at their great number—hence his claim, The misfortunes surpass the number of hairs on my head. *And my heart failed me*: I almost fainted and was not myself, so weak had all my thinking become.

Be pleased, Lord, to rescue me (v. 13): since this is my attitude, you were pleased to rescue me personally (*Be pleased* meaning You were pleased). *Lord, attend to helping me*: (246): you attended to my help (the tense being changed here as well). *Let those be put to shame and overturned together who seek my life to do away with it* (v. 14): all who devised noxious schemes against me were confounded and overturned (the tense being changed in all these clauses). *Let them be turned back and put to shame who seek to harm me,* meaning, They were turned back and put to shame. *Let them meet with shame from the outset who say to me, Aha, Aha* (v. 15): those gloating over me (the meaning of *Aha, Aha*) met with shame.

May all who place their hope in you rejoice and be glad in you, Lord (v. 16): but those who hope in you were established in great joy and happiness. *And may they say always, May the Lord be magnified*: they were brought to the point of singing your praise and glory. Who are they? *Those who love your salvation*: all who awaited salvation from you and trusted in it. *But I am poor and needy, the Lord will be concerned for me* (v. 17): since I was (247) in need of every good and short of every necessity, you were concerned for me unexpectedly. *You are my helper and my protector, Lord; do not delay*: you proved my helper and protector, at the ready in time of need.

Psalm 41

The forty-first psalm has a theme to do with the situation of Hezekiah. David develops his inspired work in the following fashion, adopting as his theme the situation of Hezekiah so as to declare blessed those zealous in treating the poor well, in the course of this producing a psalm that is both inspired discourse and instruction. That is to say, he takes Hezekiah as an example to exhort all people to be merciful so as to attain a similar reward to Hezekiah. Hence he begins the psalm with a beatitude in these words, *Blessed is the one who understands the poor and needy* (v. 1). Symmachus says, "The one who has a thought for the poor," the meaning being, That man is to be blessed who has a thought and concern for treating people well. There is a reference to King Hezekiah's being such a person and on that account receiving loving-kindness from God.

In declaring such a person blessed he proceeds to mention specifically what such a person is accorded, continuing as follows: *The Lord will deliver him on an evil day*. By *evil day* he refers not to it as naturally evil (248)—a day not being evil by nature, since if it were, the day would transfer the responsibility to its creator. Instead, by *evil day* he refers to the one on which a person is enveloped in distress, affliction, and pain, or falls victim to illness or some other hazard. So he means, When such a day comes, God who lends help is not asleep. *The Lord will closely guard him and give him life, and make him blessed in the land, and will not give him into the hands of his foes* (v. 2): not only will he rescue him from trouble, and not only guard him from every other difficult situation, but will also extend the life of such a person. Now, he is hinting at the addition to Hezekiah's life span, and presenting him as blessed and glorious. He refers to the sun's reversal and the fact that he did not surrender him to the enemy, and touches on the death of the Assyrians. *The Lord will help him on his bed of pain* (v. 3): even if he falls victim to illness, such a person is accorded God's loving-kindness, as in fact happened also in Hezekiah's case.[1] *In his illness you overturned all his sickbed,* by *all his sickbed* meaning, (249) You completely transformed his illness and restored to him to health and strength.

I said, Lord, have mercy on me, heal my soul because I sinned against you (v. 4). He cites the actual words of most blessed Hezekiah, which he spoke in his illness.[2] His instruction is that those who treat the needy well and fall victim to tribulation, if they say such things to God, receive similar help. *My foes spoke evil against me* (v. 5). He refers to what happened in the time of illness, namely, While I confessed my sin to God, those who were not well disposed to me plotted and desired to bring troubles on me—hence the possibility of hearing them voice such sentiments, *When will he die and his name perish?* They uttered such things out of the base longings they held against me. *He came to see me, he spoke idly* (v. 6), meaning, They concentrated on trickery, wishing me good health in words while plotting against me what they did not dare say, fear of royalty causing them to give no open signs of hostility. *His heart heaped up lawlessness for himself*: while uttering good things by word of mouth, (250) he planned the opposite in his mind, so that he laid up sins for himself in making unjust attempts on my life.

He went out and spoke. All my foes whispered together against me (vv. 6–7): of course, such people—namely, those who wished me well to my face—went out and leveled the wily accusations concealed within them, whispering being a furtive kind of slander just as open defamation is abuse. Blessed Paul also says in similar terms,

---

[1] Cf. 2 Kgs 19–20 and Isa 37–38.
[2] Cf. 2 Kgs 20:3; Isa 38:3.
[3] 1 Cor 4:12.

"Though abused we bless,"[3] bringing out that he was abused to his face and repaid it with a blessing. *Against me they devised troubles for me.* He is saying the same as before, that while giving good wishes openly, they went out whispering vile slander and plotting similar things. *They set up a lawless plan against me* (v. 8). He refers to the plan that was unjustly hatched against him as *lawless*: since his foes were probably also foes of godliness and said whatever occurred to them, "When are we to be rid of this godless and most savage person?" whereas on the contrary godliness and gentleness proved to be true in Hezekiah's case, he referred to the slander as perverse *lawlessness. Surely the one who lies down will not succeed in rising?* By *lying down* he refers to the grave illness, his meaning therefore being, Completely despairing of me and giving me no good chance of (251) getting up or recovering, that was the way they said and did everything.

A person at peace with me, in whom I had hope, who ate bread with me, behaved in a dastardly manner toward me (v. 9). He blames in particular his own palace friends, *a man at peace with me* meaning, The one I thought did everything to avoid causing me trouble was found a schemer at the time of my illness. *The one who ate bread with me* means, The one who shared the same table with me and the same victuals proved to be a foe the more threatening the more he concealed his malice under his close relationship. The Lord also suffered this in the case of Judas: in that case, too, it was not someone from the outer group of disciples who concocted plots, but one who gave the impression of being closely related and sharing with him table and victuals.[4] *But you, Lord, have mercy on me, raise me up, and I shall repay them* (v. 10): instead in your case, Lord, since I did them no wrong whereas they were seen to be like that to me, return evil for evil to them and turn the plan in my favor so that this very thing may result in vengeance on the wicked; nothing so distresses those addicted to vice as frustration of their desires. This, in fact, is the meaning of *and I shall repay* here, not that blessed Hezekiah was bent on vengeance—in fact, he did not (252) take vengeance—but because the affair turned out to be vengeance upon the wicked, whose desires were frustrated and who witnessed what they had not intended.

By this I knew that you were pleased with me, that my foe did not

---

[4] While the Synoptics also present Jesus speaking of Judas at table as betraying his trust, John 13:18 has him citing this verse in confirmation. Diodore implicitly acknowledges this as an instance of accommodation (only).

rejoice over me (v. 11). You notice that he hints more clearly at the repayment here in his mentioning, not vengeance by the wronged, but personal disappointment by the frustrated, which resulted in their punishing themselves on seeing the one they envied held in high esteem. His meaning here is, in fact, Show, Lord, how you care for me by their not rejoicing in the vile hopes they have for me. *But you supported me for my innocence, and confirmed me in your presence forever* (v. 12): but just as I pray that in their case their plans come to nothing on account of their wickedness, so just the opposite in my case: act in the knowledge of my innocence in their regard, providing me with help while not granting it to them.

Blessed be the Lord, the God of Israel, from everlasting to everlasting! May it be, may it be! (v. 13): so that I may be judged worthy by everyone of singing your glory and praises, God of Israel, eternal and without end.[5]

Psalm 42

"To the end. For understanding for the sons of Korah." (253) The title of the forty-second psalm indicates that the psalm was given to the sons of Korah by blessed David; they were singers or temple singers engaged in performing to the accompaniment of musical instruments.[1] The psalm is composed from the viewpoint of the people longing to see their own place, pining for it and begging God to be freed from the captivity and slavery in Babylon and to return to their own place, the memory of which had the effect of arousing them to stronger desire of the places and the holy temple.

As the deer longs for the springs of water, so my soul longs for you, O God (v. 1). This creature is said to be thirsty and, on account of

---

[5] There is no sense here that Diodore recognizes in this doxology (not part of the original poem, according to Dahood) a conclusion to one of five books of Psalms, a division harking back to the beginning of the Christian era. The distinguishing features of the respective books are largely linguistic, and so would have been lost on commentators working solely from a version.

[1] Diodore would know from 2 Chr 20:19 that the "sons of Korah" were a guild of temple singers. As with the title of Ps 32, on the other hand, he does not recognize in the LXX's attempt at Hebrew *maskil* a key to a psalm type. He does, however, betray a certain sense of the pathos of the psalm's sentiments.

[2] This piece of natural mythology about deer the later Antiochenes are also familiar with, in addition to Origen's gloss that the thirst was due to their habit of eating snakes, based on Greek animal lore.

its natural dryness, not to stray far from water.² So the meaning is, What this creature experiences by nature, I also suffer by choice, longing for the holy places from which I have been transported. Continuing the figure, he goes on, *My soul thirsted for God, who is strong and living* (v. 2).³ Then, to comment on the thirst and the excessive degree of the longing, he goes on, *When shall I come and see the face of God?*—in other words, This I long for, to see the time when I return to Jerusalem, where the temple is located and God is worshiped, and I present myself in person to God (their impression being that God really dwelt only in Jerusalem). *My tears* (254) *have become my bread day and night* (v. 3): the longing in me for the return was as great and the desire in me as pleasing as bread is pleasing to a hungry person. *As they say to me each day, Where is your God?* The enemies' taunts inflamed me more, he is saying, and those claiming that God is not helping me aroused in me the further desire to see help from you.

These things I remembered, and I poured out my soul (v. 4): I ruminated on the holy places—the temple, the liturgy, the festivals there—and the recollection inflamed my longing (*I poured out* meaning, I went to pieces, as Symmachus also said). *Because I shall pass through every corner of the wonderful tabernacle as far as the house of God*: how I used to walk as far as God's wonderful tabernacle (meaning the temple). *With sounds of exultation and praise, a roar of celebration*: I recalled also this fact, that in the temple I heard those voices raised in wonderful confession and thanksgiving, as well as those not celebrating the festival. (255) *Why are you disconsolate, my soul, and why do you disturb me? Hope in God, for I shall confess to him* (v. 5): since the memory of those events caused me unbearable pangs, and I found no one to console me in the distress, the reasons of which I alone had a personal understanding, I urged myself to find comfort in hope in God's help. *The savior of my person and my God*, *my person* meaning my reputation, my dignity: I said to myself, I hoped in God, who always cared for my salvation and my dignity.

My soul is confused within itself (v. 6): after these thoughts, however, I was again confused, the recollection of the places overcoming the consolation from the thought of them. Hence he goes on, *For this reason I shall remember you from the land of Jordan*

---

³ The Antiochene text, unlike most forms of the LXX and modern versions, contains both "strong" and "living," Dahood maintaining the Hebrew is susceptible of both meanings.

and Hermon, from a small mountain: being disturbed, I was not in a condition to remember that wonderful land (referring to it by the river Jordan and Mount Hermon). *Small* is used as a gloss to suggest again someone earnestly longing for the place, a metaphor from people fond of little children giving them nicknames. *Deep calls on deep to the sound of your cataracts* (v. 7): I remembered that while I was living there, (256) vast numbers beyond my experience assembled and were combined with other enemies, and in this fashion they gave vent to your unspeakable wrath (by *deep* referring to the vast number, and by *cataracts* to God's wrath). So his meaning is, A vast number of enemies assembled against me and gave vent to your wrath as if borne along by cataracts, as it were. *All your heights and your billows have passed over me*: yet I was the butt of all your threats and bursts of rage, which were lifted up over me like billows and encircled me. *By day the Lord will show his mercy, and by night his song is with me* (v. 8). He means the rapidity of God's help, as if to say, just as in your anger you inflicted waves of enemies on me, so in your wish to save me you brought rapid assistance, the result being that together with your commands you did not prevent my thanking you, nothing coming between your command and my enjoyment. *A prayer to the God of my life*: immediately thanksgiving arises in me directed to God, who granted me life.

I shall say to God, You are my support: why have you forgotten me? (v. 9). I promptly add that if you support me in this way, why do you allow me to suffer? It was not the mark of a friend to allow such awful punishments in this way. (257) *And why do I go about with face downcast while the foe afflicts me?* Why was I downcast for such a long time with foes besetting and distressing me? *In trampling on my bones my foes taunt me* (v. 10): the foes had the greatest pretext to taunt me on seeing the extent of the weakness to which I was reduced. *By saying to me each day, Where is your God?* They seemed even to have good grounds for taunting me in the fact that your loving-kindness for a long time passed me by.

Why are you disconsolate, my soul, and why do you disturb me? Hope in God, because I shall confess to him, savior of my person and my God (v. 11): Pondering all this within myself, then, I was again encouraged not to be alarmed, but to hope in God, who readily provides me with salvation and again makes me famous. Turning their thoughts over and over, sometimes in despair, sometimes in hope, is typical of people suffering.[4]

Psalm 43

The forty-third psalm has the same theme,[1] the members of the people urging God to judge between them and the Babylonians in the attainment of loving-kindness from God. (258) *Judge in my favor, O God, and decide for me against a nation that is not holy* (v. 1). *Judge in my favor* here means, Give me a ruling, as was remarked also in the introduction to the psalms, namely, that when he employs the accusative, as Judge him or Judge them, he means Condemn, whereas when he employs the dative, as Judge in my favor, he means, Rule in my favor and give me a just verdict. By *a nation that is not holy* he refers to the Babylonians as being unholy and defiled. *From a lawless and deceitful person rescue me.* He accuses them all in common and each of them individually for the similar wickedness of their exploits both all together and each person individually. *Because you, O God, are my force: why did you repulse me?* (v. 2) Have regard to this, Lord, that you always proved my helper and strength, and now you ought not abandon me forever. *Why do I go about downcast while the enemy afflicts me?* Do not let me be so downcast for a long period, distressed and pained by the foe.

Send forth your light and your truth (v. 3): dispatch your reliable (259) assistance (by *light* referring to the support, and by *truth* to its reliability). What happens in that case? *They guided me and led me to your holy mountain and your tabernacles*: so that your reliable help may conduct me to the holy places and your holy temple (*guided and led* meaning, You will guide and lead). *I shall go to the altar of God* (v. 4): so that I may enter and be granted attendance at the altar nearby. *To God who brings joy to my youth.* By *my youth* he means

---

[4] We are fortunate, if only because of the psalm's liturgical use, to have comment on it from all four major Antiochenes, diverse though they be and thus illustrative of the range of commentary styles these four represent. See my article, "Psalm 41 (42): A Classic Text for Antiochene Spirituality," *ITQ* 68 (2003): 25–33.

[1] The two psalms are so similar, with the occurrence of the same verse in Ps 42:5, 11, and Ps 43:5, as to suggest that they constitute one psalm (this detail escaping Diodore).

from my youth, as if to say, To your altar, O God, you who bring me joy and helped me from my youth (by *youth* referring to the people's journey from Egypt). *I shall confess to you with a lyre, O God my God*: so that on attaining this I shall thank you with musical instruments and songs.

Why are you disconsolate, my soul, and why do you disturb me? Hope in God, because I shall confess to him, my personal savior and my God (v. 5): it is clear that you will do this as well; hence I shall console myself and in the meantime not allow myself to be alarmed by my thoughts, but to hope in you my God, to whom I should also give thanks, for from you it is also possible to hope for salvation. (260)

Psalm 44

Blessed David composed the forty-fourth psalm from the viewpoint of the Maccabees. It also bears this title, "To the end. For the sons of Korah, for understanding." This very fact suggests that while it was composed by blessed David, it was given to the sons of Korah for meditation and performance to the accompaniment of instruments in the presence of the people. Blessed David presents the psalm as though coming from the Maccabees when suffering a harsh fate at the hands of the generals of Antiochus and in need of relief from the misfortunes and of attainment of assistance similar to what their fathers also received both in Egypt and in Babylon, the Maccabees' experience coming later than theirs.

O God, we have heard with our ears, our fathers have told us the work you accomplished in their days, in the days of old (v. 1): we were given an account by the ancestors, Lord, of the deep lovingkindness they received from you when the need required, and especially this. Which? *Your hand utterly destroyed nations and you planted them* (v. 2). By *nations* here he refers to the Canaanites and the five provinces in Palestine, which God afflicted one by one, (261) drove out, and replaced with the Israelites (*you planted* meaning, You led in and . . . settled). The names of the provinces are as follows: Gath, Ashdod, Ekron, Gaza, and Ashkelon.[1] *You afflicted people and drove them out*, meaning, the very ones whose names we listed. *It was not by their own sword, in fact, that they inherited the*

---

[1] In a conjecture that his successors will not adopt, Diodore (on the basis of God's words to Joshua in Josh 13:3) comes up with the five regions of the Philistines—an uncalled-for specification.

land, nor their own arm that saved them (v. 3): resisting such strong and warlike nations was not due to the strength of the ancestors. Instead, what? *Rather, it was your right hand, your arm and the light of your countenance, because you were pleased with them,* by *light of your countenance* meaning, The support coming from your manifestation helped them: it was not they themselves—that is, our fathers—who came to their aid.

You are my king and my God, commanding the salvation of Jacob (v. 4): it is you, Lord God, who now as well granted salvation to Israel as usual (*commanding* meaning granting). *Through you we shall prevail over our foes, and through your name we bring to naught those who rise up against us* (v. 5): now as well (262) through you we ward off the foe (*we shall prevail* meaning we ward off, and *we shall bring to naught* meaning we shall pursue them, worth nothing as they are) thanks to your help, Lord. *Not in my bow shall I hope, after all, nor will my sword save me* (v. 6): like my ancestors I do not trust in myself, but in your help and power. *In fact, you saved us from those oppressing us, and put to shame those who hate us* (v. 7): because you will save us from those oppressing us, and put to shame the foe (the tense being changed here again). *We shall commend God all day long* (v. 8). For *commend* Symmachus says "boast," and rightly so.² The phrase *all day long* means constantly, the meaning being, You were responsible for our boasting always. *And we shall confess in your name forever*: your name proved cause enough for us to thank you; since we always receive help from you, we consequently offer up hymns to you.

As it is, however, you rejected and shamed us, and you did not sally forth, God, with our forces (v. 9): but as it is, Lord, (263) whereas the misfortunes are numerous, help is missing—not as in the case of our ancestors, when consolation was mingled with their tribulations, whereas in our case the effect of misfortune alone is to the fore, with no effect of consolation at hand (the phrase *you did not sally forth, God, with our forces* meaning, You are not helping or assisting us—just the opposite). In what way? *You made us retreat before our foes* (v. 10), that is, you made us fugitives, turning our back on the foe. And what was the result of this? *And those hating us took plunder for themselves*: our possessions became plunder for anyone

---

² The alternative versions (Theodore cites Aquila to the same effect) suggest that the Hebrew they are reading, like our Masoretic Text, means "boast." For the first time Diodore cites Symmachus against the LXX, without giving reasons why he is right.

wanting to do so at will. *You gave us like sheep for eating, and scattered us among the nations* (v. 11): we are now ready only to be sacrificed like sheep, not to be helped. Even if anyone escapes the sword, they are taken captive, the result being that even someone alive and escaping the sword will endure a slavery harsher than execution at the hands of the nations.

Why, he asks, should so much be said? *You disposed of your people without charge, and there was no great cost in our changing hands* (v. 12), that is you sold us to the nations for nothing (the meaning of *without charge*) like useless slaves (264) of no value. And in the same sense he goes on, *and there was no great cost in our changing hands* (by *changing hands* referring again to the sale); so *there was no great cost in our changing hands* means, You caused the exchange of us to involve no cost. Worse still, *You made us an object of taunting to our neighbors, a laughingstock and mockery to those round about us* (v. 13): as a result of this even the neighboring peoples (he means Moabites and Ammonites round about)[3] taunt us with our sufferings. *You have set us as a byword to the nations, a shaking of the head among the peoples* (v. 14): and, in short, we have become a proverb to all the nations; they all recount our misfortunes, as though having nothing better to share with one another (by *shaking of the head* meaning excessive mockery: when you have high hopes of someone and then see the opposite outcome, you shake your head for expecting one thing and seeing another). *All day long my shame is before me, and I am covered in blushes* (v. 15): as for me, hearing some things and seeing others happening to me, and people taunting and shaking their heads, I am embarrassed, incapable of looking others in the face. Hence he goes on, (265) *From the sound of the one taunting and slandering me, from the aspect of foe and persecutor* (v. 16): I am embarrassed by those taunting and belittling me (the meaning of *persecutor*).

All this came upon us, and we did not forget you and did not break your covenant (v. 17): yet such awful calamities did not divert us from you nor cause us to put our hope in anyone else; we did not violate the covenant, that is, we did not transgress any of the laws under such pressure. He is referring in particular to their being unwilling to take up arms on the sabbath and choosing to be slaughtered rather than break the law.[4] *Our heart has not turned back*

---

[3] Though Theodoret will accept this reference, and even add the Idumeans, all such groups had in fact by the time of the Maccabees gone out of existence.

[4] Cf. 1 Macc 2:32–38.

(v. 18): neither were we overcome by the misfortunes nor did we willingly transgress the laws even under pressure. Instead, if we were supposed to offer sacrifices, we performed them even with the enemy at hand; if we had to observe the sabbath, we observed it to the shedding of blood; if we were obliged to be circumcised, we did not neglect it; if obliged not even to taste what was forbidden by the law, this too we observed at the risk of ultimate sanctions.[5] In no way, therefore, Lord, did we either violate your covenant willingly or forsake it under pressure. *You moved our steps from your way:* (266) admittedly, with your permission we were given the command to bypass the laws and take up weapons on the sabbath, not having begun the fighting, only defending ourselves;[6] yet we chose observance of the laws to life itself. *Because you humiliated us in a place of affliction* (v. 19). By *place of affliction* he refers to the place in which troubles were piled up on them, and by *you humiliated* he means, You allowed us to be brought very low. *And he wrapped us in the darkness of death,* by *darkness of death* meaning hazards resembling death. For proof that in all this we did not abandon ancestral and legal requirements, he is saying, we have you as witness.

If we forgot the name of our God, and if we spread out our hands to a foreign god, would not God find this out? After all, he knows the secrets of the heart (vv. 20–21): it is impossible for anyone transgressing the laws or planning to do so to escape your notice, Lord, because you so carefully occupy our minds. Are you not aware even of this? *Because for your sake we are being put to death all day long* (v. 22). He continues to use the term *all day long:* Because we consistently choose death to avoid transgressing the laws. (267) *We were accounted as sheep for slaughter:* just as sheep are handed over to butchers not to be defended but to be sacrificed, so we too handed ourselves over to the slaughterers to avoid infringing the ancestral observances.[7]

So what is the upshot of this? *Bestir yourself! Why do you sleep, Lord? Arise, and do not drive us off forever* (v. 23): since such behav-

[5] Cf. 1 Macc 4:53; 1:60–63; 2 Macc 6:18–7:42.

[6] The LXX has unaccountably omitted a negative here, which the alternative versions detect; all unaware because not checking with the Hexapla, Diodore turns to the text of 1 Macc 2:41 for evidence of a relaxation of the law (whereas Chrysostom and Theodoret will try to reconcile the two versions).

[7] Paul in Rom 8:36 cites this verse in reference to the tribulations experienced by ministers of the gospel. Diodore does not advert to it, whereas Theodore will, though classing it as just one more instance of simple accommodation of OT texts by the NT.

ior of ours, Lord, shows preference for observance of the laws to our very life, do not in your case resemble those who oversleep (Symmachus likewise rendering it, "Why be like a sleeper, Lord?"). *Why do you turn your face away?* (v. 24) Attend to us now, Lord: at this time you resemble someone who is angry and turning from us, as a result of which we were also beset with such awful disasters. *You have forgotten our poverty and our tribulations*: not even the excessive distress and lack of necessities make you turn toward us. *Because our soul is brought down to the dust* (v. 25): not even the fact that we resembled unburied corpses, Lord, brings you round. *Our stomach is stuck fast to the ground*: not even the fact that we are prostrate, ready to suffer anything for the temple and the law, leads you to have mercy on us. (268) *Rise up, Lord, come to our aid and redeem us for your name's sake* (v. 26). He did well to keep the more compelling motive for the end: If we are judged unworthy of gaining mercy for all these things mentioned, he is saying, nevertheless be faithful to yourself; Lord, on account of your name conferred on us, free us from the enemy.[8]

Psalm 45

"To the end. For those to be changed. For the sons of Korah, for understanding. A song for the beloved." "Those to be changed" means those taking a turn for the better. So the psalm title means that this psalm is recited for those taking a turn for the better in later times when the Son of God appears.[1] In fact, this psalm seems to refer to the Lord Jesus, not to Solomon, as Jews claim: even if under pressure they transfer most of the content to Solomon for being expressed in human fashion, yet the verse *Your throne, O God, is forever and ever, the rod of your kingship a rod of equity* completely shuts their mouth, since Solomon was not called God and did not reign forever. Instead, Christ alone as God also adopted the human condition for our sake and, being God and king forever, also retained his own status by nature. If, on the other hand, most of the things it mentions are human, that is no surprise, since in becoming human

---

[8] There may be a reference here to Jer 14:9.

[1] In not recognizing musical clues in the title, Diodore also fails to detect the LXX's misreading of the Hebrew direction "according to the lilies," *shoshanim* (probably a verse from a well-known melody), as connected with the verb *shanah*, "to change."

he accepted also commendation for his humanity. (269) After all, if he accepted suffering as a human being, much more also commendation as a human being, no harm transferring to his divine nature.

Blessed David, then, begins in this fashion. *My heart belched a good word* (v. 1). He means, I intend to give voice to this psalm from the depths of my mind as though belching, not as I utter the inspired works on other matters; instead, in this psalm I sing a special theme.² Why? *I tell of my works to the king*: since I intend to dedicate the psalm to the king of all (by *work* referring to the actual composition of the psalm). *My tongue the pen of a rapid scribe*. Since he had said, I utter the psalm from the depths of my mind, he says, I bring to bear also my tongue to the extent possible so as to serve the thought coming from grace in the way that a pen follows the lead of a writer's thought.³

Having thus far delivered an introduction and indicated to whom he intends the psalm to refer, he now begins the eulogy from this point. *Striking in your beauty compared with the sons of human beings* (v. 2). Clearly *beauty* refers to glory. *Compared with the sons of human beings* was well put: no member of the human race acquired this person's glory. *Grace was poured out on your lips*. After mentioning the glory, here he mentions its effect, namely, that you were invested with such persuasion as even to attract disciples merely by your lips: the extraordinary degree of wisdom required no great number of words for persuading. (270) *Hence God your God blessed you forever*.⁴ The term *Hence* is a Hebrew idiom,⁵ the meaning

---

² The LXX had done well to render a *hapax legomenon* in the Hebrew as "belch," conveying a sense of involuntariness that Chrysostom will develop at length to explore the notion of the divine inspiration of the biblical authors. Diodore, too, is combining the double elements of divine inspiration and human activity (reflecting the dyophysitism above). This psalm is a classic text for prompting patristic commentators to develop their thinking on this topic; see my article, "Psalm 45: A *Locus Classicus* for Patristic Thinking on Biblical Inspiration."

³ Whereas Bruce Vawter, *Biblical Inspiration* (Theological Resources; Philadelphia: Westminster, 1972), 25, will declare (without adequate reference to Antiochene thinking) that for the Fathers "prophecy was exclusively mantic experience and scriptural inspiration solely mechanical dictation," Diodore nicely distinguishes the role of the human author's tongue cooperating with the (divinely inspired) thought to give it expression, also nicely qualifying this contribution with the phrase "to the extent possible."

⁴ The phrase "your God" does not occur in the text of the other Antiochenes.

⁵ Contrary to the opinion of Diodore, the use of Hebrew *hal-ken* seems unexceptionable here, whereas to judge from his comment on v. 7b he thinks the Hebrew text contains no such item.

being, Since God brought you to this degree of blessing as to be both superior in glory to all human beings and persuasive of vast numbers by the abundance of virtue. If, on the other hand, as incarnate Son he refers to his Father as God here, there is nothing surprising: it is the Lord risen from the dead who says to the disciples, "I am going to my Father and to your Father, my God and your God,"[6] meaning that his Father by nature is the same God according to the incarnation. *Gird your sword on your thigh, O mighty one* (v. 3). He hints in human fashion at Christ's power, his meaning being, You possess not only beauty and persuasiveness but also power sufficient to punish unbelievers.[7] He is using the metaphor of generals with thighs girt with swords and ready to punish those they wish. *In your charm and your beauty*, that is, Combine with your charm and your splendor also the power of punishing when occasion requires.

Advance, proceed, and reign (v. 4). *Advance* means, Be brave and press forward, do not yield: everything will be straightforward for your reign. (271) *For the sake of truth, gentleness and righteousness*. He means, Everything is prepared for your reigning on the basis of truth in regard to gentleness and righteousness—that is, you truly have these qualities, it is no fiction; hence you reign securely as well. *Your right hand will guide you in marvelous fashion, will guide you* meaning will subject them to you: *your right hand*—that is, your power—will subject everything to you, as blessed Paul says, "by the power that enables him to submit all things to himself."[8] *Your arrows are sharpened, O mighty one; peoples will fall under you in the heart of the king's foes* (v. 5). The clause *peoples will fall under you* is inserted, the sequence being, Your arrows, O mighty one, in the heart of the king's foes, and then *peoples will fall under you*. As it is, however, as I remarked, the clause is inserted and causes confusion.[9] His meaning is, Direct well-aimed words, like arrows, at the hearts of the listeners, and as a result all peoples will be subjected to you as well (using a metaphor of men wounding with arrows and subjecting the wounded). He means, Your arrows are so effective that not only will they subject disciples but also fall upon enemies and bring them into subjection.

[6] John 20:17, a message to the disciples spoken to Mary Magdalene.
[7] Cf. 2 Cor 10:6.
[8] Phil 3:21.
[9] The order of clauses in the verse, puzzling also to modern commentators, gives rise to comment by all the Antiochenes.

Your throne, O God, is forever and ever (v. 6). And what should be said in particular? he asks. (272) Being Most High and reigning without interruption, you consequently have everything subject to you. *The rod of your kingship a rod of equity.* By *rod* he refers to kingship. So your kingship, he is saying, equitable as it is, brings everything under your control. *You loved righteousness and hated lawlessness* (v. 7). He explained what *equity* is, hatred of wickedness and a proper attitude to good. *For this reason God your God anointed you with the oil of gladness beyond your partners.* The term *For this reason* has once again been inserted as before:[10] it was not *For this reason* that he was anointed, that he loved righteousness and hated lawlessness; rather, it was by being anointed by the Holy Spirit that he exercised these virtues. He uses the phrase *beyond your partners* in this way, that while the others who were anointed were anointed with oil of prophecy or priesthood or royalty, he was anointed with the Holy Spirit. Here again he makes mention of the incarnation, or how he was able to call the same person God in one case as in the above verse *Your throne, O God, is forever*, and in another case *God your God anointed you*. In the above case, however, he referred to nature; here he introduces the incarnation. By his *fellows* he refers more precisely to the apostles and those who later shared his grace. (273)

Myrrh, resin, and cassia from your garments (v. 8). In these fragrances he hints at death, incorruptible ointment preserving the corpse. So since "his flesh did not experience corruption,"[11] he hints at death in such fragrances. He did well to add *your garments*: the body resembled a garment, and the fragrances are detected in association with the body. *From ivory buildings, from which they delighted you.* By *buildings* he means houses, and by *ivory* the splendor of the houses, by this implying the churches. So his intention is to say that after the death of Christ splendid and beautiful temples will be erected to him, like the churches to be seen in our day. *Daughters of kings in your honor* (v. 9). By *daughters of kings* he refers to the queens themselves. So he means, Queens also will go in procession in your honor. *At your right hand stands the queen, clad in garments of gold, of a rich variety.* In portraits they picture kings

---

[10] As in v. 2, Diodore is questioning the occurrence of a particle in the Hebrew (*hal-ken*, in fact, unexceptionable again).

[11] Acts 2:31, Peter's citation of Ps 16:10 at Pentecost. Antiochenes can use the figure of a garment for Christ's humanity that does less than justice to the hypostatic union.

seated with some women in attendance, and give as an inscription Kingship or Righteousness or something of the like. So by analogy with the portraits his meaning is, You are seated on an elevated throne, and the church will attend on you (274) in the place of a queen. The phrase *clad in garments of gold, of a rich variety* means the manifold graces of the church: of the members of the church some possessed words of wisdom, some words of knowledge, others the working of miracles, others of prophecy, still others discernment of spirits, and others tongues of various kinds.[12] So he compared the variety of charisms to the variety of the queen's garments.

Listen, daughter, take note and incline your ear (v. 10). David in person exhorts the church. And what is the exhortation? *Forget your people and your father's house.* The church was formed from pagans and Jews; so he does well to say *Forget your people and your father's house*, meaning idolatry and observance of the law, practicing instead a new life by grace. *The king will long for your beauty* (v. 11): in this way the king who united himself to you would be enraptured with your charm. *Because he is your Lord*: take account also of this, that though he is your Lord by nature, in loving-kindness he united himself to you. *And daughters of Tyre will bow down to him with gifts* (v. 12). At that time the women of Tyre had the reputation for being wealthy; so he means, Though your Lord, he united you to himself, and will subject to you all the wealthy women or those of varying degrees of magnificence so that they will also bring you gifts, the respect for the bridegroom clearly passing also the bride.[13] To make it clearer he goes on, *The wealthy members of the people will entreat your countenance.* Having mentioned wealthy women above, here he included wealthy men; and after mentioning there that they would bow down to him, here he says that they *will entreat* him, bringing out, as I said, that respect for bride and bridegroom is the same on account of the loving-kindness of the chosen one.

All the glory of the King's daughter is within (v. 13). He does well to refer to her in one place as bride, in another as daughter: to bring out that the bride is not united with the bridegroom by marriage law but by the law of approval and grace, in places he calls her bride in view of the union, in other places daughter in view of baptism and rebirth. So his meaning is, The bride herself, or the King's

---

[12] Cf. 1 Cor 12:8–10.

[13] The Antiochenes and alternative versions differ as to whether the verse should also include the phrase "Bow down to him."

daughter, possesses complete glory and wealth in the privileges of soul (hinting at the gifts of soul through mention of material things). Hence he proceeds, *In golden tassels, clad in many colors*: (276) something that is visible in the case of a king's daughter, clothed in golden finery in her garments and in that rich variety, can be seen in the case of this bride in her privileges and gifts of soul. *Maidens will be brought to the king in her wake* (v. 14): in her wake— that is, the bride's—maidens also will follow. Since virginity is the more esteemed role in the church, he indicates that the church will also have maidens to serve her.[14] *Her neighbors will be brought to you*—*hers*, that is, the bride's, as if to say, the maidens accompanying you will be the ones to follow you, drawn by reverence to pay you respect. *They will be brought in joy and gladness* (v. 15): far from practicing virginity under pressure and with complaint, they willingly choose this august role and condition, and will follow you with joy and gladness. *They will be led to the king's temple*: they also will follow so as to become in their own case a *king's temple* as well. By mention of the virginal women, in fact, he gives a clear hint also of the virginal men: it was unlikely that women practicing virginity would alone (277) be a *king's temple*, and not men at that stage, the law applying equally to men and women. After all, just as when David says, "Blessed the man who did not walk in the counsel of the ungodly,"[15] he does not exclude the woman from the beatitude, if indeed she did not walk in the way of the ungodly, and the beatitude applies equally to man and woman in that case, so here too it is not that he introduces women and expels men, but says that the same thing applies also to men if they likewise opt for virginity.

In the place of your fathers your sons were born (v. 16). Since the church's *fathers* were Jews, but were baptized in holy baptism and beneficiaries of the grace of mission, and so became actual *sons* of the church, he did well to say *In place of your fathers sons were born*. *You will set them as princes over the whole earth*: these you will appoint as priests and rulers over the whole earth. He prophesies that the message will be accepted everywhere and that the apostles will rule spiritually over the whole world. *I shall remember your name in every single generation* (v. 17): I, David, shall ever be remembered, thanks to you, Lord; though my God and Lord, you did not

---

[14] Chrysostom and Theodore will take a lead from this brief but definite encomium of virginity by the head of the *asketerion* to endorse its relative status in the church of the day. Theodoret prefers to see a reference to unadulterated faith.
[15] Ps 1:1.

disdain to be called also son of David (the phrase *I shall remember* meaning I shall be remembered).[16] (278) *Hence people will confess to you for ages of ages*: for this reason and as a result of your wonderful considerateness,[17] peoples and tribes and tongues will not cease thanking you for as long as the ages last.

Psalm 46

The theme of the forty-sixth psalm is found also in the books of Kings and in Isaiah: the king of the ten tribes, Pekah son of Remaliah, took as an ally Rezin, king of the Syrians, and advanced on Jerusalem.[1] At that time Ahaz was king of Jerusalem, reigning also over the two tribes, namely, Judah and Benjamin. So blessed David recites this psalm from the viewpoint both of Ahaz and of the two tribes.

God is our refuge and power, help in the tribulations befalling us in great number (v. 1): granted that the ten tribes have conspired together and are of one mind with the Syrians, our help is nevertheless more powerful; we have God as our refuge and strength in the tribulations besetting us. *Hence we shall not fear at the shaking of the earth and the shifting of mountains in the heart of the seas* (v. 2): for this reason we shall not be afraid of you; (279) instead, even if all the earth is shaken and the impossible happens, the shifting of mountains into the sea, like some flood of people swamping us, we are still not frightened, the help given us being greater than the assailants. *Their waters roared and were disturbed* (v. 3). By *waters* he refers to the vast numbers of the ten tribes and the Syrians. So he means, Like a rising tide they advanced upon us, but all to no avail. How and in what manner? *The mountains were shaken by his might*: his might and strength combined to topple their warriors and champions (by *mountains* here referring to their leaders and rulers).

The currents of the river gladden the city of God (v. 4). By *city of*

---

[16] His pupils decline to follow Diodore in this convenient exercise of taking the active verb in a passive sense.

[17] This is the first occurrence in Diodore of the term συγκατάβασις that we associate particularly with Chrysostom for the divine accommodation (not a demeaning notion like "condescension," though often so translated by a lazy calque) to our human limitations—demonstrated preeminently in the incarnation, as suggested here, but also in the acts of sacred history and the language of Scripture.

[1] Cf. 2 Kgs 16:5; Isa 7:1.

God he refers to Jerusalem, and calls the good things now coming from God *river currents.* So he means, God's goodness, being greater than the troubles besetting us, and bearing down on us like a flowing river, brings joy to the city. *The Most High sanctified his tabernacle.* Again by God's *tabernacle* he refers to Jerusalem for the reason of God's living and dwelling there. (280) So he is saying, He *sanctified the tabernacle,* that is, kept it unscathed and free of all harm. *God is in his midst, and it will not be moved* (v. 5). How, in fact, was the city which the Lord personally inhabits going to survive the tumult? *God will help it in the morning.* By *in the morning* he refers to the speed and rapid support:[2] For this reason, he is saying, he provides rapid help and speedy care. *Nations were in uproar, kingdoms tottered* (v. 6): at this point those warring against us were suddenly seized with shaking and alarm, and the kingdoms yielded to us and became subject. *The Most High gave his shout, the earth moved*: as an excellent general by shouting out from the city in the hearing of the enemy not only struck panic into them but also brought confusion upon the whole earth. *The Lord of hosts is with us* (v. 7): it is God who accords us help. *The God of Jacob is our support*: the God of our forefather Jacob is the one who grants us support.

Come now, see the works of God (v. 8): so assemble together, everyone, and learn what God has done for us. (281) *Portents he performed in the land*: in our land, that is, Jerusalem, he gave evidence of miracles and portents, repelling as ineffective such vast numbers of enemies. *Bringing wars to an end as far as the ends of the earth* (v. 9): he it is who routs all the enemy when he wishes and brings peace to the earth to the degree he wants. *He will break the bow, smash weapons, and burn shields in fire*: he is the God who does away with the enemy with their own weapons when he wishes.

Be at rest and know that I am God (v. 10): so consider that God will say to everyone, When you see an end of the enemy and are at rest, you will have the opportunity to know the kind of God you have. *I shall be exalted among the nations, I shall be exalted on earth*: give heed to learning this from him as well, I am exalted over all nations and the land of Jerusalem, and I arrange events as I wish. *The Lord of hosts is with us, the God of Jacob is our supporter* (v. 11): he is the God who is with us, who has authority over hosts, who is

---

[2] Diodore's text may not contain the double adverb for "in the morning" the other Antiochenes know.

the supporter of our forefather and continues his kindnesses as far as us, too.

Now, those who gave this psalm a title did not fully grasp the theme, (282) entitling it "To the end. For the sons of Korah, on the secrets. A psalm for David." The title is meant to indicate that this psalm was given to the sons of Korah for meditation and performance, and that the phrase "on the secrets" means on some ineffable matters.[3] And so it is.

Psalm 47

The forty-seventh psalm bears the title, "To the end. For the sons of Korah," that is, this psalm was also given them for singing. In fact, they did not express its theme, either, which is as follows: it is a triumphal psalm by the Maccabees on their getting the better of the generals of Antiochus. The actual text also brings out its festive nature, being full of joy and gladness.

All the nations, clap your hands (v. 1). They summon as well all the others who had suffered under the generals of Antiochus to a celebration of God's victory. *Shout to God with a cry of gladness.* A *shout* is properly a triumphal cry. So he is saying, Come now, all nations, joyfully raise a triumphal cry to God for being freed from the hardships besetting you from the enemy. So having said, Come now, everyone, sing the triumphal hymn, he gives the reasons. *Because the Lord Most High is fearsome, great king over all the earth* (v. 2): he became manifest in the events themselves, (283) by which he routed those harassing the godly and proved superior to their scheme, fearsome to the enemy and in short king like no other on earth, since he is also Lord of all.

Being like this, what did he do? *He subjected people to us, and nations under our feet* (v. 3), the generals around Antiochus and the enemy with them; they had many allies and confederates. *He chose for us his inheritance* (v. 4), by *for us* meaning us: he chose us as his inheritance, that is, he protected us as his possession and inheritance. *The beauty of Jacob, which he loved*: he kept us unharmed, since we proved an adornment for Jacob in growing into such a large number from the single person beloved by God.

God went up with a shout (v. 5). By *went up* he refers not to place

---

[3] Diodore is unaware that the LXX has committed another solecism by confusing a melody cue in the title, *'alamoth*, "maidens," with the verb *'alam*, "to conceal"—an error his successors will perpetuate.

but to action, his meaning being that just as in descending and vanquishing on our behalf, once again he took possession of his own thrones that could be seen on high. *The Lord with a sound of a trumpet*: just like a trumpet sound preceding him as conqueror, so he took possession of his own high places. *Sing to our God, sing; sing to our king, sing* (v. 6): for this reason, therefore, (284) he deserves hymn-singing and triumphal voices from everyone for being both God and king. *Because God is king of all the earth; sing with understanding* (v. 7). Since he had said *king*, he went on to say, not only ours but of *all the earth*: the one responsible for some people conquering and others being conquered, as he wishes, no matter from what quarter they mount their charge, how could he not be confessed as king of all? The phrase *sing with understanding* means, with a sense of what has been done and keeping in mind the achievements.

God reigned over the nations (v. 8). Since he had said *Sing with understanding*, he mentions also what they should take to heart while singing, that our God is both Lord of all nations and king. *God sits on his holy throne*: and that he is firmly established, secure in existing where he always is. *Rulers of the people are gathered with the God of Abraham* (v. 9). The phrase *are gathered* means will then be gathered: on the basis of what has happened the rulers of all the nations will be gathered together with us and sing the praises of the one God; the unexpected marvels in our favor will gather them from all quarters in singing the praises of the one who has given evidence of such wonderful good things. *Because the mighty ones of God are raised to great heights over the earth.* (285) By *mighty ones of God* he refers to those given strength and attention by him, namely, the Israelites.[1] So he means, We were given great help by God and lifted high above the earth, that is, elevated, since what was done in our favor made us more splendid than the whole earth.

---

[1] If this sounds like a guess, it is. Aquila and the NRSV (which divides the verse differently) render the LXX's "mighty ones" as "shields" and Symmachus and Theodotion as "protectors" (we are told by Theodoret, who accommodates the LXX more easily into his eschatological reference to the apostles). Dahood has to have recourse to Ugaritic to confirm the LXX version (after amending our Hebrew).

Psalm 48

"A psalm for singing by the sons of Korah. On the second day of the week." The title of the forty-eighth psalm indicates that this psalm was also given to the sons of Korah for meditation and performance in broad daylight, that is, on the second day of the week.[1] In including only this element of the theme in the title, they did not arrive at the psalm's whole meaning. The theme is as follows: it also is uttered by blessed David from the viewpoint of Hezekiah in triumph over what happened in Jerusalem, where the enemy were wiped out and the city saved against the odds. So he speaks in these terms, *Great is the Lord and much to be praised* (v. 2). He says *Great is the Lord* in reference to the magnitude of the happenings. Of course, after saying *and to be praised* he added *much* to bring out the greatness of what was achieved by him.

Then, since the question could arise as to where these marvels happened, he goes on, *In the city of our God, on his holy mountain.* By *city of God* he refers to Jerusalem itself by reason of God's dwelling in it and unexpectedly saving it. (286) *God rooting it firmly in the gladness of all the earth* (v. 2), the term *rooting* meaning augmenting:[2] the God of all the earth augments its joy and gladness. Hence he went on, *Mountains of Sion, sides of the north*: how surprising that, though God of all the earth, he works wonders in one place, exposed on the north, so as to bring out that the situation of the place was rather vulnerable as lying toward the north. *The city of the great king*: despite being thus situated and thought of no importance owing to its position, it was shown to be the city of the great king. *God is known in its buildings whenever he supports it* (v. 3). *In its buildings* means in the houses, that is, the dwellings: God is shown to be dwelling in it all, and from there he supports it.

He goes on, in fact, to explain what happened. *Because, lo, the kings of the earth were assembled, they came together* (v. 4). The divine Scripture normally calls the high and mighty *kings*; actually, one king advanced on it at that time, (287) Sennacherib, but as I said, it refers as *kings* to all the high and mighty ones advancing. *On seeing it, they were amazed* (v. 5): though the mighty ones assembled

---

[1] This obscure phrase in the LXX title does not occur in the Hebrew. The other Antiochenes ignore it.

[2] Diodore gives Theodore a false lead here (which Chrysostom, of whom his teacher Libanius was prouder, will reject) in suggesting the verb εὑρίζειν is derived from εὑρύς, "broad," not simply a compound εὑ-ρίζειν. The Hebrew, admittedly, is "much contested" (Dahood).

against it were numerous, they were astonished at what happened; to witness such a victory without bloodshed was without precedent. Then, also to comment on what they were amazed at, he proceeds, *They were panic-stricken, they staggered, trembling seized them* (vv. 5–6): so many strong men were no different at that time from people confused and in a state of collapse with the expectation of fearsome events. *Pains there as of a woman in labor*: unexpected travail and hazard took hold of them such as would take hold of a woman in labor.

With a violent wind you will smash ships of Tarshish (v. 7). By *Tarshish* he refers to the coastal regions, his meaning being, Just as if ships happened to be at anchor in coastal regions, and suddenly a violent gale arose, and smashed and destroyed them all, so too with the Babylonians: God's anger fell upon them and manifested itself among them like a smashing and ruin of ships. *As we have heard, so we have seen* (v. 8). He is now reciting this from the viewpoint of the city inhabitants and Hezekiah himself: Just as we heard (288) of our city that God works wonders in it, we know it from the facts themselves. *In the city of the Lord of hosts, in the city of our God*: we learned from experience that it is the Lord of hosts who is our God and who dwells in our city. *God established it forever*: and the fact that he made it immovable and unassailable. *Forever* does not mean for the whole of time: how could it, when the city was later besieged both by the generals of Antiochus and by the Romans? Instead, it is customary with Scripture often to call temporary things eternal, as it says in the case of Hezekiah himself, "He asked life of you, and you gave him length of days forever."[3] In fact, he granted him an extra fifteen years, but it refers to his past life as an age and the addition as an age, and hence said *forever* on the grounds of adding one period to another period, not speaking of the time as unlimited, but as limited in both cases.

We assumed, O God, your mercy in the midst of your people (v. 9). *We assumed* means, We know and have learned by experience your loving-kindness for your people.[4] (289) *As is your name, O God, so is your praise, to the ends of the earth* (v. 10): the reality was not at odds with the reputation preceding you, nor did you emerge as inferior to the impression we all had of you, Lord. *Your right hand is filled*

---

[3] Ps 21:4.
[4] In the local form of the LXX a scribe has evidently written λαοῦ, "people," for ναοῦ, "temple"—an error that predictably escapes Diodore's notice, as it will the later readers of that text.

with righteousness. Righteousness was well put: since he admires the retribution on all sides, he made the further observation here that it was also marked by justice; he punished the assailants and wrongdoers, not those at peace minding their own business. *Let Mount Sion be glad, and the daughters of Judah rejoice* (v. 11): you will therefore be restored to gladness, you who inhabit this mountain along with all the women of Judah (including the whole populace by mention of part of it). *Because of your judgments, Lord.* Since he had said, You will be glad, he went on to say, Because of God's judgments by which he judged in your favor.

Go around Sion and encircle it (v. 12),[5] that is, Set up groups at points where gladness is to be found. *Narrate in its towers*: and in the groups found in it let there often be narration and song about the deeds worked for us, like those that occur in such cases. *Set your hearts on its might* (v. 13). *On its might* means, (290) On the might coming to it from God. *Set your hearts* means, Always keep in mind the happenings and recount them to the extent possible. *Take its buildings one by one.* Since he had said, Set up groups in each place, he says, Let the groups also be distributed house by house so that every place may enjoy happiness. *So that you may tell the next generation*: so that the happenings may be transmitted also to those coming after us by the account and the songs of the groups. *That this is our God forever, and ever and ever* (v. 14): with the result that those coming after us will also be convinced that he it is who is both our God and the wonderworker in our fathers' case. He is making a reference to the wonders in Egypt. *He will shepherd us forever.* He cites shepherding as an example of care, his meaning therefore being, It is the same God who provides us with similar care to our fathers, unceasingly and to the end.

Psalm 49

This forty-ninth psalm teaches a moral lesson not only for Jews but also for all people. (291) You see, while in fidelity to God's purpose the inspired authors had in mind the benefit of all people, the time did not yet permit it; so they addressed most of their words to

---

[5] Olivier finds the word "peoples" following "Go around" in some manuscripts, but it is not registered elsewhere. These verses 12–13 offer the commentator some difficulties, which Chrysostom deals with by citing the alternative versions.

Jews. But in some cases they also direct their exhortation to all people, that sin and it alone is an evil difficult to abandon, and that it would be difficult for anyone to abandon their sins while persisting in their faults through money, whereas if repentance gives a lead, there is also a distribution of money to the wronged. Money, you see, is in itself of no benefit unless associated with sincere repentance.

For this reason, therefore, blessed David exhorts all people in these words. *Hear this, all nations* (v. 1). This psalm, too, like many others, is given to the sons of Korah for meditation and performance to the accompaniment of musical instruments. *Give ear, all inhabitants of the world.* He summons everyone from all quarters to a discovery of this excellent lesson that sin is fearsome in people and incapable of being brought under control by outlay of money. *Both earthborn people and human beings* (v. 2). He means the same thing, by *earthborn people* referring to those sprung from the earth, (292) his meaning being that there is no one exempt from this lesson. And to make it clearer, he goes on, *Rich and poor alike*, the result being that no one I intend to instruct will be left in the dark.

Having to this point summoned everyone from all quarters to discovery of the good, he begins his task at this stage. *My mouth will speak wisdom, and the pondering of my heart understanding* (v. 3): all wisdom comes to be known by reflection and dissemination. So his meaning is, I deliberate on some wise ideas, and with the intention of disseminating them I want you all to be hearers of what is said by me. Hence his reference to *pondering*, for each person to realize that far from coming to instruction by accident, they are brought to learn by deep pondering and much practical experience. Hence he continues, *I shall incline my ear to a parable* (v. 4), that is, I myself actually inclined my ear to a parable (a change of tense occurring). Now, what is the meaning of *I inclined to a parable*? It means, I personally was schooled in such expositions (*parable* here meaning exposition). Clearly, he was taught by the Holy Spirit and presents the idea as though learning such lessons by hearing. *I shall solve my riddle with a harp*, by *riddle* referring to the instruction itself. So he means, (293) What I myself learned from the Holy Spirit I shall with an instrument—namely, the harp—produce so that the hearers are pleased to be instructed; such a process of discovery is achieved by more extensive recall.

Having delivered this introduction so far, he now takes up the topic and treats of it in the form of a question. *Why shall I fear on an evil day?* (v. 5). By *evil day* he refers to that on which some hardship or disaster befell us. So what, then, he asks, is to be dreaded on a day of disasters? He goes on, *The iniquity of my heel will encircle me.* He calls the path *heel* from the treading of the path with the heel, and by path referring to behavior.[1] So he means, In a time of disasters and in difficult days nothing is to be feared except behavior that is vile and productive of sin. After mentioning what is terrifying among human beings, he now brings out how dangerous it is, that such an evil is not brought under control at any price, nor do relatives rescue one, be they ever so holy, nor does anyone else, the only hope being that repentance goes ahead and sways the judge to show mercy.

He begins, then, with the rich and tells them their duty, then moves to the case of the poor, and for a while discourses of the rich. *Those who trust in their power and boast of the abundance of their wealth* (v. 6): so listen, all you rich who think you have power from being rich, and glory in (294) your many possessions: you will gain nothing from money while sinning and believing security is acquired by money, whereas family connections are of no benefit to you. He explains the reason for this: *If a brother is not redeemed, will anyone be redeemed?* (v. 7). Having done well to say, *If a brother is not redeemed*, he proceeded to make the general statement, Neither will anyone else. *He will not pay God a ransom for himself, or the price of redemption of his own soul* (vv. 7–8): this alone—namely, sin—is not up for sale, nor does it get help from family connections, as elsewhere also the Lord says that even if Noah, Daniel, and Job were to rise up, they would not save their children from their crimes.[2]

Having to this point spoken to the rich and taught them not to take pride in their wealth, he now moves to the case of the poor in the words, *He labored forever, and will live to the end* (v. 9): the poor person, on the other hand, who is mindful of righteousness, even if having tribulation in this age, if he is not pressured by his poverty to do anything wrong, goes to a better life, in no way harmed by his poverty here just as the rich person is no better off for his riches. (295) *He will not see ruin when he witnesses the death of wise people* (vv. 9–10). In this he advises the poor not to be vexed or sorry at heart on seeing wealthy wrongdoers enjoying their wealth to the

---

[1] The LXX reads "heel" for a similar Hebrew form that the NRSV renders as "slanderers."

[2] Cf. Ezek 14:14, 20.

end, but to await the outcome of everything until death arrives to strip them of all their external accoutrements and reveal them to be devoid and bereft of everything—hence his saying *He will not see ruin when he witnesses the death of wise people.* By *wise people* here he refers to the rich by Hebrew idiom, mocking him with the title *wise* instead of turning the word "rich" into Greek. So his meaning is that the poor person is no longer vexed when he sees the rich meeting the same end and brought down to the same dust. After all, what then goes through his mind?

Fool and dolt will perish together: he reasons that such a person gained nothing from his wealth; instead, by his own folly he is condemned to the common death, invested in the common retribution. He calls him *fool* in what follows. How, in fact, does he proceed? *They will leave behind their wealth to strangers*: how is it that such a fool, who amassed great wealth not always on the basis of justice but sometimes even by adding to his wealth the tears of many poor people, and then, after making money from crime and (296) hatching no useful plans for himself or for someone else, did not even leave his wealth to those he wished? Hence his saying *to strangers*, since leaving it to those of one's own family and choice brings some consolation to the dying, whereas passing it on to people who are possibly foes or unknown incurs heavy condemnation of the folly of the person amassing it in this way and leaving it in this way.

So having said *They will leave behind their wealth to strangers*, he goes on, *Their graves are their homes forever* (v. 11): they occupy common graves, from which there is now no possibility of emerging; instead, they are guarded as though in a prison at the time of judgment, stripped of all they gloried in beforehand. *Their dwelling places from generation to generation.* He says the same thing, They occupy their dwellings, that is, their eternal habitation, from which it is impossible to emerge. *They bestowed their names on their lands.* He suggests the conceit they showed in their lifetime, saying that they gave their own names to their possessions—baths, houses perhaps, and other such things—so that their property was long called after them, believing as they did that they could take it with them if their name was on it.

Though enjoying a state of honor, man did not understand; (297) *he was comparable with brute beasts and likened to them* (v. 12): though accorded such dignity by God as to be rational and capable of realizing in some fashion the brevity of his life by giving the beasts names, he did not even appreciate the one who bestowed the dignity. Instead, he conducted his life like an irrational being, lacking the support of virtue, and thus occupied his grave. *This way of theirs is a scandal for them* (v. 13). By *This way* he means, Such an attitude and this conceit prevented their understanding anything of their duty; instead, they suffered the death of brute beasts, and yet those coming later gained nothing. He asks, Why? *And later they will take delight in their mouth*, that is, those coming later gained nothing from what went before, but even they took delight: *the mouths* of the departed—that is, the possessions and the things that bore the names they gave them—they made sure passed to them as successors of the departed.

What was the result? The second group with such an attitude not only gained nothing, but even suffered the same fate. He goes on, in fact, *Like sheep they were placed in Hades; death will shepherd them* (v. 14): yet they, too, were herded together like irrational sheep into one place, (298) and had death as a shepherd like those before them. What is their fate according to God's righteous judgment? *The upright will dominate them in the morning*, by *in the morning* meaning swiftly: Those who do not stray from the straight and narrow, he is saying, are found to have better intentions by comparison with them (*will dominate* meaning, Those living by wise counsel will prove better than those addicted to imprudence); their virtue makes them more secure than possessions made the others, since the wealth of fools disappears, whereas glory accompanies those showing esteem for virtue. Hence he goes further in reference to the rich, *Their help will deteriorate in Hades*, by *Their help* meaning, The help they thought to gain—from riches, I mean—proves useless for them, especially at the moment of death. How and in what fashion? *They were rejected from their glory*. The phrase *They were rejected* was well put for their being, as it were, rejected from riches as though from somebody else's house and thrown out into the grave. *But God will ransom my soul from the hand of Hades when he receives me* (v. 15): it is not so, however, with the wise person giving thought to what is righteous; many such people the Lord God recalled from death on account of their virtue and restored to life, such as Hezekiah and the like.[3]

At this point he now (299) urges the poor person not to admire the rich if virtue does not accompany being rich as well as the skill of knowing how to manage it. Hence he proceeds, *Do not be afraid when one becomes rich, or when the glory of his house is magnified*

[3] Cf. 2 Kgs 20:1–11.

(v. 16). The phrase *Do not be afraid* means, Do not be alarmed or upset or distressed when you see someone surrounded with great wealth and many possessions. Why not? *Because when he dies, he will take none of it at all, nor will his glory go down with him* (v. 17): even if rich in this life, he will not for this reason prove to be blessed after death as well. On the contrary, then, he will leave it all behind and thus present himself naked at the judge's tribunal. *He will acknowledge you when you do him favors* (v. 18b).[4] The verse involves great obscurity arising from the metaphor in the Hebrew. His meaning is, in short, One thing alone will accrue to him in the age to come, if he gave evidence of any good to anyone. So *He will acknowledge you* means, He will thank God only for this, being found to have performed something good, so as to find some reward in turn. As for the rest, he proceeds to explain.

He will go to his ancestors' generation (v. 19): the result being that if he is not found to have done any good, he will gain nothing from his wealth, and instead will join those lying in the dust until judgment. Hence he goes on, (300) *He will not see light forever*: riches will no longer be any good to him where he lies, by the law of nature incapable of seeing the light. *Though enjoying a state of honor, man did not understand; he was comparable to brute beasts, and likened to them* (v. 20). He resumed what he had said above: And so such a person, dying in this way after amassing money and not managing it properly, will be no different from a brute beast, failing to acknowledge the dignity he received from God, but resembling the brute beasts for whom the end of life means only death.

Psalm 50

The leaders of the Jews set no store by virtue, thinking instead that everything lay in learning the laws and teaching them by rote and in offering sacrifices, whereas they were not interested in knowing the reason for doing so. In fact, reading of the law and provision of sacrifices are fruits of underlying virtue, since to be sure without virtue simply doing those things is no different from anointing oneself for wrestling while neglecting the bouts themselves in the belief that the mere anointing takes the place of the contests. Those of

---

[4] Olivier's text contains nothing of v. 18a ("Because his soul will be blessed in his lifetime," in the other Antiochenes) or any comment on it by Diodore. Metaphor or not, v. 18b certainly gives rise to a range of ancient and modern versions.

this mind, then, blessed David accuses by introducing God himself reproaching the Jews and showing that in the absence of virtue he declines their sacrifices, as God says more clearly (301) in Isaiah, "The lawless person who offers a heifer to me is like someone striking a man, and the one sacrificing a lamb from the flock like someone killing a dog, and the one making a grain offering like swine's blood, the one giving incense as a memorial like the blasphemer."[1] In this sense David also says the sacrifices are of no value without virtue. As though in an image, then, he presents the whole scene and introduces God suddenly appearing from the heavens and seated in judgment, judging the very judges and rulers of the Jews.

This, at any rate, is the way he delivers the introduction in the words, *The Lord God of gods spoke and summoned the earth* (v. 1). By *gods* here he refers to the judges and rulers: since after God man alone exercises judgment, receiving it by grace as he receives from grace the role of judging and ruling, so too the person judging bears by grace the name of God. So *God of gods* means, The true God and the real judge of judges and jurors, who were known as gods by the Jews, being Lord of all, summoned the earth and addressed it. *From the rising of the sun to its setting. Out of Sion the comeliness of his charm* (vv. 1–2). Since he was about to say that he was seen on Sion and held court there, lest anyone think that he is Lord only of Sion, he did well to add *from the rising of the sun to its setting. Out of Sion the comeliness of his charm,* (302) his meaning being, The one with authority over everything and the whole earth *from the rising of the sun* to its setting nevertheless holds court for the time being not in every place but in Sion, suddenly being visible from there and from there holding court.

God will come in an obvious manner, our God, and he will not keep silence (vv. 2–3). Since he had said that he will come to judge the rulers of the Jews (his coming often referring to his activity in the sense of He shone, as when it says, "Let your face shine upon your servant,"[2] that is, By the operation of your help show me yourself), lest anyone get the impression here also that the term *will come* refers to his activity, he went on to say *He will come in an obvious manner*, that is, will show himself completely in the guise of a judge. It was mentioned, in fact, that he presents his whole discourse as if God personally were present and judging—hence his

---

[1] Isa 66:3.
[2] Ps 31:16.

addition of *he will not keep silence*, that is, he will choose to judge the judges in no other way than by personal inspection and as though by his very presence. Then, to bring out that he arrives in retribution and as a cause of deep fear, attended by sanctions like bodyguards, he goes on, *A fire will burn in his presence, with a severe storm around him*: just as the rulers of the earth have heralds going ahead to inspire submission with their shouting, so too God comes in person with fire going ahead and a severe storm to inspire fear in those due to (303) be judged. By *storm* he refers to a power capable of drawing down to Hades.

He will call to heaven above and to earth to judge his people (v. 4): on arriving in an obvious manner, then, with fire and storm as his bodyguards, he will summon everyone from all quarters as if to appoint those present as witnesses of the judgment. So whom does he summon? The heavenly powers from on high (the sense of *above*) and the whole *earth* from below, and he will hold court on them. Then, seated in judgment on this throne, as it were, he calls in the defendants and says, *Assemble for him his holy ones, who made covenant with him by sacrifice* (v. 5). By *holy ones* he refers to those considered holy for the reason of offering sacrifices, calling them not truly holy, only in those people's opinion, the result being that this name is rather a reproach to them than a commendation because they actually neglect virtue and give all their attention to sacrifices. Hence he added *those who made covenant with him by sacrifice*, that is, those thinking that the covenant with God consists entirely of sacrifices and not in doing good works. Next, when these people had been brought forward, what does he proceed to say? *The heavens will announce his righteousness, because God is judge* (v. 6): they will shout, and the heavenly powers (304) will listen to the judge speaking to those on trial.

What, in fact, does he say to them? Note that it is simple, concise, and quite full of truth. *Listen, my people, and I shall speak to you* (v. 7). *I shall speak to you* refers to what I am about to say to you and to what I am about to communicate to you. *Israel, and I shall testify against you*. By *Israel* and *my people* he means the same thing; *and I shall testify against you* likewise. So having, as it were, created deep stillness in the court through this introduction, he goes on, *I am God your God*. By the duplication he did well to bring out that the Jews, as if on a search, will not find any other God; rather, just as he says in Isaiah, "I am God first and I am God after that,"[3] so

---
[3] Isa 44:6.

too here *I am God your God*—that is, I am present in my own person, and I speak to you in my own person, so that you have no good grounds for ignorance.

What is your criticism, then, Lord? *It is not on the score of your sacrifices that I shall censure you* (v. 8): be aware of this, that I do not set great store by sacrifices, nor find fault with their neglect as though deeply wronged; on the contrary, I shall regard everything as filling the role of sacrifices. Hence he proceeds, (305) *Your holocausts are ever before me.* He says this by way of concession: Not only do I not blame you for sacrifices you do not make; on the contrary, I consider all your sacrifices are before me and I think I have them all. But hear the truth: I accept the sacrifices without having need of them, nor is it out of insufficiency that I require them of anyone, since the one who requires out of insufficiency is inferior to the one who provides. Hence he goes on in detail, *I shall not accept your bulls from your house* (v. 9), *I shall not accept* meaning on the basis of need. *Or goats from your flocks.* By *goats* here he refers to young goats.

Then he also supplies the reason. *Because all the wild beasts of the countryside are mine* (v. 10): accept proof of my not accepting these things out of need on the grounds that they are all mine. *Cattle on mountains and oxen.* After saying above *wild beasts*, he said here *cattle*, his meaning being, All wild and tame things are under my control and of my making, not only four-footed ones but also "the winged creatures in the firmament of heaven."[4] He proceeds, in fact, (306) *I know all the birds in the sky, and the charm of the countryside is from me* (v. 11): in short, if there is any good in any of it, it is all of my doing and making, and falls under my lordship (*I know* meaning I own, from owners having knowledge of what they own). So what if they are all mine, and I apportion them as I wish to those under my control? In your case, when you offer part of what you receive, it is not so much that you are grateful in giving a part as ungrateful in not returning it all.

For this reason, and by way of irony, he expresses the following in these terms, *If I were hungry, I would not tell you.* He stated the impossible: As it is not possible for me to be hungry or find myself in need of anything, so neither is it possible for me to ask for anything. If, however (just to make a point), you were to grant that I was at any time hungry, I would not broadcast the need, nor by

---

[4] Gen 1:20.

making a request hold weakness to blame. *For the world is mine, and all its fullness.* He supplied the reason for not making a request: even if I found myself in need, I have resources of my own to outlay and would not demand what I had given you in the beginning. So much, then, by way of making a point: for proof that I suffer no need and am naturally self-sufficient, listen to the following. *Surely I do not eat the flesh of bulls or drink goats' blood?* (v. 13). Surely you are not so stupid as to think I am nourished on bulls' meat and drink goats' blood? While on your part you would not be under that impression, neither would I charge you (307) with such awful inanity.

This being the case, then, he is saying, hear what it is I love and long for, and of what I confess to be in need. What? *Sacrifice to God a sacrifice of praise* (v. 14): this is what I need, for you to be grateful, offering thanks and praise for what you receive from me—not because I need this, but out of longing for you to be appreciative, so that I may have occasion to give you further favors. *And pay your vows to the Most High.* He states more clearly what I said: Be grateful for what you have received in the past, and thus later as well bring requests to me the Most High (by *vows* here meaning requests). Hence he goes on, *Call upon me in the day of your tribulation, and I shall rescue you and glorify you* (v. 15). He gave the reason for wishing people to be grateful, that when they called upon him, he would again take their gratitude in anticipation as grounds for bestowing favors.

Having to this point spoken of sacrifices and shown them to be ineffective unless accompanied by virtue, at this point he addresses the teachers and legal experts themselves, who pretended to know the law and undertook to teach others, but were themselves bereft of the good deeds of which they spoke. Hence from the beginning he called such people sinners for being wide of the mark (308) in teaching obligations but failing to perform the actions of which they spoke. This is the height of sinfulness, when deeds are not in keeping with speech; it is fine and lovely as far as words go, but falls completely short of the deeds themselves. So he continues as follows: *But to the wicked God said* (v. 16), that is, to such a teacher, with fine words but no deeds. What does he say to such a one? *Why do you outline my ordinances and take up my covenant in your mouth?* Why is this your intention, to explicate my laws and give evidence of such interest in them as to proclaim them even without reading them? What value do you get from them when you do not practice what you preach? Hence he goes on, *You hated instruction* (v. 17). By *instruction* he means lessons in good things. On the contrary, in fact, you seem not only not to love what you say, but even to hate these very things and do the opposite. Hence he continues, *You cast my words behind you*: you clearly obstruct all my commandments and commit your own actions of depravity and contempt; there is no single form of vice you avoid, you (309) who undertake to give instruction in virtue. *If you saw a thief, you consorted with him, and you threw in your lot with adulterers* (v. 18), that is, though giving instruction in virtue, you proved to be guilty of these crimes, and not only guilty but even complimentary of the crimes themselves.

Your mouth was awash with wickedness (v. 19): you did not even desist from evildoing by word of mouth. He refers to both flattery and slander, and says flattery and the harm it causes are worse. Hence he continues, *Your tongue wrapped itself around deceptions*, that is, you employed deceit, saying sweet nothings to those in your company but involving them in incurable evil, with the result that they took no precautions against your words because under the guise of friendship you hatched a dire fate for them. And to make the same thing clearer, he goes on, *You sat down to malign your brother, and put a stumbling block in the way of your mother's son* (v. 20): far from proving to be like this only by chance and casually, you even sat down and plotted against your kith and kin, and devised schemes and snares. *These things you did, and I kept silence; you assumed I would be like you where iniquity is concerned* (v. 21): my long-suffering (310) probably encouraged you and made you worse, and the fact that I did not immediately inflict punishments led you to think I was satisfied with such things.

But it is not so, not so. *I shall censure you, and bring you face to face with your sins*: realize, then, from the facts themselves that the previous long-suffering did not mean cancellation of punishment but the basis of graver accusation, because even after such long-suffering you did not improve. I shall bring you face to face with all your sins for you to be persuaded that it was not in ignorance of what was happening that I showed long-suffering, but to preserve for you the opportunity for repentance. You, on the other hand, abused the opportunity for repentance and proved to be the grounds and liability for heavier accusation of yourself.

Having to this point spoken of those who explained the laws without putting into practice anything of which they spoke, he now proceeds to deliver a general exhortation for such sins to be taken note of, and for them to be grateful, so that God will have grounds for saving such people again. So he continues the delivery of the exhortation in these terms: *Understand this, you who forget God* (v. 22): all you who have been caught up in such sins, fix in your minds what God has said to you. *Lest he ever snatch you away instead of being the one to rescue you:* (311) before he inflicts a punishment too great for any defense. Lo, what he wishes is clearly revealed. Namely? *A sacrifice of praise will glorify me; that is the path by which I shall show him my salvation* (v. 23). What is his recommendation? He says, Sacrifices are not pleasing to me; I delight in people's gratitude, which is the way I provide salvation for people (*that* taking the place of an action, in the sense, This is the way and the behavior of people for them to be saved). What way is that? Gratitude by which a person praises me and glorifies me for what has been received from me.

Psalm 51

"To the end. A psalm for David, on the prophet Nathan's going in to him when he had gone in to Bathsheba." Those who interpreted the psalm in terms of the title incurred the predictable results; they would be culpable for not grasping the complete sense of the psalm, finding its real contents and interpreting it in that fashion. The carelessness of those who gave it the title was, in fact, bound to prove a way to ignorance for the more zealous, whereas by contrast the diligence of the latter was bound to set to rights the error of the former. Admittedly the psalm, in fact, by and large suits every person who confesses and asks for loving-kindness—hence the error of those assigning the title, who thought it was more suited to the composer of the psalm in person (blessed David, I mean) as guilty of a great sin.[1] But the final verses (312) of the psalm make clear that he develops a specific theme applicable to both an entire nation and an abused city: the verse *Be good, Lord, to Sion in your good pleasure, and let the walls of Jerusalem be built*, and after the improvement of the city requesting in turn, *Then you will take pleasure in a sacrifice of righteousness, offering, and holocausts*, then *They will offer up young bulls on your altar* (vv. 18–19)—how is it not obvious that he is shown to be prophesying on behalf of Jerusalem, due to be rebuilt after the occurrence of the captivity, and in reference to the altars that they too are in turn rebuilt, and

---

[1] Cf. 2 Sam 11–12.

for the offering of sacrifices again according to the ancient regulation? What opportunity does this give the person confessing his own sins in specific terms? After all, who ever omitted raising a petition for their own sin when praying for city and altars and sacrifices? It is therefore likely that this psalm, instead of being one of confession of a single sin, proves to be spoken on the part of the people in captivity while in Babylon, and under the pressure of misfortune obliged to beg God to stay his anger against them and show them pity commensurate with his loving-kindness, restore also the situation of the city (Jerusalem, I mean), renew the sacrifices and restore to the city the former trappings of prosperity.

Such is the psalm's theme, which begins as follows. (313) *Have mercy on me, O God, according to the greatness of your mercy* (v. 1). The Israelites give the appearance of being very much improved by the misfortunes: while making a petition for great mercy, they confess to be requesting it for a serious failing. Now, nothing so wins the Lord to mercy as confession of sin, and especially when the power of sin is admitted to an unusual degree. Hence they proceed, *And according to the abundance of your compassion blot out my lawlessness.* As in the case of mercy his request was for a *great* amount, also in the case of compassion he asked for *an abundance,* since the sin could not be forgiven because of its gravity if it did not receive commensurate compassion and loving-kindness. What follows makes this even clearer; he goes on, *Cleanse me yet further of my iniquity, and purify me of my sin* (v. 2). Here again he asked for a double dose of purification in the words *Cleanse me yet further* to bring out at all points the gravity of sin.

He then mentions also the reason why he is worthy of loving-kindness, continuing, *Because I know my iniquity, and my sin is always before me* (v. 3): if I did not acknowledge my sin or daily keep it before me so that in some fashion compunction for it and repentance is prompted more readily, I would still not be worthy to receive loving-kindness. If, however, I torture myself with acknowledgment of the wrong and the sight of the deed, let it be enough, Lord, for me to (314) pay the penalty by myself, without your imposing it on your part. He next adduces another reasonable cause. What is it that he proceeds to mention? *Against you alone have I sinned, and done evil in your sight* (v. 4): have regard, Lord, to the fact that I committed no wrong against the Babylonians, who are now wronging me, sinning only against you, the Lord. So it would be right for me to be freed from their ill-treatment, and to be the beneficiary of your approval and loving-kindness. He did well to combine the two reasonable claims to be accorded loving-kindness—firstly, that he acknowledged his sin, and secondly, that he did the Babylonians no wrong, instead sinning against God but in no way wronging the Babylonians.

Hence he goes on, *So that you were justified in your words and prevailed in your judging*: for your part, Lord, if you judge in my favor, you prevail over me, having conferred many benefits and received no gratitude from us. Babylonians, on the other hand, have no grounds for upbraiding us or citing to us any reasonable excuses for wronging us. Now, note should be taken also of the idiom of Scripture in the clause *So that you were justified in your words and prevailed in your judging*: the people did not sin against God so that God might be proven righteous in giving judgment; (315) rather, since the people were ungrateful, as the object of their ingratitude he consequently had good reason to level a charge against the ingrates. So the conjunction *so that* occurs here not for purpose (even if highlighting it); instead, it explains the actual consequence, namely, that after the people sinned, God was shown to be righteous in giving judgment against them. So much for the movement of thought.

He proceeds accordingly, *For, lo, I was conceived in iniquities, and in sins my mother carried me* (v. 5). He employed remarkable thinking. He said firstly, I am worthy of receiving loving-kindness since I acknowledged my faults; secondly, I did no wrong to the Babylonians, sinning only against you, and it is you that has the right to require a heavy penalty of me for my ingratitude. In addition to this he continues, *lo, I was conceived in iniquities*, as if saying to God, So if you wish to call me to account for my sins against you, it is time for you to take account not only of my sins but also my forefathers': they did not prove grateful to you, and neither did I—rather, I inherited in some fashion the ancestors' ingratitude, and from them I draw the habit of sinning against you.[2] But you overlooked all these faults on our forefathers' part, in fidelity to yourself and recalling your characteristic loving-kindness. What is the proof of

---

[2] Theodore and Theodoret will draw from Diodore an interpretation of this verse—quite at variance with Dahood's paraphrase, "All men have a congenital tendency towards evil" (*Psalms*, 2:4)—as referring only to the desert people's infidelity and in no way implying an impairment of human nature deriving from the fall as Gen 3 presents it.

this? *For, lo, you loved truth; you revealed to me the uncertain and hidden things of wisdom* (v. 6). *You loved truth* was well put: Instead of fixing your eye on the ancestors' failings, he is saying, you were faithful to your own consistency and goodness; (316) when the ancestors sinned to the extent even of sculpting and adoring a calf in place of God, you gave laws, vouchsafed to arrange for priesthood, and introduced a godly way of life characterized also by righteousness (referring to all these requirements of the law by *uncertain and hidden things* in formerly being uncertain and hidden from human beings, but later made clear through the gift of the law, as also the prophet Baruch says, "Blessed are we, Israel, because what is pleasing to God is known to us,"[3] just as before this time human beings had difficulties even with actually knowing what is pleasing to God).

Sprinkle me with hyssop, and I shall be cleansed; wash me, and I shall be whiter than snow (v. 7). Having said, You gave us divine laws and arrangements for priesthood, he says something more significant, Grant us also some purification by the law. Blessed Moses, remember, also made arrangements in keeping with God's instructions: taking the blood of calves and hyssop, he sprinkled the people and the tent and everything else by way of purifying them and making them worthy of God's holiness.[4] He means to express, then, the extraordinary degree of God's loving-kindness: Not only did you grant laws despite the ancestors' sin, but you also purified those incapable of being purified of themselves. In keeping with your purpose, therefore, Lord, in this case as well do not fix your eye on our faults, but on your loving-kindness from the beginning, and extend it likewise to us, too: (317) you it is who is God in the case of similar sinners.

Hence he proceeds, *You will let me hear joy and gladness; bones that are humbled will rejoice* (v. 10): so now in our case grant joy and gladness, satisfied with our crushing and the humbling of our strength, and take pity (*You will let me hear* meaning, You will bring to our notice the working of your loving-kindness, and You will bring to our notice, meaning, You will provide). In other words, as we now have knowledge of what has come to our notice, so too (he said) what has been provided has come to our notice. But how will this be? If you overlook our sins. Hence he goes on, *Turn away your*

[3] Bar 4:4 (the Antiochenes' canon contained deuterocanonical works such as Baruch, Sirach, and the Wisdom of Solomon, as well as the Maccabees).
[4] Cf. Heb 9:19–21; Exod 24:6–8.

face from our sins, and wipe out all my iniquities (v. 9): if you were to provide this in your grace, you would be faithful to yourself in regard to those likewise in need of loving-kindness.

Create a pure heart in me, O God (v. 10), *Create,* meaning, Re-create: they are asking, not for a new heart for themselves, but for their own heart to be renewed (by *heart* referring to their thinking). So he means, Set to rights our thinking, Lord. *And renew a right spirit in my innards,* by a *right spirit* meaning a sound free will: Impart one to us that is no longer at fault; if you were to set to rights our thinking, you would consequently set to rights also our free will. So tell us openly what you require. (318) *Do not thrust me from your presence, and do not remove your holy spirit from me* (v. 11): so do not make me stay too long in Babylon; instead, bring me back to Jerusalem; as it is, in fact, I seem to be outside your presence, not standing in the temple and offering the accustomed sacrifices. Bring me back to my own place, therefore, and once more grant me the former grace (the meaning of *your holy spirit*). *Restore to me the joy of your salvation* (v. 12): restore to me the former things by which I was saved. *And strengthen me with a guiding spirit*: cause me to rule the neighboring and other nations as I reigned over them in the time of David and Solomon (*guiding spirit* meaning, Make me leader and ruler of the neighboring peoples again).

And what will be the result of this? If you are appointed ruler and leader of the neighbors and the nations, what will you do? He goes on, *I shall teach lawless peoples your ways, and godless people will be converted to you* (v. 13): I shall therefore convince them, too, to hold fast to godliness and ignore the idols. *Deliver me from bloodshed, God, God of my salvation* (v. 14): free me, then, Lord, from these bloodthirsty men (the meaning of *from bloodshed*). *My tongue* (319) *will rejoice in your righteousness. You will open my lips, Lord, and my mouth will declare your praise* (vv. 14–15). He says the same thing in the three clauses: Allow me, Lord, to commend and sing your praises by mouth and lip, to proclaim all your gifts to me, and do so with gladness.

He next proceeds to mention in turn reasonable grounds for doing so. *Because if you had wanted sacrifice, I would have given it; you will not be pleased with holocausts* (v. 16): if beyond these requests you had accepted sacrifice and wished to receive a sacrifice in another place, even in captivity, I would have performed it; but since the law forbids it, it is not possible for us to offer sacrifices outside Jerusalem—in fact, you are not pleased with such burnt offerings—what are we to offer you in place of sacrifices? He goes on, *A contrite spirit is a sacrifice to God, a contrite and humbled heart God will not despise* (v. 17): in place of sacrifices we offer you an attitude (the meaning of *spirit*) that is humbled and a heart that has suffered; do not ignore them, Lord, but accept them as sacrifices.

And what do you ask be done for you? *Be good, Lord, to Sion in your good pleasure* (v. 18): be pleased, Lord, to give evidence of your goodness even in the case of Sion. The result being? (320) *And let the walls of Jerusalem be built*: so that once more the walls may recover their former aspect. Then, in praying for the city, he mentions the reason why he prays for it. *Then you will take pleasure in a sacrifice of righteousness* (v. 19): I pray for the city, not idly, but for it to be a place for us to be ready to practice religion and discharge the laws. *Offering and holocausts*: to offer you what the law commands. *Then they will offer up young bulls on your altar*: so that there may also be an opportunity for us habitually to offer up on the temple altars young bulls for sin and for salvation.

Select Bibliography

Bardy, Gustave. "Diodore." Pages 986–93 in vol. 3 of *Dictionnaire de spiritualité*. Paris: Beauchesne, 1967.
———. "Théodoret." *DTC* 15:299–325.
Barthélemy, Dominic. *Les devanciers d'Aquila*. VTSup 10. Leiden: Brill, 1963.
Bourke, Myles. "Hebrews." *NJBC*, 920–41.
Bouyer, Louis. *The Spirituality of the New Testament and the Fathers*. Translated by Mary Perkins Ryan. London: Burns & Oates, 1963.
Dahood, Mitchell. *Psalms*. 3 vols. AB 16–17A. Garden City, N.Y.: Doubleday, 1965–70.
Devreesse, Robert. *Les anciens commentateurs grecs de l'Octateuch et des Rois*. Studi e Testi 201. Vatican City: Biblioteca Apostolica Vaticana, 1959.
———. *Les anciens commentateurs grecs des psaumes*. Studi e Testi 264. Vatican City: Bibliotheca Apostolica Vaticana, 1970.
———. *Le commentaire de Théodore de Mopsueste sur les psaumes (I–LXXX)*. Studi e Testi 93. Vatican City: Bibliotheca Apostolica Vaticana, 1939.
———. *Essai sur Théodore de Mopsueste*. Studi e Testi 141. Vatican City: Biblioteca Apostolica Vaticana, 1948.
Drewery, Benjamin. "Antiochien." *TRE* 3:103–13.
Fernández Marcos, Natalio. *Scribes and Translators: Septuagint and Old Latin in the Books of Kings*. VTSup 54. Leiden: Brill, 1994.
———. *The Septuagint in Context: Introduction to the Greek Versions of the Bible*. Translated by Wilfred G. E. Watson. Leiden: Brill, 2001.
———. "Some Reflections on the Antiochian Text of the Septuagint." Pages 219–29 in *Studien zur Septuagint: Robert Hanhart zu Ehren*. Edited by D. Fraenkel, U. Quast, and J. W. Wevers. MSU 20. Göttingen: Vandenhoeck & Ruprecht, 1990.
Fernández Marcos, Natalio, and Angel Sáenz-Badillos, *Theodoreti Cyrensis Quaestiones in Octateuchum*. Textos y estudios "Cardenal Cisneros" 17. Madrid: Consejo Superior de Investigaciones Cientificas, 1979.
Fernández Marcos, Natalio, and José Ramon Busto Saiz. *Theodoreti Cyrensis Quaestiones in Reges et Paralipomena*. Textos y

Estudios "Cardenal Cisneros" 32. Madrid: Consejo Superior de Investigaciones Cientificas, 1984.
Greer, Rowan A. "The Antiochene Christology of Diodore of Tarsus." *JTS* NS 17 (1966): 327–41.
Guinot, Jean-Noël. "L'*In Psalmos* de Théodoret: Une relecture critique du commentaire de Diodore de Tarse." *Cahiers de Biblia Patristica* 4 (1993): 97–134.
———. *L'Exégèse de Théodoret de Cyr*. Théologie historique 100. Paris: Beauchesne, 1995.
Hill, Robert C. "His Master's Voice: Theodore of Mopsuestia on the Psalms." *HeyJ* 45 (2004): 40–53.
———. "*Orientale lumen:* Western Biblical Scholarship's Unacknowledged Debt." Pages 157–72 in *Orientale Lumen Australasia-Oceania: Proceedings 2000*. Edited by Lawrence Cross. Melbourne: Australian Catholic University, 2001.
———. "A Pelagian Commentator on the Psalms?" *ITQ* 63 (1998): 263–71.
———. "Psalm 41 (42): A Classic Text for Antiochene Spirituality." *ITQ* 68 (2003): 25–33.
———. "Psalm 45: A *Locus Classicus* for Patristic Thinking on Biblical Inspiration." *StPatr* 25 (1993): 95–100.
———. "*Sartor resartus*: Theodore under Review by Theodoret." *Aug* 41 (2001): 465–76.
———. *St. John Chrysostom: Commentary on the Psalms*. 2 vols. Brookline, Mass.: Holy Cross Orthodox Press, 1998.
———. "Theodore of Mopsuestia, Interpreter of the Prophets." *Sacris Erudiri* 40 (2001): 107–29.
———. *Theodoret of Cyrus: Commentary on the Letters of St Paul*. 2 vols. Brookline, Mass.: Holy Cross Orthodox Press, 2001.
———. *Theodoret of Cyrus: Commentary on the Psalms*. 2 vols. FC 101–102. Washington, D.C.: Catholic University of America Press, 2000–2001.
———. "Theodoret Wrestling with Romans." *StPatr* 34 (2001): 347–52.
———. "Two Antiochene Commentators on the Psalms." *StPatr* 34 (2001): 353–69.
Jellicoe, Sidney. *The Septuagint and Modern Study*. Oxford: Clarendon, 1968.
Kahle, Paul E. *The Cairo Genizah*. 2nd ed. Oxford: Blackwell, 1959.

Kelly, John N. D. *Early Christian Doctrines*. 5th ed. New York: Harper & Row, 1978.

———. *Golden Mouth: The Story of John Chrysostom: Ascetic, Preacher, Bishop*. Ithaca, N.Y.: Cornell University Press, 1995.

Klostermann, Erich, ed. *Origenes, Eustathius von Antiochien und Gregor von Nyssa über die Hexe von Endor*. KlT 83. Bonn: A. Marcus und E. Weber's Verlag, 1912.

Mariès, Louis. "Etudes préliminaires à l'édition de Diodore de Tarse 'Sur les Psaumes.'" *RSR* 22 (1932): 385–408, 513–40.

Mowinckel, Sigmund. *The Psalms in Israel's Worship*. 2 vols. Nashville: Abingdon, 1967.

Nassif, Bradley. "'Spiritual Exegesis' in the School of Antioch." Pages 342–77 in *New Perspectives in Historical Theology*. Edited by Bradley Nassif. Grand Rapids: Eerdmans, 1996.

O'Keefe, John J. "'A Letter That Killeth': Toward a Reassessment of Antiochene Exegesis, or Diodore, Theodore, and Theodoret on the Psalms." *JECS* 8 (2000): 83–104.

Olivier, Jean-Marie. *Diodori Tarsensis commentarii in Psalmos*. Vol. 1: *Commentarii in Psalmos I–L*. CCSG 6. Turnhout, Belgium: Brepols, 1980.

Quasten, Johannes. *Patrology*. 3 vols. Westminster, Md.: Newman, 1950–60.

Rad, Gerhard von. *Genesis: A Commentary*. Translated by John H. Marks. OTL. Philadelphia: Westminster, 1961.

Rahlfs, Alfred. *Septuaginta: Vetus Testamentum graecum*. Vol. 10: *Psalmi cum Odis*. 2nd ed. Göttingen: Vandenhoeck & Ruprecht, 1967.

Rondeau, Marie-Josèphe. *Les commentaires patristiques du psautier du IIIe au Ve siècles*. Vol. 1: *Les travaux des pères grecs et latins sur le psautier: Recherches et bilan*. Vol. 2: *Exégèse prosopologique et théologie*. OrChrAn 219–220. Rome: Pont. Institutum Studiorum Orientalium, 1982–85.

Schäublin, Christoph. "Diodor von Tarsus." *TRE* 8:763–67.

———. *Untersuchungen zu Methode und Herkunft der Antiochenischen Exegese*. Theophaneia: Beiträge zur Religions- und Kirchengeschichte des Altertums 23. Köln: Hanstein, 1974.

Sprenger, Hans N. *Theodori Mopsuesteni commentarius in XII prophetas*. GO, Biblica et Patristica 1. Wiesbaden: Harrassowitz, 1977.

Ternant, Paul. "La θεωρία d'Antioche dans le cadre de sens de l'Ecriture." *Bib* 34 (1953): 135–58, 354–83, 456–86.

Vaccari, Albert. "La θεωρία nella scuola esegetica di Antiochia." *Bib* 1 (1920): 3–36.
Vawter, Bruce. *Biblical Inspiration.* Theological Resources. Philadelphia: Westminster, 1972.
Wallace-Hadrill, David S. *Christian Antioch: A Study of Early Christian Thought in the East.* Cambridge: Cambridge University Press, 1982.
Weiser, Artur. *The Psalms.* Translated by H. Hartwell. OTL. London: SCM, 1962.
Weitzman, Michael P. *The Syriac Version of the Old Testament.* Cambridge: Cambridge University Press, 1999.
Young, Frances M. *Biblical Exegesis and the Formation of Christian Culture.* Cambridge: Cambridge University Press, 1996.

General Index

accommodation, xxix, 133, 146
Adam, 28
akolouthia, xviii, xxi, xxiv, xxxv, 109
Alexandria, xiv, xxxv,
allegorical, xii, xiii, xxi, xxix, xxx, xxxv, 4, 19
alphabetic, xviii, 30, 106, 117
Anastasius, xiii
anthropomorphic, 60
Antioch, *passim*
Antiochus, 149
Aquila, xxii, xxiii, 10, 50, 118, 139, 151
apocalyptic, xxiv, xxvii, xxxv
Apollinarianism, xiii
Aramaic, xv
Arian, xxxiii, 8
Aristarchus, xxviii
ascetical, xix, xxxi
asketerion, xi, xiii, xvi, xx, xxiv, xxxi, xxxv
Assyria, 1, 3, 42, 65, 68, 82, 87, 101
authenticity, xii–xiv, xvii, 91, 125
authorship, xix, 3, 124

Babylon, 2, 16, 43, 74, 75, 77, 93, 137

Caesarea, xii
canon, xvi, 168
Chalcedon, xxxiii
Christology, xviii, xxii, xxix, xxxiii–xxxiv, 7, 26, 69–74, 77, 129, 142–48
Chrysostom, *passim*
church, 16
comprehension, xx, xxxi, xxxv
Constantinople, xi, xiii
council, xi, xiii
creed, xi
Cyril of Alexandria, xi

dating, xiii
David, *passim*

deuterocanonical, xvi, 168
Deuteronomist, xxxvii
diapsalma, xxiii, xxiv, 11
didaskaleion, xiv, xxviii
discernment, xxv, xxx, 4
dyophysite, xvii, xxviii, 143

Egypt, 3
eisegesis, xxi
eschatological, xxvii, xxxii
Eusebius of Caesarea, xv, 11
Eustathius, xii, xx, xxxv
evangelist, xxviii, 26, 72
exegesis, xi, xii xxiv, xxix, xxxiv
Ezra, xvii, 3, 91

factual, xxvi, xxxv, 48

grammatical, xxi, xxii
genre, xxiv, xxxv, 3, 19, 98, 107, 134
grace, xxxii, xxxv

Hebrew, *passim*
hermeneutics, xi, xii, xx, xxiv–xxx, xxxiii, xxxiv
Hexapla, xix, xxii, xxiii, xxxiv, 10, 93, 118
historian, xi
historical, xii, xix, xxiv, xxvi, xxviii, 4, 77
Homer, xxviii
hypostatic union, 146
hypothesis, 21

imagery, xxvii
incarnation, xxxiii, 9, 26–28
inspiration, xvii, xix, 11, 93, 143

Jeduthun, xix, 124
Jerome, xv
Jesus, xxviii, 94, 111, 113, 133
Jews, xxix, xxx, xxxi, xxxiii, 3, 4, 7, 9, 26, 27, 29, 115
Josephus, Flavius, xvi

Judaism, 5
Julian the Apostate, xi, xiv

Lateran, xi
Libanius, xxi, xxviii, 152
linguistic, xviii, xxiii, 134
literal, xi, xxvi, 4
literalism, xxvii, xxviii, xxix, xxxvi
liturgy, xvii, xx, xxiv, xxix, 124
Lucian, xii, xv

Maccabees, 3, 138, 149, 168
Manichees, 5
manuscript, xii–xiii, 85
Menander, 5
messianic, xxviii, xxix
millenarist, xxvii
moral, xix, xxvi, xxvii, 2, 5, 7, 115
moralizing, xiv
Moses, xxxvii, 60
music, xx, xxiv, 11, 19, 25, 38, 40, 69, 134, 142
mystical, xix, xxxi, xxxvi

Nestorius, xi, xiii, xxxviii
Nicea, xiii, xx
numerology, xxx, 19

Octateuch, xii, xv, xxxvi
Origen, xii, xv, xx, xxi, xviii, xxvii, xxxi, xxxv, 134
original sin, xxxii, 167
orthodoxy, xi

paideia, xxi
parallelism, xxii
pastoral, xxxvi
penitential, 19
Peshitta, xxiii
preaching, xiv
predestination, 55
prosody, xxi
providence, xxiv, 12–16, 59
rationalism, xvii, xix, 25

rationalism, xvii, xix, 25
rationalizing, xix
rhetoric, xxi, xxii, xxviii

sacramental, xxxii
school, xii
Septuagint, *passim*
Sheol, xxxii
sin, xiv, 63–64
singing, 1, 2, 11, 92, 134
skopos, xxi
Socrates Scholasticus, xi, xxvi, xxxi
Sozomen, xi, xxvi, xxviii
spiritual, xxx–xxxii, xxxv, xxxvii, 4
subordinationist, xxviii
Symmachus, xxii, xxiii, 111, 118, 135, 139, 151
synkatabasis, 148
Syriac, xxii, xxiii, 88

Targum, xv
Tarsus, xi, xxxiv
text, xv–xvii
theodicy, xxiv
Theodore of Mopsuestia, *passim*
Theodoret of Cyrus, *passim*
Theodosius, xi
Theodotion, xxii, 151
theological, xxxiii–xxxiv
theoria, xii, xxv–xxvi, xxxv, 4
titles, xvii, xix, xxii, 4, 12, 19, 21, 25, 29, 38, 69, 89, 91, 100, 103, 124, 142, 150, 165
Torah, xxxvi
trinitarian, xxxii–xxxiv
typology, xxx

Ugaritic, 68, 151

Valens, xi
versions, xxii–xxiii, 2, 33, 60, 135, 139, 141, 146, 154, 159
virginity, xiv, 147

Index of Biblical Citations

Old Testament
Genesis
1:1   10
1:20   162
1:26   26
3   167
15:13   128
16:15   xxix, 4
21:2   xxix, 4
21:9   xxix, 4
34   107
49:7   107

Exodus
3:7   128
12:46   xxix, 72
24:6–8   168

Numbers
16:6   47
16:8   47
16:16   47

Joshua
13:3   138

1 Samuel
21   103
24:17   113
26:17   113

2 Samuel
11–12   165
12:13   40
16–17   21
16:5–8   70
18:1–4   38
22   51

2 Kings
16:5   148
18–19   65
18:30–35   42, 65, 67
19:1   91

19:2–4   65
19:35   43
19:36–37   68
20   85, 132
20:6   67
20:1–11   158

1 Chronicles
15:21   19
16:41   124

2 Chronicles
16:9   37

Esther
8:14–17   xvi

Job
4:19   102

Psalms
1   xxvi, xxxii
1:1   147
1:6   118
2:8   xxxiii
3   xxiii
3:4   118
5   xx
5:1   30
5:6   30
5:10   42
6   xxix, 38
7:6   xvi
7:13   xvii, xxiii
8:6   xxvi
10:7   43
12:7   76
14   xix
16:10   145
17:13   xxiii
18:19   xvi
19   xxiv
19:1   xvii
19:12–13   xiv

(Psalms) 21:4 xxvii, xxxii, 154
22 xxviii
22:16–17 xxix
23 xxvii
24 xx
25 xxx, xxxii
27:13 xxxii
28 xxxii
29:8 xxiii
30 xxxii
30:8 xxxiv
31 xix
31:16 160
32 xxxi, xxxii, 135
33:2 xx
34 xviii
35 xxvi
35:12 xvi
35:25 xvi
36:1 43
36:9 xxxii
37 xviii, xxvi, xxxi
37:3 xiv
39 xix
39:6 xxi
40 xxi, xxxii
40:6–8 xxix
40:10 xxii
40:13–16 xxi
41 xvii, xxvi
42 137
45 xxii, xxix
45:1 xvii
45:14 xiv
46 xxvii
46:5 xvi
47:7 xxi, 2
48:8 xxvii
48:9 xviii
49 xxvi, xxxii
49:18 xvi
50 xxix
51 xxiv, xxix, xxxii
51:11 xxxiv
65:6 23, 31
66:3 xvi

70 xxi
73:13 81
93:2 102
95:4 76
110 xxxiii
115:6 xviii
115:16 60
132:1 104
133:1 115
133:3 115
140:3 43
143 xxiii

Ecclesiastes
1:14 119
2:11 119
2:14 119
2:24 119
3:16 119
4:1 119

Isaiah
6 xxx
7:1 148
14:14 xxx
36–37 65
36:8 103
36:18–20 42, 65
37:36 43
38 85, 132
38:1–3 89
38:20 91
44:6 161
53:7 67
59:7–8 43
66:3 160

Jeremiah
2:20 8
14:9 142
18:6 9
37:11–15 108

Ezekiel
14:14 156
14:20 156

Index of Biblical Citations

**Apocryphal/
Deuterocanonical Books**
Wisdom
 13:5 62

Baruch
 4:4 168

1 Maccabees
 1:60–63 142
 2:32–38 141
 2:41 142
 4:53 142

2 Maccabees
 6:18–7:42 142

2 Esdras
 14 3

New Testament
Matthew
 5:5 117
 21:8–17 26
 26:39 37
 27:24 81
 27:39–44 70
 27:46 69

Mark
 2:26 103
 15:34 69

Luke
 19:37–40 26
 23:46 94

John
 13:18 133
 15:25 111
 19:36 xxix, 72
 20:17 144

Acts
 2:29–32 48, 145
 4:23–31 7

 5:1–11 3
 13:35–37 48

Romans
 3:9–12 42
 3:14–18 43
 4:7–8 98
 8:36 141
 11:33 114
 12:1 7

1 Corinthians
 12:8–10 146
 14:15 2
 15:33 6

2 Corinthians
 3:6 xviii
 10:6 144

Galatians
 4:27–5:1 xxv, 4

Ephesians
 4:10 27

Philippians
 2:7 27
 3:21 144

1 Timothy
 3:6 xxx

2 Timothy
 3:16–17 xix, xxxii, 1

Hebrews
 1:3 8
 2:7 28
 2:8 28
 9:19–21 168
 10:5–7 xxix, 129
 11:4 xxx, 4
 12:24 xxx, 4

Index of Modern Authors

Bardy, G., xvii, xxvi, 171
Barthélemy, D., xv, 171
Bourke, M., 28, 171
Busto Saiz, J. R., xxxvi

Cross, L. xvi

Dahood, M., xxii, xxvii, xxviii, 58, 60, 86, 103, 135, 151, 152, 167, 171
Devreesse, R., xiii, xxxvi, 171
Drewery, B., xv, 171

Fernández Marcos, N., xv, xxvi, 171

Greer, R., xxxiv, 172
Guinot, J.-N., xv, xxix, xxxvi, 172

Harwell, H., xxvii
Hill, R. C., xiv, xviii, xxxii, xxxv, 137, 143, 172

Jellicoe, S., xv, 172

Kahle, P., xv, 172
Kelly, J. N. D., xii, 173
Klostermann, E., xx, 173

Mai, A., xiii
Mariès, L., xiii, xxxiii, 173
Mowinckel, S., 19, 173

Nassif, B., xxv, 173

Oden, T. C., xxxvi
O'Keefe, J. J., xvii, xxvii, 173
Olivier, J.-M., xii, xiii, xvi, xxiii, xxxiii, xxxiv, 1, 10, 32, 85, 118, 127, 154, 159, 173

Quasten, J., xi, xii, 173

Rad, G. von, 107, 173
Rahlfs, A., xv, 173
Rondeau, M.-J., xiii, xxxiii, 173

Sáenz-Badillos, A., xxxvi
Schäublin, C., xii, xxi, xxv, xxviii, 173
Sprenger, H. N., xiii, 173

Ternant, P., xxv, xxxv, 173

Vaccari, A., xxv, 174
Vawter, B., 143, 174

Wallace-Hadrill, D. S., xv, xxvii, 174
Watson, G. E., xv
Weiser, A., xxvii, xxxii, 26, 100, 174
Weitzman, M. P., xxiii, 174

Young, F. M., xx, xxi, xxv, xxx, 174

www.ingramcontent.com/pod-product-compliance
Lightning Source LLC
Chambersburg PA
CBHW031312150426
43191CB00005B/198